The
Velvet
Rope
Economy

The Velvet Rope Economy

HOW INEQUALITY
BECAME
BIG BUSINESS

Nelson D. Schwartz

Doubleday
New York

www.doubleday.com

DOUBLEDAY and the portrayal of an anchor with a dolphin
are registered trademarks of Penguin Random House LLC.

Book design by Maria Carella
Jacket design and illustration by Michael J. Windsor

Library of Congress Cataloging-in-Publication Data
Names: Schwartz, Nelson, D., author.
Title: The velvet rope economy : how inequality became big business /
Nelson D. Schwartz.
Description: First edition. | New York : Doubleday, [2020]
Identifiers: LCCN 2019021223 (print) | LCCN 2019981578 (ebook) |
ISBN 9780385543088 | ISBN 9780385543095 (ebook)
Subjects: LCSH: Income distribution—United States. | Affluent consumers—
United States. | United States—Economic conditions—21st century. |
Classism—United States.
Classification: LCC HC110.I5 S315 2020 (print) | LCC HC110.I5 (ebook) |
DDC 339.2/20973—dc23
LC record available at https://lccn.loc.gov/2019021223
LC ebook record available at https://lccn.loc.gov/2019981578

MANUFACTURED IN THE UNITED STATES OF AMERICA

1 3 5 7 9 10 8 6 4 2

First Edition

TO ANNALISE

Money doesn't talk, it swears.

—BOB DYLAN,
"IT'S ALRIGHT, MA (I'M ONLY BLEEDING)"

Contents

. . . .

The
Velvet
Rope
Economy

Introduction

....

Under the baking hot sun of an Orlando morning in August, the line at SeaWorld snakes its way past the turnstiles and into the distance toward the vast parking lots. Sweat pours down the faces and backs of the dads, while the moms vainly try to calm screaming toddlers and entertain their fidgety older siblings. Gum sticks to the kids' sneakers as parents shell out money for one more bottle of water and the loudspeakers announce yet another delay for the Dolphins Up-Close Tour. When visitors finally arrive at the front of the line, groups are quickly hustled past the dolphin pools, only enabling the weary tourists to briefly touch the captive creatures.

Two miles away, the cast of characters is the same but the atmosphere is completely different. Here, at an oasis called Discovery Cove, parents lounge on daybeds and kids play in hammocks amid lush landscaping. Lines are nowhere to be seen, and there are even private cabanas complete with towel service and fridges stocked with snacks and beverages by an artificial beach. When they are ready, families depart for a personalized Dolphin Swim Experience, with an individual trainer as their guide.

At Discovery Cove, parents and children wade into the dolphin pool, where the boldest visitors can take hold of a dolphin's dorsal fin and go for a gentle ride. Teenagers can break off from the group as part of the "Trainer for a Day" package, complete with feedings with dolphins, a behind-the-scenes tour, and the opportunity to shadow employees. Other options include a chance to wade beside otters, hand-feed parrots and toucans, or go snorkeling with tropical fish and rays. Both parks are owned by SeaWorld, so Discovery Cove's guests can always hop over to the traditional park for old favorites like the dolphin show. And, for an extra fee, they can skip SeaWorld's lines and reserve the best seats in the house to see the marine mammals.

While thousands of visitors a day throng SeaWorld, daily attendance at Discovery Cove is capped at 1,300. Why? To create an exclusive experience that an affluent family of four is willing to pay up to $1,240 for, more than three times what a visit to SeaWorld would cost. And for SeaWorld, a publicly traded company that has been battered by criticism from animal rights activists, Discovery Cove is a cash cow. So while long waits are a feature of the traditional park, at Discovery Cove there are expanded offerings aimed at a tiny slice of visitors. In 2017, the upscale park began offering its most adventurous guests the chance to swim with sharks for an extra $109 per person, or with stingrays for $59. "With no lines throughout the park, you can plan your adventure at your own pace," Discovery Cove's website promises.

This pattern—a Versailles-like world of pampering for a privileged few on one side of the velvet rope, a mad scramble for basic service for everyone else—is being repeated in one sphere of American society after another. At Yankee Stadium, holders of elite Legends tickets enter through a separate door, enjoy a private dining room with gourmet food in addition to the usual franks and popcorn, and are ushered to seats that sell for $1,000 or more, located along the first- and third-base lines. Occupants of the Legends Suite never come into contact with other people attending the game if they don't want to, whether they are far away in the bleachers or sitting in slightly less expensive mid-tier boxes a few yards back. Nor can the other fans sitting further away walk down to the field for autographs or a sight of their favorite player at bat like in the old days. The new Yankee Stadium that opened in 2009 was designed with a moat that prevents anyone except Legends seat holders from getting close to the field near home plate. What was once a quintessentially communal, American experience—going to a baseball game—has become another archetype of what I call the Velvet Rope Economy. And behind the scenes, among the purveyors of elite experiences, the business of building Velvet Ropes has never been better. It's driven by straightforward economics—as more wealth accumulates in fewer hands, attracting this wealthy contingent is essential if profits are to grow.

But this book is about more than business or economics. The rise of the Velvet Rope Economy threatens to worsen the divisiveness that plagues our politics and culture today. After all, if you never actually encounter people from a different class or social background, it's much easier to demonize them. "With growing inequality, there is an attempt by the affluent to buy their way out of public spaces and services in favor of something better and often more exclusive," said Michael J. Sandel, a professor of political philosophy at Harvard. Sandel examined these issues in his 2012 book, *What Money Can't Buy: The Moral Limits of Markets,* and the trend has only gathered steam since then. As a result, he said, "it becomes harder to think of ourselves as citizens engaged in a common project and in a shared way of life. This has contributed to the growing polarization of American life and the erosion of community."

The political and social repercussions of the spreading Velvet Rope go beyond symbolism and rhetoric—they have a real impact on government policies and fiscal priorities. For instance, when corporate decision makers, members of Congress, and especially the political donor class routinely bypass traffic jams and deteriorating trains and buses and get to the airport via a luxury helicopter service like Blade, the political impetus to improve public transit systems fades. The ease of catching a commercial flight at the deluxe new private terminal at Los Angeles International Airport—the first of its kind in America, with a $4,500 annual membership plus a $3,000 fee per trip—makes it that much easier for those who can afford it to forget about the decrepit main terminal, with its claustrophobic hallways and overcrowded waiting areas. Similarly, if wealthier consumers can jump the line at the hospital and see specialists before everyone else or employ high-priced counselors to gain special access to the Ivy League universities, health care and education reform become much less pressing. The name for the American system of government, a republic, comes from the Latin *res publica,* or public things. As the public sector is replaced by private services aimed at the elite, the very foundation of the republic is eroded.

Take Nick Hanauer, a Seattle entrepreneur worth hundreds of millions of dollars. Money provides him a private version of E-ZPass, enabling him to zip past the everyday obstacles the rest of us have to contend with. "This is my life, I see it everywhere," said Hanauer. "I haven't waited in a line in ten years." Hanauer doesn't deal with TSA lines—or even commercial airports. Indeed, as the first person to invest in Amazon from outside the family of its founder, Jeff Bezos, Hanauer now gets around in his own personal Dassault Falcon 900LX jet, which retails for $43 million. He shared Bezos's vision of the internet's potential a quarter of a century ago, and thanks to that early stake and other similarly prescient investments, Hanauer now inhabits an economic stratosphere. But for all his wealth, Hanauer said he has a gnawing fear that the widening gulf between economic winners like himself and ordinary Americans is unsustainable. "If you're not genuinely concerned about the future of the United States, you are not paying attention," he said. If inequality continues to worsen, he fears the country could face civil disorder or even revolution.

Hanauer may fly private, but for ordinary Americans, nowhere are the workings of the Velvet Rope Economy on more obvious display than at a cruising altitude of 36,000 feet. While elite fliers in the front of the plane enjoy more and more lavish amenities—flat beds, cashmere blankets, even a shower on some flights—for everyone else air travel increasingly resembles something out of Hieronymus Bosch's grisly palette. In order to expand business and first class cabins, airlines have reduced the space between seats in coach to sardine-can-like proportions, and even shrunk the thickness of the seat cushions. Meanwhile, with boarding now staggered into nine separate groups on airlines like American, fliers without elite status are condemned to force their bulging carry-on suitcases into overhead compartments in order to avoid the $25 fee for checked bags. By the time Basic Economy fliers reach their seats, finding room for carry-ons is impossible. Flight attendants nickname them Group Nines, because they board after everyone else and frequently are furious about their last-place status.

In recent years, the practice of sorting and separating customers into tiers has spread far beyond the world of jets, cruise ships, and hotels to reshape nearly every aspect of American life. No corner of society is immune, with castelike divisions appearing in realms like education where the rhetoric of egalitarianism was once the order of the day. The rise of the Velvet Rope Economy marks an end to the great democratization of American life in the post–World War II era. As the jet set faded and budget airlines were born, the rapid growth of the economy created a vast middle class, and in places like airports and theme parks even the very privileged rubbed shoulders with everyone else. Now the pendulum is swinging rapidly in the opposite direction.

On board the latest Norwegian cruise ships, the kind of rigid class distinctions famous from the era of the *Titanic* have staged a comeback. A couple might save for years to celebrate their twenty-fifth anniversary with a cruise, only to find that the best views aren't included. Those are reserved for travelers in the Haven, a ship-within-in-a-ship off-limits to most guests, where the most privileged passengers have the most desirable decks to themselves. On board ship, the Haven itself is hidden behind a locked door but the special treatment is hardly a secret. "Be pampered throughout your cruise," Norwegian promises in its marketing pitch for the Haven. "Skip the lines and be personally escorted on and off the ship at the pier and at ports-of-call." For companies able to profit from this system, the rewards are immense. The Haven is among the fastest-growing offerings at Norwegian. And Discovery Cove helped private equity giant Blackstone Group earn $1.7 billion on its investment in Sea-World, nearly triple what the firm put in.

Sometimes, the edge provided by entrée inside the rope is small. In the Legends suite at Yankee Stadium, fans can still enjoy a beer in the bottom of the ninth inning. For everyone else at the ballpark alcohol is cut off after the seventh inning stretch. Or at the airport, instead of racing from one terminal to another to catch a connecting flight, Delta's Surprise-and-Delight service ferries the most elite frequent fliers directly between planes in a Porsche.

To be sure, there are worse fates in America than having to schlep on foot from one terminal to another at the airport, or waiting for hours in line at Walt Disney World while the FastPass+ holders fly by. Nearly 40 million Americans lived in poverty in 2017, equivalent to 12.3 percent of the population. Just over 17 percent of children lived in households that earned less than $25,465, the income threshold for what the government defines as the poverty line for a family of four. But as we shall see, the Velvet Rope doesn't merely delight the wealthy—it also exacerbates the isolation and abandonment of the poor.

And the ability to pay to slip past the Velvet Rope can sometimes mean the difference between life and death. In California, private firefighters sent by insurers saved the vineyards and estates of a fortunate few during the recent spate of wildfires even as neighboring homes were reduced to ashes. For $50,000, private health care consultants can steer cancer patients into potentially lifesaving clinical trials.

The evidence of this trend isn't merely anecdotal, either: the richest one percent of Americans live nearly fifteen years longer on average than the poorest one percent, according to a 2016 study in the *Journal of the American Medical Association*. And that disparity is increasing, with life expectancy rising by 2.5 years for the wealthiest top 5 percent of Americans between 2001 and 2014, while barely changing for the bottom 5 percent over the same period.

Whatever the arena in contemporary life—health care, education, work, travel and leisure—on the right side of the rope is a friction-free existence where, for a price, needs are anticipated and catered to. Red tape is cut, lines are jumped, appointments are secured, and doors are opened. On the other side of the Velvet Rope, friction is practically the defining characteristic, with middle- and working-class Americans facing an increasingly Darwinian fight for a decent seat on the plane, a place in line with their kids at the amusement park, a college scholarship, or a doctor's appointment.

Of course, there have long been different classes for travelers and varying standards of service for customers, whether in more traditional European societies or in the same America that promised a more egalitarian life. At times in the past, the stratification was even more dramatic than it is today. In the mid-1800s, French railroads avoided putting roofs on third-class wagons to force any passengers who could afford second-class seats to cough up a few extra francs. In turn, second class wasn't made too comfortable to increase the allure of first. "The companies, having proved almost cruel to third-class passengers and mean to second-class ones, become lavish in dealing with first-class passengers," wrote Jules Dupuit, a pioneering economist in nineteenth-century France. "Having refused the poor what is necessary, they give the rich what is superfluous."

Dupuit was one of the first economists to identify what his modern counterparts call price discrimination. This describes how companies can charge different amounts for nearly identical products that cost the same to produce. In the process, they can extract the maximum price from those willing to pay the most, without sacrificing sales to customers who can't afford to pay as much. But even the wealthiest consumers don't want to pay any more than they absolutely have to, and they certainly don't want to find out someone else paid less for nearly the same thing. Not only will that leave your best customers feeling ripped off, it will also prompt them to desert you for your competitors.

The solution for businesses is product differentiation—but this basic element of modern marketing isn't as straightforward as it first appears. Edward Chamberlin, the Harvard economist who coined the term in 1933, was among the earliest in the field to test his ideas using actual experiments, rather than theorizing as earlier economists like Adam Smith or David Ricardo did. Expanding upon Dupuit's ideas, Chamberlin showed how differentiating a product doesn't necessarily mean altering the product itself—it can be as simple as a change in how it is wrapped, when and where it is sold, or how many can be bought at one time. All that matters is that buyers perceive a difference.

And with the rise of mass markets, advertising, and increased competition in the twentieth century (much of Dupuit's work focused on monopolies), sellers needed to start differentiating their products to a much greater extent. This principle doesn't just apply to luxury goods: McDonald's has been adding and pulling the McRib from store menus practically since it was first offered in the 1980s to increase the appeal of an otherwise unremarkable BBQ-flavored pork sandwich. Although it never really disappeared, in 2017 McDonald's announced the "return" of the McRib on the thirty-fifth anniversary of its introduction, even providing fans with a McRib Locator website to track it down locally.

Altering products to capture what's known as a price premium is especially critical when providers are offering very similar goods or services in competitive markets—think airline tickets or credit cards or insurance. The actual amount of differentiation can vary— after all, tickets on a train aren't really that different. Even if some might travel in greater comfort, first-, second-, and third-class passengers all arrive in the same place at the same time. The challenge is that different customers seek different things from the same item; a few are looking for a particular feature or style, some want to think they own something unique, and many just want the lowest price. Therefore, each group is willing to pay a different amount. By segmenting their markets, companies can successfully target all of these cohorts individually without sacrificing profit margins by having to design each item from scratch.

Some segments of the market behave differently from others, however. When the product is a commodity like gasoline, and not much can be done to vary it, the main differentiator is price. Cheaper goods and mass market products are largely selected on the basis of price, but sellers have more room to raise prices—and therefore increase profits—when two factors come into play. The first, as we have said, is by differentiating the product in the first place, introducing an Apple tablet with a bigger screen at a higher price, say, or adding the extra layer of foam in Casper's new, more expensive line of mattresses. The second and even more powerful condition is when fundamental limits on capacity come into play.

There are only so many slots for admission at Stanford or Harvard—and you either get in or you don't. The supply of courtside tickets at basketball arenas and front-row seats at football games is similarly limited, no matter how new or big the stadium might be. And although almost no one in the health care world wants to discuss it openly, the same goes for access to top surgeons or specialists in rare diseases. As we shall see, when these two factors—product differentiation and capacity constraints—are combined, the sky becomes the limit in terms of what sellers can charge, what buyers with the means will pay, and the profits that can be earned.

If economists have been writing about price discrimination since the nineteenth century, and businesses have been figuring out ways to differentiate their products and segment their markets since the twentieth, then what's new about the Velvet Rope Economy?

The answer lies in how both our everyday experiences as well as the destinies of our children are increasingly determined by the Velvet Rope, how starkly the Velvet Rope has divided Americans from different walks of life, and how our social fabric is fraying as a result. As the proportion of society's resources reserved for those inside the Velvet Rope increases, less and less remains for everyone else. In many cases, it's a zero-sum game.

Indeed, the trajectory of the Velvet Rope Economy has closely tracked widening income inequality. Since the early 1970s, incomes for all but the top 10 percent of American households have remained flat. Within the top 10 percent, however, salaries have been rising, and nowhere has the surge in pay been as great as among the top one percent. The top one tenth of one percent have done the best of all. Gains in disposable income, which drive consumer spending and in turn corporate profits, have been similarly confined to the very top of the income scale.

The cause of that trend is a subject of great debate but the effect is clear. From hotels and ski resorts to youth sports, banks, and college admissions, companies are following Willie Sutton's advice and going where the money is. The same holds true even in largely nonprofit sectors, like education and philanthropy, which, if anything, are more critical to sustaining the social fabric. As a result, when the common denominator is businesses seeking growth and survival in a globally competitive economy, the private and public sectors alike are happy to build an HOV lane through life for those who are fortunate enough to have the most money.

There's also much more opportunity to profit by providing products and services for the rich than there was one or two generations ago, because they own so much more of America's wealth and control a greater share of the nation's income. To put it another way, what really counts is the change in the income of the top strata relative to everyone else. "By definition the one percent is always just one percent, but that group has gotten much wealthier and their purchasing power is bigger," said Geoff Yang, a cofounder of Redpoint Ventures and one of the Bay Area's most successful venture capitalists.

A study in 2017 by the left-of-center Institute for Policy Studies in Washington, D.C., concluded that three individuals at the apex of the American income scale—Bill Gates, Warren Buffett, and Jeff Bezos—control more wealth than the entire bottom half of the American population, or 160 million people. With Wall Street demanding double-digit annual profit increases from companies and investors looking for the next big thing, the calculus for the corporate brass is simple: focus on the richest slice.

What's more, the twin engines of economic dynamism and raw capitalistic power in America today—venture capital and private equity—have discovered the profits that follow whenever and wherever the Velvet Rope is erected. In early 2018, Redpoint's Geoff Yang helped launch LaneOne, a start-up that secures the best seats at concerts and other live events, packages them with goodies like limo service, an on-site concierge, and entry and exit through separate entrances, and sells that elite experience for a premium price. The new Private Suite at LAX is partly owned by TPG Capital, one of the country's leading private equity firms. Goldman Sachs initially owned part of Legends, a joint venture between the New York Yankees and the Dallas Cowboys that effectively creates Velvet Rope enclaves at stadiums and sports arenas around the country, including the eponymous one at Yankee Stadium. Goldman sold its investment in Legends in 2012 for a healthy profit and the sports firm is now valued at more than $750 million.

"Our team was sitting around recently and brainstorming about the most interesting markets," said Yang. "I personally have a belief that a huge number of really wealthy people have been created in the last fifteen or twenty years. You'd be surprised how many of them there are. There are a growing number of people who want the best and are willing to pay for it."

Moreover, when it comes to serving the rich, the barriers to entry are lower than when you're selling to the masses. The latter requires scale and that doesn't come cheap—again, think about airlines. If the profit margin per seat is $10, you need to sell a lot of seats, and maintain a lot of planes, to make money. On the other hand, if the profit margin is $1,000 per seat, a handful of private jets aimed at a sliver of well-heeled customers will earn as much or more than dozens of 737s filled to the brim with budget passengers.

What's also new today is just how far big American companies, professionals, and institutions are willing to go to pamper the biggest spenders—and punish everyone else. Companies have become much more adept at identifying their top customers and knowing which psychological buttons to push. With algorithms and new tools like big data, companies can pinpoint and favor these wealthy customers in ways unimaginable even a decade ago. The rise of artificial intelligence and machine learning, which many technologists consider the next big things in Silicon Valley, will only speed this trend. "This is where companies are innovating and where there is demand," said Steven Fazzari, a professor of economics at Washington University in St. Louis.

While the laws of capitalism might seem to inevitably favor the rich over everyone else, there are countervailing forces. Among the most powerful of these are what Berkeley economics professor Emmanuel Saez calls social norms, which can vary from place to place. The level of wealth may be the same on both coasts, but cruising around Manhattan in a road-hogging Escalade with a chauffeur is still viewed as cool, or at least socially acceptable, while it would be seen as gauche and over-the-top in Silicon Valley.

Teslas and less extravagant options like bikes and Priuses have a cachet of their own in high-priced zip codes in Palo Alto, Atherton, and other aeries of the tech elite. There's a dichotomy in Silicon Valley, said Geoff Yang of Redpoint Ventures. "You see very few people who have drivers even though there's more than enough wealth to support it," he said. "People don't want to come across as jerks. It's almost a mark of distinction—I'm so successful in tech but let's see how sloppy I dress or how bad a jalopy I drive."

Similarly, paying extra to speed through security at the airport is a given in the U.S. but has caught on much less quickly abroad. Don't You Know Who I Am? is a phrase more likely to be heard in Los Angeles or New York than Minneapolis or Chicago, and not just because there are more celebrities on the coasts.

Along with economic factors like growing inequality, the rise of the Velvet Rope in America has been enabled by greater social acceptance of a new norm, an updating of the Golden Rule: the guy with the gold makes the rules. Whether it means paying extra to jump to the front of the line with the kids at Six Flags or Universal's theme park, or a few years later hiring a former Ivy League admissions officer to grease their way into college, money talks in a new, utterly unapologetic way, whatever the social consequences.

Traditional social norms can be tenacious. But master marketers, social scientists, and business gurus have discovered there are ways to make slipping past the Velvet Rope much less awkward for those who can afford it. Sometimes, it can even be downright gratifying and validating. And in a few cases, displaying the Velvet Rope can be used as a selling point for consumers who seem destined to stay on the wrong side of it.

For those lucky enough and rich enough to live behind the Velvet Rope, everyday existence is a smooth glide, in which life's inevitable bumps and challenges—birth, schooling, aging, and retirement—are softened by unparalleled access and special attention. But for those without significant means, these changes have meant there are fewer and fewer shock absorbers to offset life's inevitable blows. Think of it like a barbell, with the poorest on one end, the richest on the other, and everyone else in between. As the rich get richer and the poor more plentiful, the new reality consists of less attention, fewer options, and shabbier service for everybody in between. In many cases, that's by design. Ordinary experiences deteriorate in quality, and the motivation to pay more for an upgrade and better treatment becomes more urgent, even for Americans who don't consider themselves part of the elite.

With American consumers being squeezed into ever-narrower segments, and the top echelons becoming more isolated, what had been a tiered system is morphing into a caste system. Above all, the rise of the Velvet Rope Economy marks a farewell to the egalitarian impulse that once characterized American life, if not always in deed, then at least in spirit. And there is a growing suspicion among Americans from all walks of life that this is the case. A January 2018 Gallup poll showed that 36 percent of Americans were dissatisfied with their ability to get ahead by working hard, up from 22 percent in 2001. Meanwhile, according to a survey by the Pew Research Center in October 2017, 82 percent of Americans said income inequality is a major problem. The same poll showed that 65 percent of Americans also believe the economic system in America "unfairly favors powerful interests."

The result is that the United States, founded on the proposition that all men are created equal, is on its way to becoming a nation where the day-to-day experiences of the majority are as remote from the top one percent as they are in developing countries like Brazil and South Africa, where the divide between the privileged and everyone else has been long established.

From within the privileged vantage point that comes with the protections afforded by the Velvet Rope, sympathetic observers might regard less fortunate Americans as the victims of globalization or the Great Recession, left behind between the booming Silicon Valley on one coast, and Wall Street on the other. Outside the rope, millions of people are going about their daily lives, paying their taxes and trying to make ends meet, as they wait longer to see a doctor or to get through security at the airport because richer Americans are jumping the line. And many of them are boiling with rage and resentment toward what they see, often rightly, as an out-of-touch elite, with little connection to how they live, and even less concern.

"If this continues unabated, we're done," said Nick Hanauer, the early Amazon investor, who started a think tank aimed at creating a more level playing field called Civic Ventures in 2014. "This won't be a capitalist system, it'll be a feudal system. You can't shred the norms of reciprocity that make social cohesion possible and expect to have a functioning democracy. It's just not going to work."

Where does the Velvet Rope actually fall? To make it into the much talked about one percent, you need to earn a minimum $514,000 per year. The average income among the one percent stands at $1,305,000, and this small slice of the population commands about a fifth of the country's total income. To be sure, most of us spend time on both sides of the Velvet Rope at different times in our lives, enjoying the perks of frequent-flier status or occasionally jumping the line at Walt Disney World with a FastPass+ even if we can't afford up to $625 an hour for a VIP Tour of the Magic Kingdom. Treats like the latter are typically the province of the richest one tenth of one percent, which requires an annual income of at least $2.2 million to join. At its broadest point, the Velvet Rope Economy opens up to admit the top 10 percent of households as measured by income, or a minimum of $135,000 per year. All told, the top 10 percent of households account for nearly half of national income. Defining who belongs to exactly what class is tricky—what it takes to live a middle-class life in San Francisco translates into an upper-middle-class or even rich lifestyle in Toledo. For purposes of simplicity, I define the middle class broadly, from the 40th percentile of the income distribution to the 75th, with average individual salaries ranging from $35,000 to $80,000. Next are the upper middle class, with salaries up to $207,000 that place earners in the 95th percentile, and the rich above that.

The first step in dealing with the threat of limited social mobility and the fact of how divided by class we are becoming, is to identify and acknowledge it. That's hard for some, which is why the Velvet Ropes are often camouflaged, whether via frosted glass at the airport or the red blankets at Stanford Hospital that quietly signal to doctors and nurses that they are treating a VIP.

I've organized this book based on how the system works, from both the consumers' perspective and that of the people who cater to them. The first part, Inside the Velvet Rope, looks at how the top tiers are crafted, why people with means will pay so much to gain admittance, and how businesses can maximize profits as a result. Like Pavlov's dogs, consumers have been conditioned to respond to signals they recognize but don't consciously understand. These chapters explore the most potent of these: Envy, Exclusivity, Ease, Access, and Security.

Velvet Rope tactics are constantly being refined and iterated, as more exclusive spaces and services are offered up to justify more Olympian levels of pricing. The Legends dining club at Yankee Stadium is open only to holders of tickets for the first few rows of seats along the first- and third-base lines which cost up to $1,000 apiece. Within that rarefied club is the Harman Lounge, where a security guard turns most Legends seat holders away. There's nothing unique about the semi-secret lounge—just more gray suede couches, another full bar, and wide-screen TVs. In fact, the only thing that makes the Harman Lounge special is that it is restricted to fans sitting only in the very *first* row, and those tickets cost up to $1,500 each.

Fine distinctions like those evolve into much deeper divisions when the setting is Outside the Velvet Rope, as I call the latter part of the book. Here, the ability to pay determines if your child plays on the school athletic team or stays on the sidelines. Or whether they attend a school where the PTA can raise millions to pay for extra help in the classroom or after-school enrichment, even as neighboring schools struggle to afford the basics.

Unlike in the first part of the book, where business drives much of the tiering, here public policy and elected officials have at least as much responsibility for the stratification as private enterprise does. In the criminal justice system, money means the difference between going to jail or clearing one's record of any crime. As publicly funded hospitals close, poorer patients must travel longer distances for critical medical care, like delivering a baby or treating a stroke. Not that the private sector is blameless. As businesses increasingly cater to the rich, dying malls dot the landscape and there are fewer places for Americans in different classes to gather or shop. Social capital and societal cohesion erodes, and the results are the phenomena I term Exclusion, Division, and Isolation.

As with fliers sleeping on the flat beds in first class on a jumbo jet, the most privileged Americans now rarely come into contact with people from other walks of life. Indeed, just as the poor have long been out of sight for the very rich, now even middle-class

Americans are disappearing from their view. How did we get here? How can broad swaths of the country seem unfamiliar, or at least profoundly distant, to more privileged Americans? Is there any way to prevent this stratification from becoming ever more extreme? The answers lie in the Velvet Rope Economy, and this book is its Baedeker.

Inside

the

Velvet

Rope

1.

Envy

By the time lunch is served on Royal Caribbean's *Anthem of the Seas,* hungry passengers have already begun lining up for a bite at one of the cruise ship's casual spots, the all-you-can-eat Windjammer Café. Reservations aren't taken, and with more than five thousand guests on board, seats are hard to come by. But before they can grab a tray and crowd around the buffet tables, diners must first walk past the frosted glass windows of the Coastal Kitchen, which is reserved strictly for elite guests.

It's just a few feet away, but the atmosphere inside couldn't be more different from the hectic cafeteria vibe at Windjammer. There are no chafing dishes in sight at Coastal Kitchen, where the order of the day is white tablecloths and sit-down service. Reservations are recommended, but in reality there's rarely a need to wait in the bright, wood-paneled room for the California-Mediterranean fusion cuisine on the menu. Nor does the spectacle of ordinary passengers straining to get a glimpse inside seem to bother the diners at Coastal Kitchen.

When jealous refugees from Windjammer work up the courage to open the frosted glass doors and inquire about a table, they are politely—but firmly—informed that Coastal Kitchen is only open to guests in the ship's Royal Suite Class or members of Pinnacle, Royal Caribbean's version of elite frequent-flier status on the airlines.

If the walk of envy past Coastal Kitchen sounds similar to the ritual of boarding a plane and getting a peek at first class and business before reaching the sardine can that is coach these days, well, that's because it is. In both cases, the choreography is very much intentional, with experts acknowledging that even as it stirs up resentment, envy has emerged as a powerful motivator to get customers to trade up in the Velvet Rope Economy. "Airlines paved the way for this," said Michael Bayley, a top Royal Caribbean executive.

Envy also shapes how people view a particular brand, even if they're on the outside looking in, like Windjammer's patrons, or sitting in the rear of the plane. As coach passengers pile into giant 747s and A380s, for example, "a glimpse of a shower or private suite creates a marker in people's minds," said Alex Dichter, a senior partner at McKinsey who works with major airlines. For instance, while the vast majority of people who fly the Mideast airline Emirates might be packed into the back of a plane, that's not what fliers associate with the Emirates brand. Instead, it's innovations like private suites in first class, which Emirates pioneered in 2003, that have come to shape how the Dubai-based carrier is perceived.

The airline's ads feature Jennifer Aniston enjoying first-class amenities, including one spot where the actress has a nightmare that she's on another airline and flight attendants laugh when she asks where the shower is, only to wake up in the comfort of her Emirates suite, reassured that all is okay. In the latest refresh of first class on its 777s, Emirates partnered with Mercedes to create the all-enclosed private suites, inspired by the design of the German automaker's S-Class model. As if soft leather seating, mood lighting, and a high-tech control panel that's reminiscent of a dashboard weren't enough, first-class passengers are ferried to the airport and back in a Mercedes or BMW.

"A lot of brands use products like these as an aspirational tool, and class segregation can create something to which people can aspire," McKinsey's Dichter said. "Emirates is taking a page out of the luxury goods playbook. Major fashion houses put all that energy into making dresses that cost thousands of dollars for runway shows that few people will wear. Hermès makes the bulk of its money from less expensive products but you've got to create that aspiration at the upper end so people will want to participate in the brand at the lower end."

Telegraphing one's social status through spending was famously described by the economist Thorstein Veblen as "conspicuous consumption" in his 1899 classic, *The Theory of the Leisure Class*. Veblen noted how with the rise of industrial fortunes and new wealth in the Gilded Age, ostentatiously showing off became a way of asserting that you belonged to this beau monde, even for those teetering on the edge of bankruptcy.

As its place among Catholicism's Seven Deadly Sins suggests, envy is a fundamental part of the human personality, with a very long history. Indeed, envy's lineage goes back much further than Pope Gregory's inclusion of it in the Church's cardinal sins in 590. The Ten Commandments include a prohibition against coveting, and according to many Jewish commentators, the first murder in human history stemmed from Cain's envy of Abel. Despite Cain's extreme reaction, and the severity of his punishment—he was cursed by God to wander the earth—envy has probably motivated human behavior since our ancestors lived in caves. By the Elizabethan era, when so-called Sumptuary Laws limited the wearing of royal purple and lace to the nobility, commoners would line their cloaks with these forbidden materials so they could furtively signal they possessed something that was supposed to be above their station.

The need to openly display one's status or evoke envy in others waxes and wanes in different economic circumstances, according to Russell Belk, a marketing professor at York University in Canada who has spent decades studying consumption habits and consumer behavior. In times of rapid economic change and political instability, like our own, the desire to preen is heightened and shifting social norms create room for exploiting envy. In Russia after the collapse of the Soviet Union, during the reunification of Germany following the fall of the Berlin Wall, and amid China's breakneck economic growth in recent decades, Belk said, "people either wanted to shore

up their status positions or claim a higher status through conspicuous consumption."

In the Velvet Rope Economy, the ostentatious behavior described by Veblen is no longer limited to the flaunting of posses-
sions. Of course, luxury goods makers frequently take advantage
of envy to sell their wares, but that's nothing new. What is new is
how the manipulation of envy and status is being used to sell services, a much bigger market that includes everything from air travel
and cruises to financial advice and entertainment. And sometimes
it's not the service being sold that brings envy into play—it's how
these services are delivered, whether that means a faster check-in
line that's side by side with the slow lane at the airport or being
called by name to board before everyone else.

The problem is, while businesses may not be above using envy
as a tool to sell their services, it can be a risky proposition. This isn't
theoretical—a 2016 study on air rage by Katherine A. DeCelles of
the University of Toronto and Harvard Business School's Michael I.
Norton found a surprisingly robust link between onboard incidents
and what they call "physical and situational inequality." To arrive at
their conclusion, the authors obtained a private database from an
international airline detailing every incident of air rage over several
years, circa 2010. They did not identify the airline, but it operated
between one million and five million flights per year.

What the researchers discovered as they sifted through the data
was remarkable—when passengers boarded at the front of the aircraft and had to walk through the premium cabin to get to coach,
the odds of an outburst in economy doubled. Nor was the anger
limited to the back of the plane. On those flights where coach passengers traipsed their way through first class upon boarding, unruly
behavior among elite passengers was nearly 12 times more likely,
hinting at discomfort among the gentry, too, over their very visible
privileges.

Even a little air rage, of course, can make for some seriously
bad PR, as United Airlines executives found when a viral video sur-
faced in 2017 showing aviation security officers violently dragging a

coach passenger off a plane on the runway in Chicago. David Dao, a doctor traveling home to Kentucky, had been minding his own business, but when he refused to give up his seat to make room for a United Airlines crew member, all hell broke loose on board. Dr. Dao eventually received an apology from United's chief executive, Oscar Munoz, and an undisclosed monetary settlement. United also announced it was revamping its policies, raising what it pays passengers who voluntarily give up their seats while calling on police only to remove fliers who pose a threat to security or safety.

So is this all likely to reduce the proximity of haves and have-nots in the skies? Far from it, according to DeCelles and Norton. "We posit that the modern airplane is a social microcosm of class-based society, and that the increasing incidence of 'air rage' can be understood through the lens of inequality," they wrote. "As both inequality and class-based airplane seating continue to rise, incidents of air rage may simply climb in frequency." And as far as many companies are concerned, stoking envy is simply too valuable a tool to give up because of a few incidents of bad behavior or some bad PR. Instead, the trick for big business is knowing when to use envy openly, when to use it covertly, and which form of envy to cultivate in the two groups of customers marketers think about in class-based situations like these—targets and bystanders.

Today, Niels van de Ven, a forty-year-old Dutch academic, is one of the world's leading experts on how envy intersects with marketing and consumer behavior. But it was only after he spent a semester studying in the United States that he got interested in the subject that would become the focus of his academic career.

"I was working with a professor at Cornell on the subject of regret," recalled van de Ven, who holds a PhD in social psychology from Tilburg University, where he now teaches. "I heard people say to me on campus, 'I envy you.' As a Dutch person, I would never say that but I realized they meant it in a benign way. They didn't hold a grudge against me, it was more like they admired me."

Envy, van de Ven realized, comes in more than just one flavor, and he has been teasing out those different elements ever since, first in his PhD dissertation and then in research that blends social psychology, linguistics, and behavioral economics. To explain his theory, van de Ven draws on two different words for envy in his native Dutch. *Benijden,* or benign envy, corresponds to a desire to move up and improve one's own position, or "leveling up," as van de Ven calls it.

"Benign envy seems to be a big motivator for people, inspiring them to attain more for themselves," van de Ven wrote in a 2009 paper, "Leveling Up and Down: The Experiences of Benign and Malicious Envy." "What's more, this emotion could be the driving force of phenomena such as 'keeping up with the Joneses.'" Malicious envy, or *afgunst* in Dutch, is fueled by resentment and brings with it the urge to pull down the object of one's feelings, as Cain did.

To figure out why some situations produced benign envy and others malicious envy, van de Ven showed research subjects videos of students with gleaming iPhones, then a fairly new product in the Netherlands. When subjects were informed the student had worked long hours to buy the phone, and therefore "deserved" it, the result was *benijden,* benign envy. In cases where they were told the phone was simply a gift from the student's father, malicious envy quickly reared its head. To van de Ven's surprise, however, malicious envy wasn't entirely negative: it did produce the desire to buy a phone, but not an iPhone, the original trigger for the *afgunst.* So if merchants are going to use envy, van de Ven concluded, they need to first make sure it is the benign form, envy for something that seemed deserved. "There is a pang of frustration there, but marketing always creates this kind of desire," he said. "Benign envy helps us deal with it."

Russell Belk, the business professor and scholar of consumption habits at York University, agrees with van de Ven's taxonomy, with the caveat that some cultures favor one form of envy over the other. In China, he said, financial success is admired and emulated, and showing off isn't necessarily bad form or a spark for resentment. That's among the reasons the signature Mercedes star medallion is larger on cars produced for the Chinese market, and the pony on Polo-brand shirts can be as big as a foot vs. an inch or so in North America. In the United States, Belk said, the key to keeping envy benign and not malicious is that the object of desire should seemingly be within reach. "The American dream is about not feeling resentful because we have the outside hope that we can acquire what we want," he said. "Even if it's a vaguely attainable fantasy we tend not to be resentful."

When American executives publicly describe how they deploy envy to market their services, this is usually the context. "It's about transparency," said David Clarke, who works with leisure industry giants as a principal at PricewaterhouseCoopers. "What customers hate is when you're trying to hide stuff and are not being honest with them." As long as service providers make clear why they are favoring certain customers over others, showing bystanders exactly what the targets did to earn their status, the thinking goes, rage in the air, on land, and at sea will be averted and something close to harmony can be achieved.

At Royal Caribbean, executives maintain that they've cracked the benign envy code. "The idea of segregating people into a class system is un-American," said Michael Bayley, the company's president. "But if you live on Central Park, you are going to pay more. That's how the system works."

A native of Wales who is more comfortable talking about the finer points of class than most Americans, Bayley isn't from a posh background himself. He grew up in Cardiff, the son of a coal miner, and started out at the bottom as an assistant purser on board ship before working his way into the company's top ranks. If Bayley speaks without a hint of the defensiveness that characterizes some other gatekeepers in the Velvet Rope Economy, it's with the knowledge that a little envy has proven enormously beneficial to Royal Caribbean's bottom line. That's obvious from the publicly traded company's financial results—in 2018, Royal Caribbean's profits totaled more than $1.8 billion, over twice what it earned in 2014. Over the last five years, shares of Royal Caribbean Cruises have tripled, far outpacing benchmarks like the Standard & Poor's 500 index or the Dow Jones Industrial Average.

Delivering that kind of financial performance explains why Bayley makes the big bucks—he earned over $8 million in 2017, more than double his total compensation in 2016. "I think society is prepared to accept that if you pay more for certain elements, then you deserve them," he said. "It's the American way." Suites aimed at elite travelers are among the fastest-growing offerings for Royal Caribbean, and they carry much bigger profit margins than standard rooms do. With a week in a top Royal Suite costing upward of $30,000, compared with $4,000 for an ordinary cabin, he said, the focus is on "very affluent travelers, and we have no trouble filling these rooms."

Different classes aboard cruise ships, of course, are nothing new. On board the *Titanic* more than a century ago, at the height of the Gilded Age, third class passengers in what was then called steerage were separated from their supposed betters by metal gates that barred circulation between different sections of the vessel. That made it much harder for them to reach the upper decks where lifeboats were waiting after the ship struck an iceberg in the North Atlantic on the ship's maiden voyage. As a result, first-class female passengers on the *Titanic* were twice as likely to survive as women traveling in third class in the 1912 maritime disaster.

Fast forward a century. Just as the *Titanic* has come to symbolize the rigid class structure of the Edwardian era, cruise ships are a microcosm of how the Velvet Rope Economy has evolved in recent years. In the decades after World War II, as tens of millions of Americans moved into the middle class and their disposable income increased, the leisure, travel, and entertainment industries adapted to their needs. Resolutely middle-class hotel chains like Marriott, Hyatt, and Hilton emerged as the face of an industry that formerly catered to aristocrats and millionaires as seen in Depression-era movies like *Grand Hotel* or *A Night at the Ritz*. The cruise industry underwent a similar democratization in the postwar era. Instead of being the setting for Hollywood glamour among the smart set in movies like *Now, Voyager* or *An Affair to Remember,* television's *The Love Boat* redefined cruising as an escape for the masses in the 1980s.

Richard Fain, Royal Caribbean's chairman, saw that dynamic play out on board ship. A thirty-year veteran of the industry whose ability to keep profits rising in the face of hurricanes, terrorism, and volatile fuel prices has made him a legend on Wall Street, Fain is quieter than Bayley and other travel execs. He's lived in Miami, Royal Caribbean's base, for decades but retains the New England accent of his native Providence, Rhode Island. At Royal Caribbean events with investors and tour bookers, he isn't followed by a retinue and doesn't identify himself as the boss when he asks millennial employees for demos of the high-tech entertainment options and drink-serving robots being rolled out on new ships.

Fain's gift is an unerring instinct for where consumer tastes are headed. By the early 1980s, *The Love Boat* was one of ABC's top-rated shows and the industry was on its way back from the slump that followed the rise of jet travel in the 1950s and 1960s. Between 1970 and 2013, the number of Americans who took a cruise each year rose from 500,000 to more than 20 million. Middle-class characters rubbed shoulders with upper-crust types on *The Love Boat,* and though guest stars like Charo and Joan Collins now make the show seem like the height of 1980s camp, the mix accurately reflected how common areas of cruise ships were organized at the time.

Throughout the 1970s and 1980s, in dining rooms, theaters, pools, and fitness centers and on deck, the onboard experience of a cruise ship passenger in the equivalent of suite class today wasn't that much different from a guest occupying a windowless room in the bowels of the boat. "For a long time there was an acceptance that outside the door of your room, you were on an equal footing," said Adam Goldstein, Royal Caribbean's vice chairman. "We didn't attempt to have any differentiation in how services were delivered."

But as the richest fifth of American households pulled away in recent decades, the design and atmosphere on cruise ships has evolved in parallel. Not only are the gaps between the classes greater than ever, they're also more obvious, bringing the envy factor right out into the open. "We're not independent of society," said Fain. "It's a societal move."

Beginning in the late 1990s, Royal Caribbean introduced dedicated concierge lounges for suite occupants. It was a tentative process, Goldstein recalled, and executives carefully monitored guests for any sign of pushback. Initially, repeat Royal Caribbean customers in regular rooms were irritated that the concierge lounges for suite guests were off-limits to them. In response, management retrofitted ships to create additional lounges earmarked for the top tier of frequent cruisers, wherever they were staying on board the ship.

Since then, Royal Caribbean has steadily become more comfortable with heightening the contrast between the treatment meted out to ordinary passengers and the level of service reserved for upper-class passengers. "We didn't go from day to night in terms of stratification," Goldstein said. "We went from absolutely no differentiation outside the stateroom to some, and slowly but surely the guests who had the resources to do so showed they were willing to pay for it."

In addition to expecting larger rooms and softer sheets, big spenders also want to feel special nowadays—a desire companies like Royal Caribbean are happy to indulge. For example, room service requests from Royal Suite occupants are automatically routed to a different number than the one available to regular passengers, who get slower, less personalized service. "In our sector and others, people paying higher amounts have become more conscious about receiving a higher level of services and amenities," Goldstein said. "They are looking for constant validation that they are higher-value customers. That's now accepted as the norm in today's society. This is what people have become habituated to."

But essentially telling ordinary passengers "you get what you paid for" is not a simple proposition. As new tiers of luxury and service are rolled out, Royal Caribbean is always watching to ensure that stoking a customer's aspiration to splurge on the next cruise doesn't curdle into disappointing them with a present one.

If the gap in service grows too wide, and envy tips into resentment, you risk turning off a large number of customers and losing them forever. Diminish the differences between classes, however, and there's much less incentive to trade up to a more expensive room. "Somehow, people who work here are genetically programmed to be nervous," Goldstein said. "We constantly innovate and are running scared at the same time." That's among the reasons Royal Caribbean has always closely studied the habits of its guests. "We have to be very careful to do it right."

Indeed, as Goldstein admits, consumer-facing companies like Royal Caribbean that sell experiences, rather than a physical product like a handbag or a car, walk a very fine line. "Where we risk a guest's discontent is if special services are delivered in people's faces," Goldstein explained. "If it's made too obvious, if they're actively sacrificing for other guests, they are likely to be disappointed. If guests have a wonderful time, and somebody else who paid a lot more money for a suite is getting a special amenity, I don't think it's a problem."

What does that mean in practice? After all, standing in line to grab a tray at a crowded buffet table while suite guests sit comfortably behind frosted glass across the way certainly sounds "in your face." But that's not how passengers perceive it, Goldstein told me. Separate restaurants for different classes, even if they are adjacent to one another as in the case of Windjammer Café and Coastal Kitchen, don't bother people nearly as much as special seating for a few swell guests in the same restaurant. "If you have areas within a restaurant that are perceived as the choicest table, that's a level of visibility we feel less comfortable with," he said. "During your whole time at dinner, you are conscious of it." Or as Professor van de Ven would say, it's a classic case of *afgunst,* malicious envy.

The cruise line has continued to add more and more high-end experiences for big spenders off the ship, while retaining cheaper options for price conscious travelers. On cruises to Cozumel, for example, Royal Caribbean offers a four-hour trip to the island on a small party boat for $79. It also pitches a private catamaran tour for a family of four for $1,000. On trips to Alaska, the luxury options are even more extravagant, including a helicopter ride to a glacier or a day trip from the ship in a seaplane for fishing and a salmon bake on shore. Budget travelers watch orcas from the deck. That said, the system does make for some odd, occasionally uncomfortable juxtapositions. When Royal Caribbean ships call at Labadee, the cruise line's private resort in Haiti, elite guests get their own special beach club—an enclave within an enclave in the Western Hemisphere's poorest country.

"It was prime," said Bob Schillo, who visited Labadee with his wife, Bobbie, during a Royal Caribbean cruise in 2018. "As a suite guest, they had a special section, and there was a person there to serve you food and whatever toys you wanted like rafts and snorkels. It was all provided."

On board ship, Schillo said he particularly liked that the best seats at shows were reserved for travelers in the biggest rooms. "You get spoiled," he said. "I didn't have to make a reservation and you don't have to fight for a decent seat. At every show, you'd just show up and sit in the first couple of rows."

When their Caribbean cruise was over and the ship returned to port in Fort Lauderdale, the Schillos were escorted off ahead of the thousands of non-suite-guest passengers. "When you leave the boat, you are walked right through customs," he said. "It took less than ten minutes to get off the boat and into a cab. Wham-bam."

As long as ordinary passengers are politely told that suite passengers and the most frequent cruisers have priority, or can dine at Coastal Kitchen, and it's not a secret who gets to go and why, perks are transformed into what Goldstein calls "aspirational opportunities." And there are plenty of other restaurants to choose from for lunch besides Coastal Kitchen; Johnny Rockets and Michael's Genuine Pub are open to all passengers. As far as Royal Caribbean is concerned, Goldstein said, "It's hard to imagine someone would think they're prevented from having a diverse culinary experience just because they can't have lunch at Coastal Kitchen." Voilà, benign envy!

. . .

For Jules Dupuit, the economist who described how railway operators in nineteenth-century France extracted the maximum amount passengers in second class would pay by leaving the roof off of third class wagons, inequality was not merely an academic interest. Trained as a railroad engineer, he watched as the Industrial Revolution created what his contemporary Karl Marx would term the bourgeoisie and the proletariat. This was the era of *Les Misérables,* and Dupuit lived through the revolutions of 1830 and 1848, when the barricades made famous in Hugo's classic went up, and urban workers fought for control of Paris and the French government. Marx published the *Communist Manifesto* in early 1848, just as the revolutions that would sweep the continent that year broke out.

In Paris that same year, a scholar was born who would follow a strikingly similar professional path as Dupuit but take his research much further. Like Dupuit, Vilfredo Pareto was trained as a civil engineer and he spent the early part of his career working for a railroad company. By the time he was in his forties, Pareto would move from engineering into economics, as Dupuit did, and go on to tackle one of the biggest issues in the field, then and now: who gets what and why? To answer the first question, Pareto showed that in one society after another in history, roughly 80 percent of the land was owned by 20 percent of the population.

Now known as the Pareto principle, or the 80/20 rule, this insight has been applied in fields as varied as technology, medicine, and criminal justice. Microsoft's former chief executive Steve Ballmer improved the performance of Microsoft Windows and Office by telling his engineers to focus on the fact that 80 percent of crashes and errors were caused by just 20 percent of code. Studies have shown that a majority of crimes are committed by a small number of chronic offenders, providing the statistical groundwork for what's known as the broken-windows approach to policing in New York City. In the health care system, 20 percent of patients consume about 80 percent of the resources.

The Pareto principle applies to the Velvet Rope Economy as well. For our purposes, it means that a disproportionate share of profits come from a relatively small group of customers, in this case the ones who are the richest and can spend the most. For example, in the airline industry, first and business class may take up one third of the plane or less but they account for roughly half of profits. Break it down in terms of fliers, rather than seats on a plane, and in Delta's case it turns out that 5 percent of the airline's customer base is responsible for 26 percent of earnings. Widening inequality, combined with the huge concentration of wealth at the top of the income scale, has only made this group more sought after in the travel, leisure, and entertainment industries.

Vilfredo Pareto never had the opportunity to take a Royal Caribbean cruise—he died in Switzerland in 1923. But he lent his name to another concept that is fundamental to how economists think about the distribution of resources and inequality today. Known as Pareto optimality, it's the intellectual backbone behind Goldstein's contention that the existence of Coastal Kitchen doesn't have to subtract from the experience of diners at Windjammer Café. A Pareto optimal situation is the point after which it becomes impossible to improve the condition of one participant without harming the condition of another. It doesn't mean dividing the pie equally. Instead, it refers to distributing resources in a way that doesn't require a sacrifice from one member of the group to better the fortunes of another.

Many economists and management experts argue it is possible to create a better experience at the front of the plane without harming passengers in coach. In other words, there is a Pareto optimal way of organizing the plane into very different levels of service and pricing the tickets accordingly. Like a lot of things in economics, interpretations of what this actually means vary. For free-market-oriented economists, expanding business and first class and squashing everyone else in the back of the cabin can be Pareto optimal if it allows those coach passengers to fly for less than they otherwise would have had to pay.

"When an industry is able to create a richer line of products for people looking to spend their money, in theory that makes everybody happier," said Steve Tadelis, a professor of economics at the Haas School of Business at Berkeley. "But getting it right in reality is very, very hard."

Social psychology plays a big role in determining what customers will—or will not—endure to get a better deal. If people are willing to tolerate more discomfort in exchange for a lower price, what is called the Pareto frontier expands.

As the gaps between the classes have become more commonplace in American life, it's become more acceptable to offer even more basic levels of service, in return for slightly lower prices. "At the low end, people's expectations have fundamentally changed," said David Clarke of PricewaterhouseCoopers. "Because it's a fraction of the cost, people say, 'I'm willing to take some discomfort because my wallet is staying full.'"

For executives, Clarke's Pareto-derived argument is reassuring. By being transparent, companies can allay feelings of malicious envy and ensure that bystanders aren't turned off as wealthier targets pay more for preferential treatment. After all, they've earned it. But what if it turns out that the psychology of the envied is completely different from that of the envier? And the peaceable kingdom of Pareto optimality is a fantasy economists and executives tell each other to assuage a guilty conscience?

It's hard, if not impossible, to satisfy all of the customers all of the time. But a personal experience with the Velvet Rope Economy can trigger groundbreaking insights into consumer psychology. That's the story behind the remarkable research of Raphaëlle Butori and Arnaud De Bruyn, two professors at ESSEC Business School near Paris, one of France's Grandes Écoles. In Butori's case, it was very special treatment at a restaurant where her friend knew the owner. As it turned out, the lavish service, off-the-menu dishes, and envious glances from other patrons at the restaurant left Butori so embarrassed she swore never to return. Butori's friend, on the other hand, was delighted. For De Bruyn and his wife, the purchase of an expensive piece of luggage at an airport store came with an added benefit: they were ushered to the front of the security line and avoided a ninety-minute wait. Madame De Bruyn was thrilled, but Professor De Bruyn now refers to it as "the walk of shame."

Those wildly different reactions to similar situations prompted Butori and De Bruyn to undertake a systematic study of how customers respond to what they call DPTs, or discretionary preferential treatments. Rather than guaranteed benefits like a king-sized bed in a hotel or a room with a porthole on Royal Caribbean, a DPT might be a surprise upgrade upon check-in, a reserved parking space for certain customers, or an escort to the front of the security line for an elite flier who is late for a flight. In academia, equity theory has been conventional wisdom since it was proposed in the early 1960s by J. Stacey Adams, a behavioral psychologist. He posited that everyone involved in an unequal transaction would be left uncomfortable and would want to reduce the inequity. Ordinary customers who get passed over might experience envy and resentment. Meanwhile, the beneficiaries of the special treatment could feel shame and guilt, especially if the favoritism was visible and hurt others, like jumping the queue and causing everyone else to wait a little longer.

To test that hypothesis, Butori and De Bruyn created two scenarios. In one, a hotel guest is granted a favored table at the hotel restaurant. In the other, a shopper at a computer store is whisked to the front of the line after they've selected a laptop. To drill down further, the authors introduced four variables into each scenario: surprise, justification, imposition, and visibility. Escorting the laptop buyer to the front of the line in full view of other shoppers was a high-visibility scenario as it was for the hotel guest when the restaurant made it clear the best table had been specially reserved for them. To test imposition, in some cases the restaurant was half empty, in others it was filled with other parties waiting for a table. Similarly, sometimes jumping the line meant literally going in front of everyone else, while in the low-imposition scenario, a cash desk was opened for the privileged customer.

Per equity theory, and good manners, the French academics hypothesized that imposing on others in a highly visible way would generate an overwhelmingly negative reaction among the favored consumers. *Mais non*—the opposite turned out to be true. Forcing others to wait created the most favorable response of the four factors, and the ideal DPT is one that is justified, imposing, visible, and surprising.

"Most customers prefer imposing to non-imposing DPTs, which violates one of our core hypotheses and contradicts Adams' equity theory," the authors wrote in a paper published in 2013. The delight the envied took in the suffering of the enviers was present even when the advantage conferred was small. "Imposing DPTs carries a higher symbolic value," Butori and De Bruyn concluded. "The firm demonstrates its willingness to sacrifice its other customers' well-being to delight the recipient. Although imposition might cause some negative emotions, it also triggers a strong positive feeling of being special and valued, and we suspect that the latter effect might be stronger than the former."

As the pleasures of imposition and jumping the line show, in the Velvet Rope Economy admitting a small group of customers into the most elite category and then counting the profits as aspiring members pay extra to upgrade isn't always sufficient. For envy and a sense of privilege to function most effectively at the high end of the market, others must be kept out.

That's the premise behind the Haven, cruise ship giant Norwegian's answer to the Royal Suite Class on archrival Royal Caribbean. A ship within a ship, the Haven occupies the top decks of Norwegian's newest liners, where rooms are much more spacious, commanding premium views for premium prices. With a dedicated concierge and twenty-four-hour butler service, the Haven's 275 occupants enjoy their own private pool, sun deck, and restaurant. The Haven is off-limits to everyone else—no upgrades allowed, which as we shall see, is one of its selling points.

What makes the Haven so attractive to its customers is that the rest of the ship's four thousand or so passengers can't crash the party. Access to this oasis comes only with the click of a gold-lettered key- card. If Haven passengers do venture out of their rarefied environs to see a show, a flash of that gold keycard gets them the best seats in the house. A special Haven representative meets guests at the dock, escorts them past the long lines of regular passengers, and lets them board before everyone else. When the ship returns to port, they dis- embark first.

Special treatment for Haven passengers isn't a secret, however. For example, while luggage-toting passengers board gigantic liners like Norwegian's *Breakaway* and cram into a handful of elevators be- fore the ship leaves port, there is always ample room in one elevator bank. Look more closely and you see the ropes that make clear it is reserved for Haven guests going to the top decks.

It's also a key message in Norwegian's marketing material to ac- tive cruisers considering an upgrade. On its travel blog, Norwegian tells prospective Haven passengers, "Gone are the days of elbowing through buffet crowds or fighting for the last deck chair because The Haven offers exclusive venues only accessible by Haven members." Executives like Royal Caribbean's Michael Bayley studied the Haven concept and acknowledged its success, but until recently they shied away from creating an outright ship-within-a-ship. The danger of malicious envy seemed high and in 2016 Bayley told me, "That's not the mojo or the culture of Royal Caribbean." But there's no denying the market, and customers told Royal Caribbean they hungered for a separate, more elite area à la the Haven. So when the company's Celebrity line launched its newest ship, *Celebrity Edge,* at the end of 2018, there was a sanctuary just for suite guests called the Retreat. "We are giving suite guests what they want," said Lisa Lutoff-Perlo, Celebrity's president. "They want to know they will have a place by the pool."

The story of the launch of the Haven shows how keeping the hordes at bay helps persuade the upper crust that they are getting something very special for their money. Just listen to Kevin Shee- han, the former Norwegian chief executive who turned the concept from a nascent marketing pitch to a full-blown, highly profitable ship-within-a-ship for affluent passengers. "We needed to fill the Haven by getting the right people on the ship," said Sheehan. He stepped down as chief executive of Norwegian in 2015, and now serves on several corporate boards. "That segment of the population wants to be surrounded by people with similar characteristics," Sheehan added.

Like Royal Caribbean's Michael Bayley, Sheehan wasn't to the manor born. A product of Catholic schools and a working-class Queens neighborhood, Sheehan earned his bachelor's degree at Hunter College, part of the City University system of New York. He played basketball in high school and then at Hunter, facing off against sharp-elbowed players from other New York colleges like Fordham and City College. When he wasn't studying or on the basketball court, Sheehan drove a taxi to help pay the bills, and eventually qualified as an accountant. Sheehan may have come up the hard way but he nonetheless possessed an instinctive feel for what elite passengers wanted—and didn't want—when they ventured aboard a cruise ship. "It's a more selfish world that we live in, everyone is self-important and wants to be catered to," he said.

If Sheehan had any doubts that this was the case, they vanished after the experience he had with elite passengers when the Haven debuted in 2010. The supposedly exclusive section was immediately swamped by tourists from regular quarters who paid $200 to upgrade and book any free Haven rooms left as the ship left port, Sheehan recalled. The upscale patrons sniffed that parvenus were ruining the elite aerie they'd paid so much more to get into. So he ordered an immediate halt to the upgrades. Not only did they undermine the Haven's main selling point, namely, that it was off-limits to the hoi polloi, they also undercut profit margins. "People know how to game every aspect of the ship," he said. "My mantra became: No Upgrades Allowed."

Essentially, it was either keep the arrivistes out or lose the rich passengers the Haven was designed to attract in the first place. "When the masses overwhelmed the group in the Haven, guests didn't have the experience they were looking for," Sheehan explained. "It destroyed the whole experience." The focus on wealthier travelers proved prescient, and as the Haven's appeal grew, its footprint on Norwegian's ships expanded. On Norwegian's newest vessels, the Haven has become more defined—with its own pool, lounge, bar, and restaurant—and more isolated from the rest of the ship. For the company, the financial rewards are indisputable: depending on the season, a room in the Haven might cost a couple $10,000 for a weeklong cruise vs. $3,000 for an ordinary stateroom elsewhere on the ship. Yet the Haven fills up fast and is frequently sold out months in advance.

With the launch of the 4,100-passenger *Epic* in 2010, "a guest could enter the Haven, and never leave," said Andy Stuart, Norwegian's present chief executive. And by 2015, when the *Escape* sailed on its maiden voyage, the Haven's ninety-five staterooms were located so high up in the forward part of the ship that guests in rooms below deck might remain unaware of its existence. Until they come across the locked doors that bar them from entering, that is.

The opulence of the Haven and Royal Suites, like locating Windjammer next door to Coastal Kitchen, has a unique ability to induce envy. But it's not because the suites are exclusive or cost far more than ordinary cabins do. (Exclusivity, as we will see later on, pushes different psychological buttons.) The secret to their effectiveness is how these cosseted worlds sit cheek-by-jowl with economy berths and cafeteria-style dining aboard ship. And while there are occasional complaints in online travel forums and from less privileged passengers who are on the outside looking in, one common response isn't to rebel. It's to pay even more for an upgrade.

Just as the rigid class separations on the *Titanic* reflected the social mores of the Gilded Age more than a century ago, the modern equivalents on cruise ships show how accepting—or resigned—Americans have become to what amounts to a new caste system for a new Gilded Age. "We are living much more cloistered lives in terms of class," said Thomas Sander, who directs a project on civic engagement at the Kennedy School at Harvard. "We are doing a much worse job of living out the egalitarian dream that has been our country's hallmark."

What if there were a way for companies to easily identify that elusive fifth of customers who Pareto found contribute 80 percent of income, target them with the right mix of benign envy, imposition, and visibility, and then analyze the response in real time? Actually, there is. It's called the frequent-flier program.

Loyalty and rewards programs existed long before American Airlines created the first mass frequent-flier program, AAdvantage, in 1981. The idea of having consumers collect coupons in the form of Betty Crocker box tops for rewards during the Great Depression helped transform General Mills, an otherwise ordinary Minneapolis flour maker, into one of the world's most powerful food companies today. But the genius behind AAdvantage, as travel industry veteran Tim Winship noted, was both "psychological and financial." The airline industry had recently been deregulated, with new competition suddenly a fact of life on many routes, and airlines were scrambling to differentiate themselves from one another and avoid having to compete directly on price. American's internal reservation system, SABRE, was able to identify the top customers of the airline and track their mileage. With free trips as the lure for more miles flown, American was able to boost their loyalty and win additional business. Moreover, mileage awards typically involved seats on the least popular routes or at inconvenient hours and might otherwise go unfilled. So with AAdvantage, the airline took what had been a costly liability—unsold inventory—and turned it into a powerful marketing tool at little or no cost.

It was an instantaneous hit—United Airlines introduced its own version, MileagePlus, less than a week later in May 1981—and by the end of the decade, AAdvantage membership had grown from an initial base of 130,000 to 20 million. "In the early 1980s, a new form of social stratification emerged in consumption settings," said Aarti Ivanic, an associate professor of marketing at the University of

San Diego. "Businesses increasingly stratified customers into 'status tiers' or 'classes' based on their demonstrated loyalty, i.e., spending." Rewards programs that were initially the preserve of airlines quickly came to encompass hotel chains, car rental companies, casinos, and even hipster coffee shops in places like Brooklyn and Berkeley, where status is conspicuously played down.

Today, AAdvantage has more than 100 million members. That explosion, combined with the rise of the internet and the ability to crunch the huge amounts of consumer data created by digital commerce, has put the already emerging Velvet Rope Economy of the 1990s on steroids since 2000. But over the last decade, frequent-flier programs have evolved to be more of a boon for the rich than for ordinary travelers. That's because most major airlines now dole out awards based on the dollar value of the ticket, rather than miles flown. In many cases, the lowest-price tickets generate no miles at all for the purchaser. It's another example of the winner-take-all nature of consumer life in the Velvet Rope Economy era.

At the same time, big data analysis has made it much easier for companies to focus their marketing efforts not merely on Pareto's top 20 percent of customers, but on the top 10 percent, and in turn, the elusive if much talked about 1 percent. In fact, companies can pinpoint and favor the wealthiest customers in ways unimaginable even a decade ago. "At the high end, we can get into real psychographics and know who spends more time at the concierge or goes skiing in February," said Bjorn Hanson, a lodging industry researcher and consultant. United Airlines, for example, introduced a new app for flight attendants in 2017 that lets them know who the elite frequent fliers are on each flight and where they are sitting so they get more personalized attention.

"There's been a confluence of forces," added Robert Palmatier, a professor of marketing at the University of Washington's Foster School of Business. "In the past, you couldn't identify your best customers. Grocery stores didn't know who you were, you'd buy and leave. When people buy online, it gives you way, way more information and because firms have this data they're more able to target segments."

Palmatier doesn't just study this phenomenon—as research director for the university's Center for Sales and Marketing Strategy, he also helps companies fine-tune their rewards programs. Some firms, he said, are willing to lose boatloads of money when they set up loyalty programs, because collecting all that data ultimately pays off as the best customers are identified, rewarded with better treatment, and in turn, spend more.

Even better, as these programs become more sophisticated, companies can favor the wealthiest customers while sidestepping malicious envy. That's caused an explosion in the number of different service tiers: the Royal Bank of Canada, for example, had three tiers of customer service in 1992. By 2018, it had eighty, which are updated monthly and guide all of the bank's marketing strategies. And thanks to loyalty programs, status means more than simply getting a better seat on the plane or disembarking first from a cruise ship. For the hapless Dr. Dao, it meant getting dragged off an overbooked flight by airport security in Chicago in 2017. If he'd had elite status on MileagePlus, the cabin crew would have found someone else to boot from the flight and someone else would have been left bloodied by security officers.

It's tempting to think that when you call the bank or another financial service provider and you are put on hold for twenty-five minutes, it's simply because it's a peak time of day and many other account holders are calling at the same moment. Tempting, but wrong.

In reality, the wait time likely has nothing to do with timing and everything to do with your CLV, or customer lifetime value. This is a calculation of how much your business is worth to whoever you are calling, and the higher the number, the better the service. At a bank or credit card company, it might be determined by your balance. Frequency of travel and spending levels help set your CLV at airlines and hotels. More and more, as soon as you call any consumer-facing company, according to Palmatier, the company's first step is to identify your phone number and then determine your CLV. "If it's high," he explained, "they might take your call more quickly, or direct it to one of their best-performing or most highly trained representatives. We call this heterogeneity in customer service, and it's driven by the profit motive."

Until now we've focused on examples of the Velvet Rope Economy where the emphasis is on the wealthiest customers to the exclusion of everyone else—a ship-within-a-ship, a seat at the elite restaurant on Royal Caribbean, and a private suite on Emirates. But CLVs have allowed the Velvet Rope phenomenon to metastasize into the rest of the economy. "We discuss very high-end wealth and services but I think this phenomenon is prevalent much deeper into the wealth pyramid," Palmatier told me. "I even think the term 'customer lifetime value' is very telling. You're judging a person on their economic value and it's like you just don't want to deal with them if it's low."

Ever since caller ID was first introduced for landlines in the 1980s, an individual banker could avoid a call from a pesky customer, just as a doctor could duck a hypochondriacal patient. But in the last few years, powerful new digital technologies like big data and sophisticated algorithms have transformed what was once an individual decision into standard practice by the biggest companies, according to Palmatier. "When you didn't have data, CLV wasn't that big of a deal," Palmatier said. "With loyalty programs or by ordering things online, huge amounts of data are created that can pinpoint consumer behavior." Beyond varying levels of customer support, CLVs can also enable what Palmatier terms micro-targeting, rolling out the red carpet for some customers and ignoring others altogether. "If I have enough data, I can predict how much individual customers are going to spend over their lifetime," Palmatier said.

Harrah's, the casino operator, spent millions to upgrade its hotel revenue management system and link it with their telephone reservations department to take advantage of CLVs. When loyalty program members called, the combined system would automatically recognize the phone number of top customers, enabling operators to present them with lower prices for hotel reservations on busy weekends, based on their gaming history and the offers they'd received in the past. On the other hand, rates would be raised for lower-value customers looking for a room on a Saturday night. "If you're a student of the Old Testament, you know that God said all people are created equally," the former chief operating officer of Harrah's, Gary Loveman, told an audience in a YouTube video. "But she never said that all customers were created equally."

What are the factors used to determine CLVs? Besides individual data points reflecting consumer behavior, zip code, income, educational level, job type, and age can instantly determine the order in which your call is answered. "We talk about discrimination in other contexts, but people will be left out of the economic system as more and more information accumulates," Palmatier said. At this point, CLV's are not like credit scores, which are set by independent firms like Equifax and determine everything from credit card rates to the likelihood of getting a mortgage. Instead, each company calculates its own CLV's for individual consumers. And in a few cases, companies are going beyond the CLV and putting better treatment up for sale outright. Optimum, which provides cable and internet service in the New York suburbs, promises buyers of its Protection Plan "priority status in the call queue when calling Optimum Support."

Like envy, the desire for status is hardwired into the human brain. And as the opportunity to flaunt one's position has become more widespread and more socially acceptable for Americans, businesses are more than happy to oblige them. "Companies prey upon people's need for status," said Joseph Nunes, chairman of the marketing department at the USC Marshall School of Business. "People look up to figure out where they are in the hierarchy, and they look down in general to feel better about themselves," he added, citing what's known as social comparison theory.

Nunes, who has consulted for giants like Nestlé and Southwest Airlines, has spent the last twenty years examining how that natural human impulse to gain status plays out in the business world. "Status matters because the need to compare oneself with others is pervasive and often occurs whether or not individuals intend to do so," Nunes and a colleague, Xavier Drèze, wrote in a 2008 paper in the *Journal of Consumer Research*.

Studying existing loyalty programs and using experiments with students at USC and Wharton, Nunes developed a series of principles outlining how to leverage status-conscious consumers and help companies maximize the envy factor as they refine and expand rewards programs. Among the rules:

- The fewer people granted elite status, the more superior these people will feel.
- Firms can offset a dilution in perceptions of status as the top tier grows by creating a second elite level just below it.
- The second elite tier will elevate perceptions of status among consumers in the top tier.
- The smaller the size of the second-highest group, the greater the perception of status among consumers in the top tier.
- The presence of additional tiers below the second elite level will not affect perception of status among consumers in the topmost tier.

What does this mean for us as consumers? For starters, it forces companies to create ever-more exclusive classes at the very top of the pyramid, so the envy factor remains constant all down the line, even as the top tiers expand over time. As more fliers achieved elite status in the late 1990s and early 2000s, airlines knew they needed to develop something more exclusive than the conventional silver, gold, and platinum levels. United created the Global Services category, choosing the top eighteen thousand fliers in its 10-million-member MileagePlus program. American responded with ConciergeKey, its own ultra-elite category. As Nunes noted, "we predict that perceptions of status will increase as the group size, or number of elites, decreases."

A second elite tier right below the top one can bring other psychological benefits. Research has also found that even as social comparison theory allows people to look down and delight in their superior status, it simultaneously triggers fears of downward mobility and the loss of status. According to Nunes, a "second elite tier may appear as a safety net for those at the top." Lastly, Nunes concluded, "a program with two elite tiers is chosen over programs with either one or no elite tiers by prospective members—regardless of whether they are eligible for status and into which elite tier they would qualify." Call it the Groucho Marx rule: consumers mostly want to join clubs that won't have them as members.

Adding new tiers further down on the prestige chain—bronze or below—with additional gradations doesn't threaten the status of the elite at the top, but it does reinforce the envy effect at the bottom. That helps explain why having nine separate groups board an American Airlines flight doesn't have to be bad for business.

Fostering envy, in the final analysis, is about more than just offering tangible benefits like entrée into a special restaurant like Coastal Kitchen or taking a special elevator up to the lofty heights of the Haven. It is every bit as important to make some passengers feel like they are being rewarded more than others. Nunes and other marketing experts actually divide the perks of loyalty programs into two categories: hard benefits and soft benefits. The former consist of concrete rewards, like twice as many frequent-flier miles for the same flight or lounge access. Soft benefits are less tangible but can be even more effective in building brand loyalty. Think of separate check-in counters, special luggage tags that advertise your status, and above all, when the cabin crew recognizes you by name as you board the plane, even before you take your seat or display your ticket. Super-elite fliers, like those in American's ConciergeKey program or in Global Services on United, can get all of the above.

"Soft benefits are even more important because they help you figure out who you are, not just how others see you," said Nunes. "Soft benefits can be a signal to the self in what we call identity formation." For example, he said, United gives out luggage tags marked 1K to passengers who fly at least 100,000 miles a year. "The bags themselves don't get priority because of the tags but when I see them it reminds me that I've achieved that status." These kinds of status symbols are especially powerful in the United States, which never had a titled aristocracy or inherited symbols or crests like Europe, Nunes explained. "We're supposed to be a meritocracy, so when we see these 1K tags and other soft benefits, we say to ourselves, 'Well, we earned it.'"

For airlines and other service industries seeking to entice a well-off clientele, it's also vital to identify and anticipate what these consumers want, sometimes before the customers themselves are conscious of it. Three types of passengers occupy the premium cabin, according to one aviation sector consultant, and the airlines are keenly aware of the psychology of each segment. "Some are corporate road warriors like me," he said. "We don't want champagne. We just want to be left alone so we can work or sleep." The second group, he said, consists of truly wealthy people who can't or won't travel any other way.

But the fastest-growing cohort are passengers who paid out of pocket for their premium seats or cashed in hard-earned frequent-flier miles—and they're determined to enjoy every minute up front. "They want to splurge and stay up watching movies and eat everything in sight," he said. They might take selfies and put them on Facebook or Instagram so their friends can envy them. Premium cabin menus play to these customers, the consultant said. "You're never going to impress the true rich people with food or wine," he said. But the third group is impressed by offerings like duck, scallops, and shrimp. "It's what they think rich people eat," he said. "It's hard to prepare duck at 36,000 feet so it doesn't taste good but duck sounds fancy to people."

Meanwhile, to give coach passengers a hint of the good life up front, Delta has started serving free sparkling wine to everyone in the back of the plane after takeoff on international flights. "It's cheap as shit, but it's been a huge hit," the consultant confided.

When it reaches its apotheosis, maximizing envy in the Velvet Rope Economy is about much more than always rewarding the most frequent travelers with the best seats or constantly doling out upgrades. If that were the case, the psychology behind loyalty programs would be as simple as the conditioned response of Pavlov's dogs, who salivated as soon as they heard the bell that announced it was feeding time. There's certainly a bit of Pavlov at work in these programs, but there's a lot more going on behind the curtain. The American psychologist B. F. Skinner, working several decades after Pavlov, discovered an even more powerful way of conditioning animal behavior: intermittent reinforcement. When animals were rewarded for certain behaviors only occasionally, not only was the response stronger, it also persisted even as the period between the rewards grew longer.

Recipients of Delta's Surprise-and-Delight service probably wouldn't appreciate the comparison to Pavlov's dogs or Skinner's rats, but the underlying dynamic is identical. As the name suggests, the Surprise-and-Delight treatment can't be booked with Delta in advance, nor is it ever guaranteed. Instead, if the stars align, elite Delta fliers with connecting flights will be met at the gate by an airline representative and whisked across the tarmac in a Porsche to their next flight. Delta launched Surprise-and-Delight in 2012 and it quickly became the talk of sites like flyertalk.com and thepoints guy.com, prompting United to roll out a version of its own with a Mercedes the following year. Not to be outdone, American followed up with a Cadillac transfer program in 2014. Like the Delta offering that spawned the trend, transfers are bestowed at the discretion of the airline, rather than according to a set formula. "When that Porsche pulls up next to your plane people really notice," said Gary Leff, a frequent traveler who writes about his experiences in a blog called View from the Wing. "Faces contort and people say 'Who is this person?'"

Whether they are riding in the Porsche, the Mercedes, or the Cadillac, it's typically not a member of the very top tier shown on each airline's frequent-flier website, like Executive Platinum on American or Diamond Medallion Status on Delta. Instead, these envy-inducing doses of intermittent reinforcement are reserved for members of the semisecret, invitation-only circles created by the airlines to distinguish the crème de la crème of elite fliers. Otherwise rational investment bankers and consultants discuss these secretive societies in the hushed tones Harvard undergraduates reserve for membership in the Porcellian Club or Yalies use to describe being tapped for Skull and Bones. The first of these was United's Global Services, followed by American's ConciergeKey and most recently Delta introduced Delta 360°.

Besides the usual upgrades and other perks, members of this elite cohort are showered with personalized attention. "It doesn't cost the airline much but the whisper factor is huge," says one consultant who belongs to Global Services and ConciergeKey. Another member, a Wall Streeter who earns several million dollars per year, can barely contain his glee as he describes being summoned by name to the American gate and allowed to board first as a ConciergeKey flier, long before run-of-the-mill Platinum status holders, let alone families with small children or active members of the military. In other cases, if a flight is canceled, an American representative will meet him and escort him onto the first available alternate flight. Sometimes, the extra attention, he admits, can be a little creepy. "They call me when I'm on the way to the airport and ask if I have luggage and do I need a hand? I don't." Other times, he revealed, "American will have someone walk with me from the luggage carousel to the taxi stand at LAX. In Brazil fine, but I don't need that in L.A. You end up having to make small talk with a stranger."

What the Surprise-and-Delight service shares with super-elite Ivy League clubs is that the standards for admission are opaque—and that's intentional. Besides the element of intermittent reinforcement, the unexpected and mysterious way these favors are handed out creates what Palmatier has found to be another powerful emotion that drives customer loyalty—gratitude.

"Rule clarity diminishes the positive effect of a reward on target customers' gratitude," Palmatier and coauthor Lena Steinhoff wrote in a 2016 paper. Moreover, "Surprise triggers emotions for customers, because events that deviate from expectations elicit strong emotional responses. Compared with rule-based, contractual rewards, discretionary non-contractual rewards then should create stronger feelings of gratitude." If all that weren't enough, the fear of losing that mysterious super-elite status and being relegated to the ranks of more typical travelers keeps beneficiaries very, very loyal. Every year, the consultant said, the airlines receive hundreds of letters of appeal from crestfallen fliers who've been dropped from ConciergeKey and Delta 360°, begging for a second chance.

For the airlines, there are additional advantages to keeping these clubs invitation-only, with no set criteria for admission. Promotion through conventional tiers like silver, gold, and platinum is done by computer according to miles flown and money spent. But when it comes to inclusion in Global Services, ConciergeKey, and Delta 360°, "there is significant managerial oversight about who they let in the door," according to one Wall Street analyst who covers the airlines. "These programs are about influencing the people who influence travel at companies." That might mean including a Hollywood studio boss in ConciergeKey, on the assumption that if she talks about her great experience on American, more junior colleagues will follow her lead. Or reaching deep into the organization chart of a *Fortune* 500 client and inviting the person who oversees travel and entertainment spending to join Delta 360°, even if he flies less than some other executives.

As befits a hierarchy built on envy, these secret programs have one final advantage—by being so mysterious and behind the scenes, they minimize malicious feelings among bystanders. While studies like the one by the professors at France's ESSEC Business School suggest visibly imposing on lesser customers boosts loyalty among the favored ones, big companies remain wary of doing this too openly, Palmatier said. In his opinion, "providing visible rewards to target customers at the expense of bystanders (making them wait while others get services) might be a dangerous strategy. The strong negative effects generated among bystanders overwhelm the relatively smaller positive effects from targets."

Whether via envy or gratitude, the Velvet Rope Economy's fusion of technology, loyalty programs, and the age-old human need for status has changed the game for consumers. And that's left even some veterans of the marketing world deeply uneasy with what they see as the rise of something approaching a caste system for customers.

Russell Lacey is one of them. A marketing professor who worked in the corporate world before entering academia, Lacey now teaches at Xavier University in Cincinnati, a Jesuit school that has shaped his thoughts on fairness, and yes, the power of envy. "I teach in an environment that encourages faculty to consider the moral dimensions of business and the greater good," he said. "Consumers are becoming increasingly divided." As the ranks of customers become more fixed, and the Velvet Ropes rise in more and more spheres, Lacey has become increasingly uncomfortable. Companies that once balked at these practices in earlier marketing efforts, he said, are now either leading the charge or reluctantly going along.

"Intentionally or unintentionally, we are creating an economy that benefits some people while putting others in a lower tier that provides them with less service," Lacey said. "It's divide and conquer. And in this time of division, emboldened companies are much more overt about treating people differently. We are asking, 'How do I get in that special lane, how do I get in that inner circle? I deserve it.'"

The result of this unease has been a shift toward exclusivity, the topic of the next chapter. Delta opened a separate airport entrance for Delta 360° members and other premium customers at LAX, so their fast lane isn't even visible to fellow fliers stuck in the slow lane. It's not just an American phenomenon. Among the most sought after secret air societies internationally is Lufthansa's HON Circle. What makes it so special? Not merely separate lounges or even a Mercedes for passengers switching planes, which the German carrier provides, just like its American counterparts. What sets the HON Circle apart is a separate *terminal*, in Frankfurt. These elite travelers may take the same flight as everyone else, but they wait separately and are ferried directly to the plane when it's time to board.

First-class ticket holders on American Airlines now enter through a special door at New York's John F. Kennedy International Airport and other terminals across the country. From there, they proceed to a separate check-in area to drop off their bags or print boarding passes. Then it's off to the front of the security line, and for these select customers, an elevator ride up to the lounges for elite passengers. All of this takes place away from the prying eyes of coach passengers, who board after elite passengers have found their seats.

First and business class passengers on American are directed to the new Flagship Lounge. Craft beers, locally sourced farm-to-table food, La Colombe coffee, and plush armchairs await. Even here, however, some places are still off-limits to all but a few. Behind another pair of frosted glass doors is the Flagship First dining room, and its gleaming marble floors and white tablecloths are reserved strictly for first-class passengers. Like a Haven for the haves and have-mores, the Flagship First dining space was created by American so first-class fliers felt they had something exclusive for themselves that mere business class travelers couldn't partake of at John F. Kennedy International Airport in New York.

Unlike the envious but mostly resigned main cabin passengers who accept their fate as they file through business and first class, these well-heeled business class customers have a habit of exploding when they are barred from the Flagship First dining room. American Airlines employees have been trained to gently talk them down, or at least steer the envy from malicious to benign. "Never say 'You aren't allowed in there,'" one veteran employee confides. "Always say, 'Your ticket doesn't give you access.' You have to be careful to never personalize it." It's true—the Velvet Rope isn't personal—it's business.

2.

Exclusivity

L ong before I take my seat just steps from the field in the exclusive Legends section of Yankee Stadium on a picture-perfect fall Sunday, it's obvious that the experience won't bear the slightest resemblance to my memories of seeing the Bronx Bombers as a kid in the 1980s.

The setting is the same—the South Bronx—although this neighborhood, once synonymous with urban decay, arson, and crime, has finally been touched by gentrification's reach in the last decade or so. Craft beers and micro brews are on tap at the Bronx Draft House near the stadium, which also serves up quinoa and farm-to-table salads, a far cry from the pizza parlors, burger joints, and bodegas that used to be the only dining options in the area. But neither hipster pleasures like those nor the now safe walk from the No. 4 subway station to the game could have prepared me for the gleaming edifice that replaced the House That Ruth Built. Opened in 2009, the new Yankee Stadium is as scrubbed and bright as an upscale mall, with some of the same amenities, such as its own Hard Rock Café.

But unlike a mall, where anyone can walk into even the most expensive stores, my day at the game will be as tiered and exclusive as a visit to a Manhattan nightclub—all that's missing are models and bottle service. Indeed, while nightclubs represent the original Velvet Rope experience, the experience and allure of exclusivity is as powerful at stadiums today as it was at Studio 54 back in the day. The old Yankee Stadium had nineteen luxury boxes and suites—its successor has seventy-eight. If that weren't enough, there are also 4,700 premium club seats at a myriad of different price points and levels of exclusivity.

At the apex of this pyramid is the Legends Suite. That's clear as my friend Jared and I walk past the long lines of fans waiting to go through security and enter the stadium. As soon as we flash our Legends tickets, the guards welcome us like old friends and wave us through the exclusive Suites Entrance by Gate 4, where the queues melt away. For a moment, I remember going into the old stadium with my grandfather—a sea of humanity pressed shoulder to shoulder passing through turnstiles into a dark, dank tunnel edged by concession stands. Only after that ordeal could fans make their way to their seats, and whether the ultimate destination was a skybox or the bleachers, everyone made the same not-so-grand entrance.

My grandfather is long gone, and so is the egalitarian spirit of the old stadium, which opened in 1923 when he was a student nearby at Morris High School and tickets to a game cost 25 cents. Legends seats run $500 to $1,000 each, among the most expensive in Major League Baseball, and for that you are whisked past the metal detectors that have replaced turnstiles into a bright hotel-lobby-like space where greeters are waiting. They direct fans to exclusive, minutely tiered sections, from entry-level boxes on the mezzanine level to midlevel suites in the Champions area, and finally to Legends. There, extending outward from home plate toward first base on one side, third base on the other, and taking up the first several rows up from the field itself, are the best seats in the house.

But before the first pitch, it's time to partake of the food in the Legends Suite, an upscale dining room with stations from some of the best Manhattan dining spots. Everything is free, and the usual ballpark fare like hot dogs, hamburgers, and ice cream is available for kids. But their parents make a beeline to the buffet for more refined offerings like swordfish ceviche, a raw bar overflowing with shrimp, or Italian specialties from the day's featured restaurant, Fresco by Scotto. Jared heads for the sushi as I try out the brisket and, with my grandfather in mind, a kosher hot dog. The game is starting but few fans are rushing out to see the action on the field, even though they can have the food delivered by waiters to their seats. Instead, they sit at tables or lounge on couches and sample the delicacies and drinks, only occasionally looking up at the game now playing overhead on huge screens.

I experience a brief flashback to the grimy concession stands at the old stadium, where lukewarm frankfurters emerged from a bath of cloudy water and the floors were caked with blackened chewing gum from games past. The truth is, for all my nostalgia and egalitarian impulses, the Legends Suite is pretty nice. But before I head down to finally see what I've come for—the game—I notice there's an area that's off-limits even to fully paid up Legends ticket holders like us. I glimpse a bar, gray suede couches, and more TV screens, before the guard closes the frosted glass doors. It turns out that when it comes to exclusivity, there always has to be a sanctum sanctorum to remind you that you really haven't reached the pinnacle. In this case, it's the Harman Lounge, which the guard tells me is reserved for fans sitting in the very front row of the Legends sections. We're in the second row, and though the Harman Lounge is nearly empty, there are no exceptions.

Not that anything is wrong with the second row, it occurs to me as I take my padded seat. It's calm, there is ample room to spread out, and no one is shouting or cursing or spilling beer on me like I remember. In fact, many of my fellow Legends fans aren't even watching the game—they're looking at their phones. Still, like almost all exclusive Velvet Rope settings, the experience is *very* seductive. Not only do I have amazing views of the game, but I feel special. That's the thing about the Velvet Rope Economy, I realize, then and there. Even as I see how segmented and stratified the Legends section is and acknowledge I could never afford to take my kids there, life inside the Velvet Rope is pretty good. (As a reporter for *The New York Times,* I'm not allowed to accept free tickets or other favors. I paid $700 apiece for my Legends seats—covering the Velvet Rope Economy can be expensive.) And the seductiveness of it all—addictiveness may be a better word—makes it easy to push away any thoughts of just how thoroughly sealed off we are from the other 50,000 or so people in the park.

Research scientists have discovered ample evidence that the impulse for exclusivity runs deep, and directly tracks the evolution of the human brain. The dean of these academic experts is Robin Dunbar, a British anthropologist and evolutionary psychologist. After initially studying the frontal lobes of nonhuman primates like the gelada baboon, Dunbar broadened his research to better understand the social habits of Homo sapiens. As brain size increased, he found, so did the maximum number of relationships primates could successfully manage. Dunbar's number, as it has come to be known, represents the maximum number of other human beings with whom we can have what Dunbar calls "a genuinely social relationship." The human brain is larger than that of its fellow primates, so as this limit expanded, it conferred an evolutionary advantage when we were still hunter-gatherers and moved about in clans or bands.

For contemporary humans, this theory is known as the social brain hypothesis. Dunbar places this limit at around 150 people. And as he and other scientists have shown, that figure crops up in a host of different historical eras and human contexts. In extant hunter-gatherer societies studied by anthropologists, the size of a typical band stands at 148.4, which is not much different from archaeologists' estimate of the population of a typical village in ancient Mesopotamia. The basic fighting group in most modern armies—a company—falls in the same range. Given the human brain's inherent capacity to remember and process information, the theory goes, larger groups end up being unmanageable and prone to fissure.

Since Dunbar's research in the early 1990s, he and other researchers have delved into what he calls the layers or circles that exist within and beyond that broad group of about 150 people. The smallest group includes three to five people, which Dunbar terms a support clique, and provides "personal advice or help in times of severe emotional and financial distress" to its members. The "sympathy group" is the next largest circle with twelve to twenty members, and "characteristically consists of all the individuals with whom one has special ties; these individuals are typically contacted once per month." Next are thirty- to fifty-member bands, followed by the clan or regional group numbering up to 150. Above these are the megaband (500 individuals) and the tribe (1,000–2,000 individuals). It's these findings that illuminate why more limited, exclusive gatherings are so appealing to even the most modern, tolerant human beings.

In the last five years, Dunbar and his colleagues have found this pattern of groupings repeated in everything from layers of friends on Facebook to Twitter followers to players in online computer games. In a 2016 paper, "Calling Dunbar's Numbers," scientists analyzed the mobile phone records of six million customers at a European cell phone carrier, then divided their contacts into groups according to how frequently they talked. The dialing habits matched up with the patterns outlined in the social brain hypothesis. It turns out that suites and skyboxes at modern stadiums closely follow the evolutionary blueprint laid out by Dunbar for the most evolved primate, the human being. At Levi's Stadium, home of the San Francisco 49ers, suite capacity typically tops out at about twenty, in line with Dunbar's sympathy group.

These findings suggest that the need to keep a certain number of individuals close to us, while driving everyone else away, is something we're born with. And just as cruise ships and airlines utilize feelings of envy for their own benefit, so marketers in the Velvet Rope Economy profit off the deep human need to divide the world into us and them. Sporting events, musical performances, and other live events increasingly reflect this phenomenon. Proximity to the game is only half the appeal—the rest lies in being in a club that others can't afford to join.

If the desire to separate one's own group from the rest of the population goes back to prehistory, the link between sports and exclusivity goes back almost as far. The Roman Colosseum, erected at the whim of the emperor between A.D. 70 and 80 and built by slaves, was as segregated by class as the Roman Empire itself. The antecedent of today's skyboxes was a reserved box for the emperor on a raised tier above the action, which was called the cubiculum. There, in full view of the audience, Caesars could recline and watch gladiatorial combat between man and beast and other fare.

Nearby, Roman nobles and senators had slightly less elevated boxes of their own, some of which bear the names of their former occupants to this day. Plebeians, or commoners, sat higher up in the stands, with the poorest of the lot way up in what we now call the nosebleed seats. Former gladiators were forbidden to enter the Colosseum, as were actors and gravediggers. We're a little different: the closest thing to former gladiators we have today, retired pro football players, are not only welcome at modern-day versions of the Colosseum, they're a frequent attraction for autograph seekers in the elite suites and clubs that dot American stadiums today.

Despite this ancient historical precedent, until relatively recently American stadiums were remarkably egalitarian. That was true both in terms of ticket prices and how fans rubbed shoulders at the game. During the 1963 World Series, when the Yankees faced off against the Los Angeles Dodgers at the latter's new stadium, bleacher tickets cost just $2, or $16.50 in present-day dollars. The most expensive seats sold for $12, equivalent to $100 now. Glassed-in skyboxes, corporate suites, and the club seats that are a hallmark of stadiums now simply didn't exist.

A 1955 visit to Rome by a Houston lawyer turned mayor turned entrepreneur named Roy Hofheinz would change all that. Determined to bring big-time sports to Houston but knowing local fans would never want to sweat out games in a hot, humid stadium during the city's fearsome summers, Hofheinz discovered the answer— wait for it—in the Colosseum. To block out direct sun or rain during gladiatorial contests and other games, he learned, Roman engineers would extend what was known as a velarium, or awning, over the crowd. Inspired by this, as well as by those boxes reserved for the emperor and other nobles, Hofheinz spearheaded construction of the Houston Astrodome. "The bread and circuses of Rome made for an apt symbol of what Hofheinz hoped to achieve for Houston," Robert C. Trumpbour and Kenneth Womack write in their history of the stadium, *The Eighth Wonder of the World: The Life of Houston's Iconic Astrodome*. "Hofheinz hoped that the profound luxury of the new indoor sports facility would build pride in a fast growing Houston."

When it opened in 1965, not only was the Astrodome the first covered, climate-controlled American stadium, it was also the first to feature glassed-in, exclusive skyboxes. Tickets to the original Colosseum may have been free, but seats at its modern-day Texas successor were anything but. The Astrodome's fifty-three skyboxes helped cover the cost of Hofheinz's dream—they retailed for $15,000 each for the season, or $122,000 today—and they were quickly snapped up by Houston's business elite. "Hofheinz boasted that the Astrodome had a higher percentage of fans from the upper income brackets than you'd find in any other park," said Benjamin D. Lisle, a professor of American Studies at Colby College and the author of *Modern Coliseum: Stadiums and American Culture*. Lisle said the opening of the Astrodome redefined how Americans watch sports. Prior to its construction, a combination of low ticket prices and little segmentation made stadiums "a place where a lot of people could afford to go and recognize each other as part of the broader urban community," he explained. "That is certainly no longer the case and it started with the Astrodome."

Hofheinz was keenly aware of the role of exclusivity as he designed his stadium and marketed what would be the first skyboxes.

In a nod to the Caesars who had inspired him, Hofheinz created a Presidential Suite, and managed to get President Lyndon Johnson to come to an opening exhibition game against the Yankees in April 1965. (Hofheinz had worked on Johnson's Senate race in the 1940s.) "People wanted to be part of that luxury and it was a transition point," Trumpbour said. "A real president had been in the suite, and people were thrilled to say they had been up there even if the views were better on the ground." It was an important lesson— sometimes exclusivity trumps quality.

Opening night for the hockey season was two weeks away and Jim Nagourney had a problem. Actually twenty-four problems. It was September 1985 and Nagourney, the vice president for administration of the New York Islanders, had spent the summer overseeing the construction and marketing of twenty-four new luxury suites. Fans of the Long Island hockey team were snapping up the suites, which featured two rows of four seats each—plus a bar and a sofa. The $50,000 price tag, or more than $6,000 per seat for the season, didn't seem to be causing any sticker shock. Most of the suites had already been sold and paid for when Nagourney got a call from the team's architect at the Nassau Veterans Memorial Coliseum, where the Islanders played.

"I made a mistake," the architect told Nagourney. "We can get four plush theater seats in the front row but only three in the back row." Decades later, remembering the call still gives him chills. "My heart skipped several beats," he recalled. "I had sold them as eight seaters and couldn't go back and say sorry, you only have seven."

Then Nagourney had a brilliant idea. "I told the architect to use four fixed theater seats in the front row and scatter four high-end leather desk chairs around the living room area. There will never be a time when people in the suite pull all four of those chairs into the second row to watch the game." It worked—Nagourney said he never received a single word of complaint about the improvised seating plan.

"Luxury features have little to do with watching the game," he said. "Ever notice those TV shots of an NFL owner in his suite, maybe three people with him in the front row? The rest of his guests standing in the living room area, sipping drinks and paying little attention to the game? Being in that suite, or any suite, makes one a member of the elite but not necessarily a member of the fan club."

The timing of the Islanders' decision in 1985 to install luxury boxes wasn't an accident—the team had just come off four consecutive Stanley Cup victories. But it also coincided with a turning point in the development of the Velvet Rope Economy. In 1981 and then again in 1986, President Ronald Reagan signed legislation that not only lowered taxes overall, but sharply cut the tax rate for the highest earners. By making the tax system less progressive, the rich suddenly had more money to spend. Meanwhile, the stock market was booming in the mid-1980s, further adding to the spending power of the richest Americans.

And perhaps most importantly, the Reagan years fostered a profound shift in what Professor Emmanuel Saez calls cultural norms. In this case, it was American attitudes toward privilege, exclusivity, and the ability to pay to jump the line. "The Reagan administrations radically changed not only policies but more deeply social norms regarding inequality," he told me. "The combination of policy and social norm changes unleashed a surge in income inequality. What we learned is this: greed is good when you have the power to exercise it for your own benefit and bad when you are on the receiving end."

The reverberations would be felt throughout society, from housing and shopping to rock concerts and theme parks, but nowhere was the shift as fast or dramatic as in sports. In spite of the initial success of the Astrodome, luxury seating and elite suites caught on only slowly amid the economic malaise of the 1970s and the deep recession of the early 1980s. The boom of the Reagan years would change that, as would the reluctance of local taxpayers to foot virtually the entire bill for new stadiums. Combined, these forces turned pro sports arenas into the Velvet Rope Economy's playground.

They also explain why 1985 marks a fault line between what

sports marketing professors Dennis R. Howard and John L. Crompton term the Public Subsidy Era and the Transitional Era in stadium construction. Besides the macroeconomic forces outlined above, two smaller changes in public policy at the time contributed to the shift. Beginning in 1984, funds from the sale of tax-exempt bonds could no longer be used to finance luxury boxes. Even more significantly, the same 1986 tax reform legislation that further cut rates on high earners also forbade local governments from using tax-exempt bonds to fund stadiums built for a single occupant, i.e., a professional sports team. These changes were intended to force rich team owners to put up more of the money for construction themselves, instead of relying on public largesse. It didn't work out as planned— the teams turned to their richest fans to fund most of the construction costs, and many sports-hungry local governments continued to chip in for ancillary expenses.

The first two venues to be (mostly) financed privately were Joe Robbie Stadium, which opened in 1987 and hosted the NFL's Miami Dolphins, and the Palace of Auburn Hills, which opened the following year as the home of the NBA's Detroit Pistons. These were the first to feature what would soon become standard—private suites overlooking the game, luxury boxes, and premier individual seating. The new facilities broke the mold, Howard and Crompton write. Until then, sports venues were all pretty much the same and featured few amenities. Most seating was bench or bleacher style. Space was tight, too, just sixteen to eighteen inches allocated for each seat.

The Palace would be as significant for the stadiums that followed as the Astrodome had been a generation before. With 180 suites and two thousand club seats, the options for fans were unprecedented. Even better, all of the construction costs were covered by the sale of premium seating. Envious team owners and the Big Four professional sports leagues—the National Football League, Major League Baseball, the National Basketball Association, and the National Hockey League—immediately saw dollar signs. "The success of the Detroit Pistons' arena precipitated what might be called a Palace Revolution," as Howard and Crompton put it. "The Palace was the first to demonstrate the income-generating capability of a fully loaded sports venue. Its success prompted owners across all leagues to seek their own sport palaces." For sports fans and stadium goers, the Transitional Era in stadium design was over. The Fully Loaded Era was about to begin.

Building on what Roy Hofheinz started in Houston, and what individual execs like Jim Nagourney did in the mid-1980s, the extravagantly tiered Palace struck a nerve with fans even before it hosted its first game on November 5, 1988. The appeal of those early exclusive seats and suites—and their even more expensive successors today—can be explained better by economics than athletics. They are what economists call "positional goods." Enlarging upon Thorstein Veblen's theory of conspicuous consumption, economist Fred Hirsch used this term in the 1970s to describe products whose price was determined by their scarcity and desirability rather than their underlying utility. In fact, the most expensive positional goods may actually be inferior in some ways to lower-priced versions of the same product, but the status they confer on the owner more than makes up for it.

Think of Roy Hofheinz's Presidential Suite at the Astrodome— the views were much better from seats lower down near the field, but they lacked the exclusivity of the elite presidential perch. The most extreme positional good in sports, according to Victor Matheson, a professor of economics at Holy Cross, may be the black upholstered chairs the Boston Celtics roll out each game. These are placed on the floor of Boston's TD Garden for deep-pocketed fans who want seats next to the bench where the players sit. To tell the truth, the view is better from conventional courtside seats—seats five rows up from courtside at basketball games actually provide the best views, but don't bother telling that to Jack Nicholson, Spike Lee, and other courtside habitués. Whatever they lack in utility, selling these seats on the actual floor has, for the Celtics, proven to be

very smart: they cost $2,500 each and are invariably sold out. Typi-
cally they are reserved for owners, season ticket holders, corporate
sponsors, and VIPs.

"When you get that seat, someone else doesn't," said Matheson.
That makes it even more appealing than the usual positional goods,
like Mercedes cars or Louis Vuitton handbags, which are always
available if you can afford to pay enough. "There's only a couple of
these and everybody sees that person sitting on the floor. And one
single chair is equivalent in price to a whole section of seats in the
upper deck."

What if there were a way to apply the exclusivity of that chair
on the floor of the Boston Garden to a more widely available positional good like those two thousand premier seats in the Palace?
A sports marketer by the name of Max Muhleman in a second-tier
sports venue discovered there is. The personal seat license, which
guarantees a specific seat for the season in perpetuity, has come to
be loathed by many fans. But it started as many misbegotten things
do, with good intentions.

Muhleman came up with the idea of granting seat rights as a
way of saying thank you to fans in Charlotte who put down deposits
for prospective season tickets when the city was vying for a new
NBA franchise in the mid-1980s. It was all very informal by the
standards of the sports business, then and now. The rights consisted
of a personal letter from the team's owner, George Shinn, informing
the first ten thousand season ticket buyers that they now possessed
charter rights to their seats in a new arena.

Whether these Charter Seat Rights, as they were called, could
be sold or transferred wasn't addressed, and after Charlotte landed
the team that would become the Hornets, Muhleman didn't think
much about them. That is, until he glanced at the classified section
of *The Charlotte Observer* over coffee one weekend a couple of years
later and stopped short. The new team had led the league in attendance during the first season, eventually selling out 364 games in a
row, and Hornets tickets were now a hot commodity. Looking at the
tiny classified print, Muhleman saw an ad from a fan offering those

Charter Seat Rights—and the opportunity to buy two sold-out season tickets—for $5,000 each. Curious, he dialed him up on the spot. "Is this right?" he asked. "It's right," the rights seller responded. "And I should have asked for $10,000 each because you're the fifth or sixth caller and I'm tired of answering the phone." It was a revelation for the courtly southerner. "I thought to myself, What hath we wrought?" he told me in an interview some three decades later.

When another area businessman, Jerry Richardson, decided to really put Charlotte on the map with an NFL expansion team in the early 1990s, and asked Muhleman for marketing help, seat rights were a natural step. Selling the rights quickly became make-or-break when the aspiring owners found out the league wanted a $140 million fee from the lucky city that would win the new team, much more than they had anticipated. That left almost nothing to build the stadium where the as yet unnamed team would play. "We didn't have time to try and go for public funding and we didn't want to use public money anyway," said Tamera Green, then a senior vice president at Muhleman's company. "This was our only chance—it was a Hail Mary."

Richardson's lawyers suggested renaming the seat rights personal seat licenses and they proved critical to Charlotte's bid. Still, the rights were controversial. As Aaron Gordon noted in his *Vice* article in 2015, "Franchise owners were already skeptical of Charlotte's privately-financed stadium plans, and PSLs had never been used to raise money for a construction project before." To overcome local suspicion, Richardson called a press conference to announce the PSL sale, and took out full-page ads in *The Charlotte Observer* detailing how rights holders would be uniquely entitled to their seat. There was skepticism initially—even Tamera Green found her own family to be among the doubters. "My husband said it would never work," she recalled.

It worked, though. Boy did it work—Muhleman realized it the day after the deadline to sign up and buy the PSLs had passed. "We knew we had to get at least $10 million out of the barn door," he recalled. "After going through the envelopes, we had $40 million on the first day. We were blown away." So was Roger Goodell, who was overseeing the expansion process as a young executive at the National Football League, and is now the NFL's commissioner. PSL prices ranged from $600 for a corner seat in the upper deck to $5,400 for a seat down near the 50-yard line. Muhleman's firm eventually sold 62,000 seat licenses. That enabled Charlotte to beat out rival bidders from Baltimore, Jacksonville, Memphis, and St. Louis. Looking back, Muhleman said, "I'm astounded by it. I never dreamed PSLs would be such a phenomenon."

For professional sports teams, the PSL opened the floodgates for a new source of fan dollars, and in turn, stadium construction. By the time the Carolina Panthers played their first game in 1995, boffo PSL sales had set the stage for a stadium building boom. Between 1990 and 1994, $4.2 billion was earmarked to build fifteen new sports venues. Between 1995 and 1999 that number had more than doubled, and thirty-four stadiums and arenas would be erected at a cost of nearly $11 billion. The cost of a stadium began to rise, too. Adjusted for inflation, Bank of America Stadium, the Panthers' new home, cost $222 million when it opened in 1996. Less than a decade later, in 2003, new stadiums would open for the Chicago Bears and the Philadelphia Eagles—each costing more than half a billion dollars. By 2008, the Indianapolis Colts' Lucas Oil Stadium would cost nearly three quarters of a billion dollars.

With each new stadium, the arc of rising PSLs and ticket prices put attending a game further out of reach for more fans. Although PSLs are now widespread in pro sports, nowhere has the impact been greater than in football, where the limited number of games and intense fan bases have made PSLs a gold mine. And whatever the blue-collar roots of some teams—think Pittsburgh Steelers and Houston Oilers—most working-class fans find it all but impossible to afford tickets for an actual game in the PSL era.

The irony isn't lost on Muhleman.

"The fan base in football was always blue-collar and we spent a lot of time figuring how to price tickets and PSLs so people weren't priced out," Muhleman recalled. "Owners would say to me, 'Are we leaving anything on the table?' I'd say, 'Yes, we are.' I suggested leaving some seats without PSLs so the average fan could afford to buy them as one ticket for one game, not a season ticket. Greedier owners, and there have been some, would never go for that. But it's inevitable that sooner or later you will lose fans, even in the NFL. And if you read comments online about PSLs from fans now, it sounds like war. I'm afraid some PSLs are hurting the attitude of fans."

Chad Estis couldn't believe his ears. Early in his career, he'd sold premium seats at the Palace of Auburn Hills for the Detroit Pistons, and learned exactly how to court rich fans. Later, he was chief marketing officer for the Cleveland Cavaliers when LeBron James was rookie of the year—rendering the need to actually market the team all but superfluous. But as Estis listened to Dallas Cowboys owner Jerry Jones describe his vision for the team's new stadium, Estis couldn't help feeling nervous. "I was uneasy," said Estis, who'd joined the Cowboys as their top sales executive in 2006 just as Jones and the Cowboys were gearing up to raise the money to build their next stadium. Initially, the budget was set at about $700 million but the estimated cost quickly blew past $1 billion and no one seemed to know how high it would eventually go. "Jerry just kept adding amenities as the revenues came in," said Estis. "I was wondering, 'Is this whole plan going to work?'"

By the time the first fan walked through the door, Cowboys Stadium had been nicknamed Jerryworld. And the success of America's Team, as the Dallas Cowboys like to be known, did as much to change sports as the Houston Astrodome did two generations earlier. In Estis's view, the new Cowboys stadium took many of the innovations in earlier iterations of sports luxury and propelled them to the next level. As a result, the already rising Velvet Rope was much more imposing than ever before. The arena's eventual price tag—$1.3 billion—cemented its ranking alongside Yankee Stadium as the most expensive American sports complex when the two facilities opened in 2009. What's more, the Cowboys and the Yankees, with some help from Goldman Sachs, would go on to spread this version of exclusivity and over-the-top luxury to football stadiums, basketball arenas, and baseball fields across the country in the decade since then.

Before we can understand why the opening of Jerryworld was such a watershed, it's critical to see what made it different from all the other sports venues that had come before it. Simply put, the team's decision to focus their marketing efforts not on the merely prosperous or even wealthy upper-middle-class fans, but on the very rich.

This elite cohort goes by different names—the one percent, the superrich, the mega-wealthy—but whatever you call them, the top PSL price of $150,000 per seat made clear who the target audience was and why everyone else was shut out. The timing couldn't have been better: Estis went to work in Dallas soon after huge new fortunes in technology, energy, and finance had begun altering what it meant to be rich in America but before the collapse of Lehman Brothers and the Great Recession temporarily stopped the music.

"We segmented from premium to super-premium," said Mike Rawlings, who served as chairman of Legends. "A special bar, special treatment, hot and cold running waiters. We wanted people to feel like they were at a high-end hotel, not just getting access to good food in a separate area." As in Houston during Roy Hofheinz's time, sports and politics have a way of mixing—Rawlings was elected mayor of Dallas a couple of years after the new stadium opened. But although he now has to appeal to the masses in that public role, he's refreshingly candid on the subject of catering to the very, very rich. "The key is not to be afraid of market segmentation," Rawlings explained. "There was a belief in sports, especially football, that it was outdoors, you bring your thermos and put your parka on, and that's how you participate."

Jerryworld—now officially known as AT&T Stadium—offered a very different vision. "We had forgotten a segment that liked football and wanted to be part of it but didn't want to be tailgaters," Rawlings said. "There are circles of intimacy and you're selling that intimate experience to a tighter circle. You can't do it for thousands of people, but there are hundreds of people that want it and will pay for it." If Robin Dunbar were to exchange studying primate behavior for sports marketing, he couldn't have said it any better.

Finding—and closing—that kind of elite ticket buyer was the task of Estis, the Cowboys' top sales representative. Despite his initial doubts, and to his own surprise, he found there were plenty of willing customers. "I was in Cleveland selling for seven years and I literally knew all the wealthy people that could afford to buy those seats. I could go around the floor and tell you their names and companies." Dallas was a different story, Estis told me. "When we started creating these concepts for the stadium, the wealth of a city like Dallas blew me away. It was a little shocking that people were coming into the center and spending $600,000 for four PSLs."

Six-figure PSLs were a whole new price point in professional sports. But what Estis calls the "value proposition" at AT&T Stadium is more than comfy seats with great views of the game. "People from elite demographics are used to convenience in all the other aspects of their lives," he said. "They want good service and quality food, to get in and out of the stadium easily. Once it starts in one area, they want it elsewhere and so the football stadium is going to offer something similar."

The Cowboys' stadium was designed to physically accentuate exclusivity. In addition to separate entrances and parking zones for elite ticket holders, entire premier sections were now off-limits to ordinary fans. So while members of elite tiers like the Founders Club or the Owners Club could mix with each other, they don't—and can't—mix with the hoi polloi. "We are creating spaces where people can interact with people from other clubs," said Estis. "You can go in the elevator from the valet parking area straight to the suite and the club. You can see people you know, mix, network, and go watch the game."

The Founders Club and Owners Club are the elite of the elite. With a total capacity of 93,000, Cowboys Stadium features 15,000 club seats, and PSLs range from $150,000 for the top clubs to an entry-level $16,000 license. That represents a high-water mark for professional sports, according to Howard and Crompton, the authors of *Financing Sport*. "The Dallas Cowboys were the first team to take full advantage of seat license sales in 2008," they write. "Up until that time, PSL prices had remained relatively modest, averaging around $2,000, with premium seat licenses generally in a range from $5,000 to $10,000."

Football season ticket holders everywhere are also obligated to buy individual tickets for eight regular and two preseason games, which in Dallas cost $350 each for a typical club seat, so in addition to the initial investment in the PSL, holding on to a pair requires an annual payout of $7,000. Considering that the median household income in Dallas stands at $64,000, the caste system on display at AT&T Stadium gives the Roman Colosseum a run for its money. "I've been doing this for twenty-five years and I started out getting paid $16,000 a year to make cold calls," said Estis, who is forty-eight. "I've seen the shift in my career. People's willingness to spend on the top tier has grown significantly."

In early 2008, as the billion-dollar stadiums that would house the Cowboys and the Yankees were nearing completion, a Goldman Sachs banker named Gerry Cardinale sat down with Jerry Jones on the Caribbean island of St. Barth's. Technically, the two met just offshore on the waters of Gustavia Harbor, aboard the yacht of Mike Ovitz, the Hollywood agent and dealmaker. Cardinale was familiar with both the sports and entertainment worlds, having helped launch the Yankees' YES cable TV network, and later negotiating Alex Rodriguez's $300 million deal in 2007 to stay with the team. "I said to Jerry, 'We've got to figure something out,'" Cardinale remembers telling the Cowboys owner. Cardinale suggested they find a way to capitalize on what he termed the intellectual property of the two soon-to-open, billion-dollar arenas. "That's a fancy way of saying let's monetize the fans that are coming in and out of those stadiums," Cardinale said. The objective, he explained, was to bring together the two most valuable sports franchises and create a new, premium product.

Jones loved the idea, and soon Cardinale was crafting the business plan for what would become Legends. This firm would essentially do to the rest of sports what the Yankees and the Cowboys had done at their own new stadiums—erect a Velvet Rope everywhere in sight, with a myriad of tiers, and then watch fans respond. Each team would own a third of the company, with Goldman Sachs controlling the final third and putting up the cash to get Legends off the ground. The timing was tricky—the mortgage meltdown was gathering speed and within months of Legends' launch, the collapse of Lehman Brothers would bring Wall Street and the economy to its knees. But Goldman being Goldman, and with the Yankees and the Cowboys being the most iconic teams in their leagues, the deal came off. Chad Estis, who blew the doors off in the PSL selling campaign for the Cowboys, would be the sports start-up's top sales executive. "We just airlifted Chad and his group into Legends," said Cardinale.

The result has changed the experience of going to a pro or college game in America. In one city after another—Minneapolis, Atlanta, Los Angeles, San Francisco and for college teams like Notre Dame and the University of Oklahoma—the Legends' formula of exclusive sections, elite amenities, and increased ticket prices and revenue are now a fact of life. More recently, Legends has moved beyond its initial expertise in hospitality and ticket pricing to also oversee project management, making sure the concrete is delivered on the right day and the stadium opens on time. All told, the company envisioned by Cardinale and Jones on that yacht in St. Barth's is now worth more than $750 million. And Cardinale is not done—as we will soon find out.

Gerry Cardinale has since become an apostle of the Velvet Rope Economy in sports. He's not a jock in the conventional sense, although he was on the crew team at Harvard and later rowed at Oxford, where he was a Rhodes Scholar. But Cardinale recognized the financial rewards that raising the Velvet Rope in sports could bring before anyone else on Wall Street did. And as the head of private equity investing at Goldman Sachs, he had access to billions in capital and could do more than any particular team owner or investor could. "There had been an unbelievable escalation of asset values in teams," said Cardinale. Stadiums and infrastructure hadn't kept up with those valuations, he said, "and I come in and close that gap. We wanted to create a new paradigm."

There are certain telltale signs of a Legends stadium, all of which were pioneered in Dallas. Separate entrances for premier seat holders and a plethora of different clubs, each one more elite than the next. In the most exclusive one, the players run through on the way from the locker room to the field just before the start of the game. So when Legends takes on a new project, those proven winners are incorporated into the design of the new stadium, along with additional bells and whistles to justify the ever higher ticket prices and stadium construction costs. "The Cowboys rewrote the rulebook," said Al Guido, who served as a sales manager on Estis's team. "Hundreds of millions of dollars in seat license revenue in Dallas woke up the league. People started coming to us for help but we got tired of giving free advice. With Legends, the feeling was: Hire us."

The first paying customers for Legends were the owners of the San Francisco 49ers, the DeBartolo and York families. They were eager to find a new home for the team after decades at aging Candlestick Park. It was built in the late 1950s and had virtually none of the profitable amenities a new stadium would offer, like club seats and high-end food and dining options. Naturally, using fan money in the form of PSLs to pay for new stadiums is good for owners, but the peculiar economics of professional sports magnify the appeal. Football teams, for example, must share 40 percent of the revenue from television rights and ticket sales with the league, while retaining the other 60 percent. But according to Roger Noll, a Stanford economics professor, teams get to keep 100 percent of the revenue from high-end restaurants, as well as amenities like valet parking. "If I'm going to spend an additional $1, it's much more profitable to expand concessions or install Michelin-starred restaurants," said Noll, one of the nation's top experts on the economics of sports. "You get to keep it all and the stadium becomes a marketing device."

To keep the 49ers, the city of San Francisco wasn't willing to go beyond a $100 million subsidy voters had approved in 1997, so the team looked further afield and settled on Santa Clara, forty miles to the south in the heart of Silicon Valley. Santa Clara kicked in the equivalent of $130 million and Goldman Sachs and other big banks provided crucial loans. But the biggest chunk of funding for the new stadium would come from the sale of seat licenses, which Al Guido of Legends would oversee. The 49ers were the NFC divisional champs in 2011 and 2012, which made Guido's sales job easier, as did a geyser of new wealth from the boom in tech stocks like Apple, Google, and Facebook and a host of fresh IPOs. The stage was set for an epic event in Velvet Rope sports, with the team itself committed to raising over 90 percent of the stadium's $1.3 billion cost.

PSL inventor Max Muhleman's admonition to owners to "leave a little on the table" for fans was quickly forgotten in the burgeoning Legends era. "The success of the Cowboys program encouraged the San Francisco 49ers to adopt an aggressive seat license pricing structure," Howard and Crompton write in *Financing Sport*. "Although well under the Cowboys' highest prices, the 49ers imposed seat license fees on 61,500 seats—virtually all of the reserved seating for sale in what is now Levi's Stadium."

The end result is a facility whose layout and atmosphere have more in common with a country club than a raucous sports arena like Candlestick Park. At Levi's, the entire stadium is honeycombed with elite clubs and gathering places with price points that vary according to comfort level and the view of the field. The east side of the stadium is dominated by suites and club seats, which are more padded and puffed out than their ordinary, hard plastic counterparts. There are several entrances designated solely for premium seat holders, and valet parking is available. There is a wine club, Appellation 49, where oenophiles can sample the top vintages from nearby California vineyards and beyond. Fans looking for a slightly grittier experience—but still within a few yards of their suites and club seats—can head down to Bourbon Steak and Pub, the stadium outpost of San Francisco chef Michael Mina. Here, for $5,000 per season, the Michelin-starred chef re-creates a tailgate party on game day, minus the cars, plastic cups, George Foreman grills, and everything else normally associated with a barebones stadium parking lot tailgate.

But pride of place goes to the BNY Mellon Club. With its hardwood floors, plush gray carpeting, and recessed lighting, it resembles a corporate conference center. Stanchions keep out fans from the nearby East Field and Citrix clubs so only BNY Mellon Club members can watch the team's players run from the locker room and out onto the field. Once that running-of-the-bulls-like show is over, members can then stand nearby in what local wags have taken to calling the "Tequila Bunker," or take seats in a partially glassed-in area a few feet from the sidelines.

At the old Candlestick Park in the 1980s, all tickets cost a uniform $64 per game, according to Andy Dolich, a veteran front office executive who worked for the 49ers from 2007 to 2010. At Levi's, he said, "the prices range from 'That's really expensive' to 'Are you shitting me?'"

Al Guido and other team executives say they are keenly attuned to making games special for all fans, not just the nine thousand or so who sit in elite seats and suites. The stadium's design does make it surprisingly intimate for an arena with nearly seventy thousand seats, and even spots high in the upper deck provide a fairly good view of the field below. For all the high-end watering holes, there are dozens of concession stands where a high ratio of servers to guests keeps wait times short during games, team officials point out. It's whistle-clean, family-friendly, and was among the first in football to have gender-neutral bathrooms. As Guido points out, the stadium is also easily accessible via commuter rail from Oakland and San Jose, which benefits all fans, no matter where they sit. The same goes for ultra-fast free WiFi and other tech touches aimed at making the experience of a piece with always-on, wired Silicon Valley. It's certainly been a success for the owners. After Levi's Stadium opened in the summer of 2014, the value of the franchise rose 69 percent to $2.7 billion, the biggest one-year jump ever for an NFL team. "Presto!" *Forbes* wrote in its annual Most Valuable Teams in the NFL survey in 2015. "The team's revenue from ticket sales, sponsors, concessions, luxury suites and non-football events jumped 160% from the previous season."

But since the move from Candlestick Park in San Francisco, fans have murmured that on any given Sunday in the fall, something's missing. "A stadium is a team's heart and soul but there are more velvet ropes at the game than at the Oscars," said Dolich, the former 49ers executive. "The stratification and the slicing and dicing has changed the tenor of live spectatorship, as has the inability to walk around a venue." What's more, after a series of losing seasons in recent years, the 49ers discovered that deep-pocketed fans aren't as loyal as their middle-class brethren during the inevitable lean years. Although Legends and Al Guido's sales team found buyers for every seat in the house when it was built, on some Sundays in recent years, the stadium sits half empty. Die-hard team supporters call these fair-weather friends "bandwagon fans"; indeed many seat holders on the fortunate side of the Velvet Rope admit they've stopped going for the most part. "If someone offered me $10,000 each for my PSLs, I'd take it in a heartbeat," said Jonathan Coslet, a Bay Area investment executive who holds three seat licenses that he bought for $30,000 each in 2014. "The team has gotten crappy and it's no fun going anymore."

That hasn't lessened the pressure to drum up new revenue opportunities.

Through its "Golden Opportunities" program, the 49ers invite the most loyal fans to purchase special experiences like attending the postgame press conference, walking on the field before the game, or even flipping the coin to see which side will get the ball after kickoff. An empty area behind one of the end zones is being converted into on-field seating. "I can only create so much beachfront property," said Guido.

. . .

Back in New York, on the refrigerator door in the pantry of RedBird Capital Partners, there is a picture of Gerry Cardinale at Super Bowl 50 in 2016. He is standing next to John Elway, the legendary former quarterback who now serves as general manager of the Denver Broncos. Cardinale is gripping the giant Super Bowl trophy the Broncos just won. For Cardinale, holding that trophy at that moment on the field moments after the big game was what the psychologist Abraham Maslow called a peak experience. But for Cardinale, it wasn't just a personal peak—it was a business epiphany. After the initial shock of holding the trophy wore off, he thought, "How do I monetize that? How do I create a business around that? It's a work in progress but I'm in the business for the long term. The best businesses are the ones where the fan comes first."

In 2012, Cardinale left Goldman to start his own firm, Red Bird Capital. Friends, he said, "thought I was having a midlife crisis." But the subsequent success of RedBird Capital assuaged their fears. With an initial investment from the Ontario Teachers' Pension Plan, plus contributions from many of the families Cardinale worked with at Goldman, RedBird now has $2 billion under management.

RedBird's success underscores how the rise of the Velvet Rope Economy is no longer propelled just by companies like Royal Caribbean, Norwegian, Delta, or other members of the *Fortune* 500 out to improve their bottom lines. In the last five years, hedge funds, private equity giants like Carlyle, and Silicon Valley venture capitalists have all recognized how profitable catering to the top one percent of households can be. Their reach and financial resources are just as great, if not greater, than the *Fortune* 500. And in many cases, they are more agile and willing to push the envelope in terms of market segmentation than old-line corporations.

Cardinale is using that financial firepower to spread the Velvet Rope Economy one sporting event and concert at a time. The vehicle is a private company called On Location Experiences, which began as a small-time subsidiary of the NFL and was located in the basement of their Manhattan headquarters. Cardinale saw the potential and persuaded the league to broaden its horizons. Now a stand-alone company with RedBird as an investor, On Location Experiences has moved out of the NFL's basement. And it's got its eye on much more than PSLs or seats at games.

Officially, On Location describes itself as a "premium experiential travel & hospitality company that partners with iconic rights holders to offer once-in-a-lifetime experiences." In reality, it's more like a pure play on exclusivity. For the Super Bowl, On Location offers up a week of events to coincide with the big game. One night it might be seats up close at a concert with Jennifer Lopez and P. Diddy, as in Minneapolis in 2018, followed by the Dave Matthews Band the next night. Or stepping onto the field during the half-time show and rubbing shoulders with players. In other words, the Super Bowl is no longer about just the game but a series of experiences, all of which are choreographed by On Location, from wheels-up and rides to hotel rooms to meet-ups with NFL Hall of Fame members.

To capture a bit of Hollywood glamour, On Location worked with *Vanity Fair* to create a Super Bowl version of the magazine's famous Oscar party for the San Francisco game in 2016. On the guest list were celebrities like Amy Adams and Jon Bon Jovi, athletes like Alex Rodriguez, tech luminaries like Susan Wojcicki of YouTube and Uber's Travis Kalanick—along with purchasers of On Location's $15,000 weeklong Super Bowl package.

"We brought *Vanity Fair* to the Super Bowl and threw a party," Cardinale said. The Super Bowl may be one day of the year, "but we are selling it all year long." With the NFL as a minority partner, On Location receives 9,500 tickets to the game. That limits the supply available to ticket brokers in the secondary ticket market, he said, making it less of a Wild West–type process for fans while yielding a bigger profit for On Location and the NFL. "I look at the Super Bowl as content and I own 15 percent," Cardinale said, referring to those 9,500 seats.

Is there really demand for this kind of thing? The answer is yes, according to Roger Noll, the Stanford economics professor. "Busi-

nesses create subsets of the population that gain some sort of exclusive right if they pay enough," Noll said. "The reason you have
all this segmentation is because people are willing to pay not to be
ordinary. I don't find it to be something I'd pay for but I know I'm
in the minority." Cardinale agreed, but he puts it in a more positive
light than Professor Noll. "People want choices and they are willing
to pay for those options," he told me. "People are dying for the Velvet Rope." The numbers for On Location back him up. In 2018, On
Location's revenues from the Super Bowl and associated festivities
totaled more than $150 million, quadruple the haul two years before
in San Francisco.

The way Cardinale sees it, supplying exclusivity and one-of-a-
kind events in conjunction with games and concerts is a natural
response to the way normal content has been "commodified." He
means that in the age of Sonos and streaming, Netflix and chill,
when you can watch games at home on a giant 75-inch LED flat
screen TV that sells for less than the cost of a $2,000 PSL, you
have to give people something *very* special to get them off their
couches. "Technology has screwed everything up," Cardinale said.
"It has changed the way fans consume content and made the live
event more valuable. Experiences are the one thing that can't be
commoditized—the live event cannot be TiVoed."

It's a few hours before Beyoncé takes the stage at the Coachella
Valley Music and Arts Festival near Palm Springs and the desert heat
is rising. But inside the Safari Lounge tent, the vibe is languid and
the air is cool. Guests sit in lounge chairs under palm trees, enjoying cocktails and air-conditioning provided by industrial-strength
chillers. There's a widescreen TV showing the warm-up acts, and in
between sets a DJ spins vinyl, but the millennial crowd is too busy
flirting and looking at their phones to pay much attention. Bar service begins at 8 a.m. with mimosas and continues until 1:45 a.m. the
next morning. In between there are foodie favorites to choose from,
like BBQ pulled-pork sandwiches and a never-ending supply of fruit

water to beat the heat outside. Except for headliners like Queen B, there's almost no reason to venture outside the soaring tent into the General Admission scrum.

This isn't the VIP zone at Coachella (we'll get to that) but the people here would certainly qualify as VIPs as far as the other 125,000 festival goers are concerned. Hidden away in a corner of the Empire Polo Grounds, where Coachella takes place, the Safari area is far from the rest of the Coachella crowd. The latter either stay in hotels or camp in the jam-packed parking lots, but this zone is where glamour meets camping—better known as glamping. For $9,500 each, festival goers can book a deluxe individual tent, which sits on a slight platform so their queen-size bed doesn't even have to touch the ground.

Then there's what's known as the Resort at Coachella. The festival is well known for drawing a trendy Hollywood crowd and any of them would feel comfortable in one of the Resort's ten yurts, which cost $35,000 for a three-day weekend. Putting the tents to shame, the yurts feature king beds and a sitting area, along with private showers and a dedicated golf cart driver on call. With passes that provide guests entrée to a viewing area by the stage, the fortunate few in the yurts might as well be staying at the W or another hip but luxurious hotel.

There's plenty of demand: the tents and the yurts sold out by Christmas, even though tent prices jumped by $1,000 between 2017 and 2018, while the going rate for a yurt was bumped up $10,000. The man who makes sure the Safari tents and the yurts are ready for demanding guests is Dan Berkowitz, a rumpled forty-year-old music promoter and former band tour manager who is the chief executive of CID Entertainment. A unit of On Location Experiences, CID (it stands for Consider It Dan) oversees the luxury accommodations, handles sales and bookings, and generally makes sure the golf carts are waiting and the champagne is cold when yurt guests arrive.

On Location has been gobbling up firms that handle live events and acquired CID in 2017, extending the firm's reach into live music.

The company offers what they call "enhanced experiences" at Metallica concerts, as well as the Bonnaroo festival, and introduced the concept of a VIP area to country music concerts. "In many respects, music might be a bigger opportunity than sports," said John Collins, a veteran sports executive who is the chief executive of On Location.

If those invite-only tents and exclusive amenities go against country and rock music's anti-authority, stick-it-to-the-man roots, well, that's a contradiction Berkowitz is willing to live with. "It's a very sensitive issue," Berkowitz acknowledged as we drove through the sprawling festival grounds, describing how many music fans already suspect that promoters, venue operators, and concert managers are out to make every last buck they can. "If you prove them right, and you don't care about the general admissions experience, it's over."

"We're not pretending," he added. "I bought general admission tickets for Phish and Bonnaroo and I know that experience intimately. But there was a time I wanted more. When I was in my twenties and following Phish, I'd sleep in a dorm room on the floor. Now I'm not." Festivals like Coachella were born in the late 1990s and early 2000s, and although fans in their twenties may still make up the base, older, richer concert goers now want something luxurious and exclusive. But in contrast to cruise ships or the boarding area at the airport, where special treatment is designed to be noticeable, Berkowitz said the key to exclusivity at Coachella is to do it in an unobtrusive way. That way, ordinary ticket buyers are less aware of what they are missing.

This is why the Safari tents and Resort yurts are so secluded. "You can't find them," he said. "There's a speakeasy vibe." There are no accommodations in the official VIP ticket zone, which is a gated area away from the main stages. VIP passes cost $999 each as opposed to $495 for general admission tickets, and holders can spread out around picnic tables and chairs or grab drinks at one of several bars and watch from afar. Major hipster food groups like kombucha, poke, and organic sausages are available from pop-up restaurants.

Just as significant to the democratic vibe, exclusive access during the actual performances is limited to a small roped-off area just off to the side of the stage, not a big velvet rope smack in the middle of the venue. Tent and yurt dwellers receive artist passes to enter—the hordes of lesser VIPs don't. "You don't take over the front row," said Berkowitz. "That detracts from the experience." And unlike Levi's Stadium, where even the main gates are named for corporate sponsors like Toyota, Intel, and Dignity Health, Coachella's organizers have kept the branding away from where the music is performed. "They want to be the best festival on earth for the next twenty years," Berkowitz said. "It's a long-term vision, and it's why the VIP section is further away than the general admission area when the artist is onstage. To close that deal, you go there. If you want to get down and dirty, come up front."

It's a few minutes before David Byrne takes the stage and Berkowitz and his wife, Dee, are surveying the crowds and looking beyond at the palm trees, sand, and mountains that ring the Coachella Valley and lend the festival much of its appeal. Although Berkowitz is as responsible as anyone for the Velvet Ropes at Coachella, he feels he's found that elusive Pareto optimal balance that delivers exclusivity to those who want it without taking away from everyone else's experience. "The energy of the collective experience leads people to needing, wanting to go to Coachella," Berkowitz said. "They're dying to go. How sad would that be if there were a barricade there?"

For the most part, Coachella and Berkowitz do manage to walk that fine line. The one percent can enjoy their tents and yurts and air-conditioning in seclusion, while ordinary fans still have the opportunity to make their way to the front of the stage for Beyoncé if they like. In the Legends section at Yankee Stadium, people sitting further back can no longer walk down to the field with their kids for a close-up view of the players or the chance to get an autograph. What fans call "the moat" seals off the Legends section from everyone else; guards and stanchions ensure no one sneaks past. Just as America has become less egalitarian, so has big-league baseball.

"I was obsessed with getting players' autographs as a little kid," said Keith Petrower, who is now thirty-three but remains devoted to the Yankees. "Of all the things in the new stadium, the moat outraged me the most. Even if you didn't have seats close to the field, you could always walk down for autographs."

On weekdays, or when the Yankees aren't facing a feared rival like the Boston Red Sox, Legends can be nearly empty, Petrower said. Some of that has to do with ticket prices but in other cases "it's because most people are prone to spend one inning in their seats and eight elsewhere." In fact, the section right behind home plate belongs to Legends, so on TV it can look like no one is at the game. "It's one thing on an airplane or a cruise ship," Petrower said of the rigid stratification that Yankee fans are now subjected to. "But this is sports, it's supposed to be America's pastime. They don't have to rub our noses in it."

Even some Yankee players have complained that the end result of all that tiering is a deadened experience for everyone concerned. In his memoir, *The Closer: My Story,* pitcher Mariano Rivera wrote, "It doesn't hold noise, or home-team fervor, anywhere near the way the old place did. . . . The old Stadium was our 10th man—a loud and frenzied cauldron of pinstripe passion, with a lot of lifers in the stands. Maybe I'm wrong, but it's hard to see that the new place can ever quite duplicate that."

Incredibly, the wave of stadiums that opened most recently could make Yankee Stadium seem downright democratic by comparison. Nowhere are the extremes in wealth in America more obvious than in San Francisco, where even Silicon Valley millionaires feel puny compared to their billionaire peers. The home team of the latter are the Golden State Warriors. In 2019, they moved out of the old Oracle Arena after half a century in Oakland and into a sparkling new $1.4 billion arena in San Francisco, the Chase Center. One of the best teams in basketball, the Warriors were national champions in 2015, 2017, and 2018—a run that coincided with tens of billions in stock market riches flowing into the Bay Area. The team's majority owner is Joe Lacob, a partner at the famed venture capital firm of Kleiner Perkins Caufield & Byers. And the list of minority owners reads like a Who's Who of Silicon Valley.

For wealthy fans who don't have a shot at a license because they weren't season ticket holders in the Oracle Arena, theater boxes have been created in the Chase Center. These four-seat mini-suites between the lower and upper bowls in the new arena can be had starting at $350,000—*a year.* It's an eleven-year commitment, with that annual bill rising to $470,371 by the end, bringing the total sum due to $4,482,629. "There are a lot of things in life and in Silicon Valley that are mechanisms for absorbing all the wealth in the world," said Fred Harman, a hugely successful venture capitalist with Oak Investment Partners. "Modern art is one. Floor seats are another."

Just as going to a game shifted from being a blue-collar pursuit to a white-collar one a couple of generations ago, now even well-off professionals and midlevel executives find themselves priced out, with only the top one tenth of one percent left in the desirable seats in the stands.

David Smith, a San Francisco ad man, had been a season ticket holder at Warriors games with the same group of friends since 1974. They had good seats at the Oracle Arena—five rows up from the court, directly behind the bench. "When you yell at the coach, he hears you," Smith said. Years ago, the tickets cost less than a hundred bucks per game, but that rose to $370 in recent years at Oracle, an increase he was willing to live with.

From his home six blocks away, Smith could watch the gleaming new Chase Center in Mission Bay going up, so he had high hopes when he went with his pals to meet with the Warriors sales team and get a preview of what he hoped would be their new digs. First, Smith said, they were told the Warriors were no longer a basketball team but an entertainment company. Then came the sticker shock, not to mention the suite shock. The seats they would be assigned were a full section further back than before, having been moved to make room for a suite that previously sat higher up. To add insult to injury, the cost of the seat license was $36,000, ticket prices were hiked to $600 per game from $370, and there was a thirty-year commitment that he was pressured to sign on the spot. Otherwise, they would offer the seats to the next group that walked in the door.

Then and there, Smith and his friends walked out. As much as he was tempted, there was no way he could justify laying down that $36,000 plus $25,000 per season, even if he split it with a friend. Smith owns a media buying company with thirty employees but as far as the Warriors were concerned, fans like him no longer mattered. "It's the end of an era," he said. "I'm a normal, affluent guy, but you have to be extraordinarily affluent to play in this game."

With prices like that, even technorati who can afford to pay that kind of sum worry that the Chase Center will just be another showcase for the wealth of an extremely tiny sliver of the population. Fred Harman is one of them. But he's not just another tech titan— he's a co-owner of the Warriors, both under Joe Lacob and the previous owners. He's seen the team's fortunes wax and wane over the years—he recalls when the most expensive Warriors ticket cost $400. But unlike many in Silicon Valley, he acknowledges something is amiss, both in sports and in the broader society. "I've been going to Oakland for games for years," he recalled. "It's a sea of humanity cutting across all socioeconomic boundaries. I can't imagine how it's going to maintain that diversity."

3.

Ease

For as long as he was the boss, Dick Kinzel fought the good fight. As chief executive of Cedar Fair, one of the nation's largest theme park operators, Kinzel watched as rivals like Six Flags and Universal began charging customers for what industry insiders call front-of-the-line access. Compared to the standard profit margins in the amusement park industry, these companies were minting money with products like the Universal Express Pass or the Flash Pass at Six Flags, which cut wait times by as much as 90 percent for the select few who can afford it.

Kinzel first encountered front-of-the-line access charges at Universal in Orlando in the early 2000s and he didn't like it. To him it was nothing more than paying to jump the line, and that rubbed him the wrong way. "I didn't want people to feel like they were second-class citizens because other people had paid a higher price and were passing in front of them," Kinzel explained. "I was always afraid it would be Joe Sixpack vs. the wine crowd."

Kinzel comes by his sympathy for blue-collar Americans naturally. He grew up in Toledo, where his father owned a tavern, back when the city was known as the glass capital of the world. After a year of college in Wisconsin, he dropped out and worked at a vending machine company for a decade. "I just filled the machines and went where they told me to go," he said. Later, he worked his way up from the bottom at Cedar Point, the company's original park in Sandusky, Ohio, starting as an assistant manager in food service in 1972. By the time Cedar Fair went public in 1987, he was on the inside track for the top job. "I was purely an operations guy," Kinzel recalled, noting how he'd walk through the park every morning before going to the office, picking up litter or pulling an operator aside if something on a ride looked amiss. "When we did our IPO, I was an executive who knew nothing about finance. I was put in as CEO by the New York bankers."

Over the next quarter century, Cedar Fair grew by leaps and bounds, acquiring Knott's Berry Farm in California, Paramount's chain of parks, and other properties. But the company never lost touch with its midwestern, working-class roots, hosting special days for autoworkers from the Honda factory in Marysville, Ohio, and other nearby auto plants. The company's stock was a lackluster performer during much of his tenure as CEO but Kinzel was more focused on pouring Cedar Fair's limited capital into bigger and badder roller coasters.

"Highest, steepest, fastest—people just loved it and it worked," he recalled. When the Magnum XL-200 ride opened, it was the tallest and steepest roller coaster in the world, and the lines, naturally, were long. Kinzel kept Cedar Point open till 2:30 a.m. on the busiest nights so everyone who waited was guaranteed a ride. Despite pressure to compete with archrival Six Flags, which began charging more aggressively for front-of-the-line access after a 2009 bankruptcy filing, Kinzel stuck to his guns. "We could see it coming and my team said we got to do it economically, but I fought it all the way to the end," Kinzel said.

Within days of Kinzel's retirement in January 2012, his Disney-trained successor, Matt Ouimet, called the troops together at Cedar Fair headquarters. An accountant by training, Ouimet spent years in the finance and business development departments at Disney before working at Starwood, the hotel chain, and Corinthian Colleges, a for-profit education chain that later went bankrupt. Among the very first action items on Ouimet's list was a charge for front-of-the-line access, and Cedar Point's Fast Lane pass quickly debuted. It made for a much less egalitarian experience for guests—but the charges were a gold mine for Cedar Fair, and Ouimet proved to be an able financial steward for the company. By the time he stepped down as chief executive in early 2018, Cedar Fair's shares had doubled.

Indeed, the privilege of jumping the line commands a very high price in the Velvet Rope Economy. Take the helicopter service Blade—for ordinary New Yorkers getting to the airport can entail a two-hour schlep via congested highways. For $195, or three times the price of a taxi, Blade's choppers bound over the traffic and get deep-pocketed travelers from midtown Manhattan to John F. Kennedy International Airport in minutes.

These and the other companies we will meet in this chapter are selling something more subtle than jumping the line. No bottlenecks, no traffic jams, no long waits on the phone for customer service—when ease is for sale, all these can be bypassed for a price. So it has become a central strategy of American business to provide a means to make the hassles melt away for those who can afford it. And the desire for ease has proven to be what economists call price inelastic—no matter what the price, affluent consumers are still willing to pay up for it.

"The premium customer doesn't want to be asked questions," said David Clarke of PricewaterhouseCoopers. "They don't want friction. They want things to happen through osmosis."

Dick Kinzel may have been the last theme park executive to believe all guests should be treated equally but he had a highly distinguished predecessor: the man who invented the modern American amusement park, Walt Disney. Well before the opening of Disneyland in Anaheim, California, in 1955, Disney had ruled out creating different classes of guests, or making life easier for a favored few. Disneyland was meant to be "the happiest place on earth," and there was no room for class conflict in Walt Disney's idealized world.

"If you look at the message of Walt Disney from the beginning, it was that we are all alike," said Todd James Pierce, author of *Three Years in Wonderland: The Disney Brothers, C.V. Wood, and the Making of the Great American Theme Park.* "We all deserve a place at the table, we all deserve a meaningful type of equality. Walt's ethos was pervasive in his lifetime and the park was never meant to be a place where people were stratified." Pierce tells the story of how the Reverend Billy Graham toured Disneyland with Disney and remarked how nice it was to see people from different races and ethnicities and classes all visiting the park. "This is the real world," Disney told the evangelist. "The fantasy is out there in the world."

In the decades since Walt Disney's death in 1966, financial realities in the form of corporate raiders, impatient investors, and demanding Wall Street analysts have gradually eroded the founder's egalitarian vision. But the company has resisted the temptation to openly stratify the customer experience the way the Yankees and other sports teams have, or as Royal Caribbean does on its cruise ships. It's not that Disney doesn't make life easier for guests who have more money to spend—they do. But Disney's tiers are unobtrusive enough or so expensive as to make them go virtually unnoticed most of the time.

"Disney has perfected the art of the soft sell," said Robert Niles, editor of *Theme Park Insider,* a news site devoted to the industry. "Disney is always looking for ways to make money but they don't want it to look like they're doing it aggressively." Admission to the parks certainly isn't cheap—from $104 to $149 per person for Disneyland in California, or $109 to $125 at Walt Disney World in Orlando—but inside the parks "the goal is to segment in a way that everybody still feels special," Niles said. "People are buying a fantasy here, they're buying an escape, and they don't want to be confronted with class division while on vacation."

Disney's pas de deux begins with FastPass, originally a paper-based system, but now a digital platform with a phone-based app. The version at Walt Disney World, known as FastPass+, allows visitors to make bookings for rides at specific times weeks or months in advance. California's Disneyland has a more limited version, simply known as FastPass, with same-day reservations only. At each attraction, whether it's a classic like Pirates of the Caribbean or a new hit like Avatar Flight of Passage, visitors are presented with two lines. One is the standby queue, where the waiting time can easily take an hour or more. The other is a line clearly marked as FastPass+ at Walt Disney World or FastPass at Disneyland, which guests are ushered through in about ten minutes or less.

It feels like a manifestation of the Velvet Rope Economy. But there's a twist that lets the company cling to Walt Disney's commitment to treating everyone the same way: three FastPass+ bookings are included in the basic ticket price at Walt Disney World. As we shall see, there are ways for higher-spending guests to make things easier for themselves, or get extra shots at the most popular rides, and generally skip just about every line in the park. But giving everyone at least three FastPass+ rides at no extra charge reduces resentment at what's known as the "merge point," the place where the standby and FastPass+ lines come together. After all, FastPass+ allows everyone to skip the line somewhere.

Like the personal seat license at sports arenas, the FastPass idea began with egalitarian intentions. Lines had bedeviled Disneyland from the moment it opened, as *The New York Times* headline the day after made clear: "Disneyland Gates Open: Play Park on Coast Jammed—15,000 on Line Before 10 a.m." Orlando's Disney World was similarly swamped after it debuted in 1971, except now the hordes were stuck in line sweating under the blazing Florida sun. Too many customers might seem like an enviable problem to have, but that was never the feeling at Disney headquarters. On the contrary, they worried that too many guests were dissatisfied because of the long lines.

Within the industry, Disney is seen as the gold standard—it is to theme parks what Boeing is to making aircraft or Coca-Cola is to selling soda. Like General Electric in its prime, Disney executives are frequently poached by competitors and have gone on to run smaller chains like Cedar Fair. One of the keys to success has always been data. Disney surveys its guests most days of the year, carefully monitoring overall guest satisfaction, as well as their intent to return in the future and willingness to recommend the park to friends.

"You have to manage by data," said Steve Brown, a onetime Disney executive who went on to run Accesso, the main provider of virtual queuing systems that enable rivals like Six Flags and Cedar Fair to charge for front-of-the-line access. "On a cruise ship you've got two thousand people—that's a piece of cake. At Disney you can have fifty to sixty thousand people at one time."

The busiest time of day in the park, according to Brown, is between noon and 2 p.m., when visitors who came in the morning have yet to leave even as families are starting to pour in for the afternoon. "All that people remember is that hump in the middle of the day," said Brown, who carried a clipboard and walked around surveying visitors early in his career, before rising to the post of vice president of revenue management and product development. "They go home and tell their friends about it."

Lines have other drawbacks, too. "If people are in long queues, they're not spending on food or toys," Brown said. "Take them out of a line and they can access the cash register and spend money." What's more, having guests stuck for hours waiting for a few popular rides meant capacity on all the other attractions was being wasted. "All those hours were spoiling, like unsold rooms in a hotel," Brown said. "We had to push people into the corners of the park." At the same time, Disney's data revealed that as visitors were able to take more rides and participate in more experiences, their satisfaction rose, as did their intent to return. That made Disney's engineers even more desperate to limit the lines. "Everything else—food, rain, you name it, it's noise," Brown said. "How do I boost rides per capita? How do we take people who are stuck in line like cattle and get their butts in a ride?"

If Bruce Laval didn't happen to be a skier, FastPass might never have been born. Laval joined Disney World as an industrial engineer in 1971, after a brief stint in the aerospace industry at Cape Canaveral, and he was among the first at the company to put the then new technology of computers to work in managing the park. Laval made a name for himself in the 1970s by using a computer simulation to show that adding more trains to the monorail wouldn't save time, but would actually increase delays. Higher-ups were skeptical at first, but Laval's computer models demonstrated that fewer trains operating at higher speeds were the way to go if the park wanted to increase the monorail's capacity. Despite that success, longer waits for rides were becoming a pressing problem for Laval. Each year in the 1980s and early 1990s, as park attendance surged, Disney executives feared the growing queues would undermine guest satisfaction.

Walt Disney himself may have been gone but his prohibition of special treatment lived on, so simply charging to jump the line was out. Laval contemplated creating a computer-based reservation system, but if visitors made reservations and then failed to show up, unused seats on rides would pile up. Then one winter Laval went skiing in Colorado and noticed that there were two parallel queues for the ski lift. One line was for groups, the other was for single skiers going up the mountain alone. Each gondola could hold four skiers, so when there was a spot left over from a group of three, someone from the singles line would fill that extra seat. Every gondola headed up the mountain full, with no wasted space.

"That was the key to making it work," Laval told me. "If you had a standby line at the ride, you could always fill any capacity left over from the virtual queue created by a reservation system." Working with a team of engineers, Laval created a computer program that would assign a portion of visitors individual ride times, freeing them up to shop, eat, or try out less popular rides before they got aboard Big Thunder Mountain Railroad or the Jungle Cruise at the appointed hour. Meanwhile, the standby line would let people simply roll up to the ride and wait if they so chose, in the process filling in any gaps left over as holders of what would become FastPass boarded.

"There was a tremendous amount of skepticism," Laval recalled. "Nobody believed that you could successfully have a reservation system for attractions." Laval employed a gambit he first used during the monorail episode—he suggested a test to his superiors. "The only way I would be able to convince them would be with a series of tests," he said. "Tests allowed me the opportunity to try something controversial while eliminating threats to the status quo and the people who created the status quo. You're giving them an opportunity to prove that they're right. Even though I was 99 percent sure what I was suggesting was going to be successful, I figured the best way to get management to try something was by testing it."

In this case, that meant creating two cohorts. Both groups were given a coupon for dinner as an incentive and asked to keep a detailed diary of everything they did in the park, which rides they took, where and what they ate, and how much stuff they bought. At popular rides, the first group was given a ticket with an assigned time and told to come back and show it to a Disney employee so they could get on immediately. The second group, the control, would wait to get on with everyone else. "It was very dramatic," said Laval. "We tested it at Animal Kingdom, which was the newest park at the time, and people with FastPass saw 25 percent more attractions and their wait time was reduced by 50 percent. What they did was eat more, shop more, and see more entertainment. Their satisfaction level went off the charts and their intent to return was higher. The data proved it worked, and that was the justification for what was a very expensive system to implement."

Then and now, there was debate within the company about whether to charge for FastPass, but at the time Walt Disney's lingering influence was strong enough to discourage it, according to Steve Brown. "The legacy of Walt was powerful," he said. "It was different in the 1990s. There were people at the company then who had actually worked with him and embodied that culture. FastPass was never about the Velvet Rope."

There were kinks at first, to be sure. At the merge point, workers had to be trained in how to board guests from each line onto rides. Frustration builds when hot and sweaty people get to the front of the standby line after a wait of forty-five minutes or more, only to see dozens of cool FastPass holders blithely pass by in front of them. The key, said Laval, is letting two or three FastPass families go, and then immediately let a standby group proceed, rather than let dozens from either side stream on at one time. "I fought very hard to get people trained in how to work the merge point because not everybody is qualified." For Laval, whose name is on Disney's patent for FastPass, it's a point of pride that the service was and remains free. "When we sold the system, we were selling it on guest satisfaction," said Laval, who retired in 2001 but spends part of the year in Orlando and visits the park frequently. "That's more important than making an extra twenty bucks today. It will generate an extra visit."

FastPass may not come with an extra charge but that doesn't mean all park guests are equal. In the years since Laval retired, Disney has crept ever closer to monetizing FastPass, while also creating different tiers, albeit in a much more understated way than rivals like Universal. For example, Walt Disney World allows guests at its hotels to book FastPass+ reservations up to sixty days in advance of a visit vs. thirty days for everyone else. "It favors the people who have the money to stay at one of the Disney properties," said Martin Lewison, an associate professor of business management at Farmingdale State College who has studied the amusement park industry. "They can snatch up all the reservations for the most desirable rides." More recently, Disney launched a pilot program at Walt Disney World that allows guests on the club floors of its hotels, where rooms can cost $650 a night, to receive three additional FastPasses per day. Hotel guests enjoy other benefits, too, like being able to book meet-and-greets with Disney characters, along with dinner reservations at park restaurants, well in advance of other visitors to the park. Hotel-based perks like these are a sign, Disney-watchers say, of how the company is much more willing to segment within its resorts than at its parks.

Florida's Disney World continues to grow in popularity, nearly a half-century after it opened, as does Disneyland in California, which is nearing its sixty-fifth birthday. In 2017, Disneyland welcomed 18,300,000 visitors, compared with 16,769,000 in 2014. The Magic Kingdom, the oldest of the four parks that make up Disney World and the most popular attraction of its kind in the world, hosted 20,450,000 attendees, a jump of more than one million from 2014. As overall attendance rises and more Disney hotel guests take advantage of FastPass—there are more than two dozen hotels spread throughout Disney World—the lines for both FastPass and standby are growing. But for the truly rich, Disney has a little-known way around that problem—or really any problem.

It's called the VIP Tour and it doesn't come cheap. For $425 to $625 per hour, well-heeled guests can reserve an individual VIP guide who is something of a magician: she or he can make lines disappear. Disney doesn't heavily promote its VIP Tours, which have to be booked for a minimum of seven hours and can accommodate up to ten people. It doesn't have to—there's plenty of demand, even though key details like the price or the seven-hour minimum engagement are buried deep in the fine print on Disney's website.

My family's tour began with Kelly picking us up at Disney's Contemporary hotel in a white Chevrolet Suburban that she'd decorated with rainbow and star magnets to delight my four-and-a-half-year-old daughter, Willow. The gates to the Magic Kingdom are five minutes away, but we don't head for the main entrance to the park, where crowds have already formed, waiting to get in. Instead, Kelly takes us around to a back entrance, where she drops off the car in an employees-only parking lot, but not before a group of other guides meet us with water and stickers for Willow. Kelly escorts us to the Town Square Theater, where there's a forty-minute wait to meet Mickey Mouse—but not for us. VIP guides possess an unlimited number of FastPasses so we breeze on in, and before I know it Willow is hugging Mickey.

Next up is Cinderella Castle and the Bibbidi Bobbidi Boutique, "an enchanted beauty salon that offers magical makeovers for young princesses and knights." Reservations sell out quickly and usually have to be made months in advance, but VIP guides can often secure them just days in advance. While Willow is busy picking out a pink costume and glitter and choosing between a bevy of hairstyles, Kelly ducks out to retrieve coffee from Starbucks for my wife, Annalise, and me. With Willow suitably attired in princess gear from head to toe, we head across the way to the popular Seven Dwarfs Mine Train ride. Willow's never been on a roller coaster, and Annalise is already queasy at the prospect of getting aboard, but Kelly assures us it's tame enough. There's a 115-minute wait for the three-minute ride, but we cruise to the front on the FastPass line. I look back at the standby queue snaking its way into the sun and feel a twinge of guilt. But it's already time to board, and the merge point is handled so smoothly we barely notice the two groups coming together.

Kelly tells us that FastPasses occasionally run out on popular rides at peak times like noon or 1 p.m. "It's like Black Friday," as she puts it, but that's never a problem on the VIP Tour. At a handful of hot attractions, though, like the Haunted Mansion, the Dinosaur ride, and Flight of Passage, the wait on even the FastPass line is too long. In these cases, Disney "backdoors" special guests through entrances normally reserved for cast members. Disney has also created what they term "perceived value entrances" for VIP Tour members. In other words, a way to bypass the shortcut when that's no longer short enough.

The VIP Tour is an exercise in ease. Kelly points out where the hard-to-find but all-important park bathrooms are, leads us through one restricted area after another to maximize our time, and secures a table when it's time for lunch at the crowded grab-and-go restaurant we choose. Later, we zip through employee-only back alleys in the white Suburban, so getting from the Magic Kingdom to Epcot takes a fraction of the time it would for regular guests. "It's supposed to be seamless," she said, using a term that seems to always crop up when it comes to the Velvet Rope Economy. "We take care of all the decisions so they don't have to think."

When it comes time to meet Minnie, which my daughter has been waiting for, there's no secret entrance and the lines are long.

Kelly huddles with a Disney colleague—she seems to know every-one in the park—and we are hustled through a red door and up the exit line, where we are not-so-discreetly inserted into the front of the queue. As Willow smiles and chats with Minnie, I think about how children are affected by experiences like this. As a kid visiting Six Flags in New Jersey in the early 1980s, we were all thrown together on the same line, which proceeded at the same snail's pace for every-one. Even if there had been an option to pay to go to the front—it would take new technology and twenty more years to arrive—my otherwise prosperous parents or grandparents would have insisted that I could wait just like everyone else.

Would I make the same call if I could afford it for Willow and her toddler sister? Nope—front-of-the-line favors seem like a life-saver as a parent today. But I don't want Willow to get the idea that the lines will always part for her, or that she's entitled to this kind of special treatment. My reverie is interrupted by Kelly, who has taken to carrying Willow around so she doesn't lose energy before it's time for the afternoon parade. Kelly escorts us up the stairs and past a rope marked Reserved to a prime viewing area just for members of VIP Tours. As we watch the characters dreamed up by Walt Disney so long ago float by—Minnie, Mickey, Snow White and the Seven Dwarfs—I wonder what Walt would think about the exclusive aerie from which we watch the show, and gaze upon the crowded throng down below.

The VIP Tour is just one of a number of offerings that come under the umbrella of Disney's new Signature Services division, which provides concierge-level attention for a small coterie of deep-pocketed guests. Although the VIP Tours themselves have been around for decades, they are growing in popularity, despite the fact they cost at least $3,000 per day. As a result, Disney has been pour-ing resources into Signature Services, offering an expanded slate of what it calls Enchanting Extras. For an extra $125 per person, there's Disney After Hours, which lets guests stay three hours past the regular closing time of 10 p.m. "When the crowds clear and the gates close, rediscover the Magic Kingdom park after dark," Enchanting Extras promises.

For a few hundred dollars more, families can get a Sense of Africa at the Animal Kingdom, dine with an animal trainer, or take a dive with the fish and marine mammals in Epcot's 5.7 million gallon saltwater aquarium. All of these options are on top of the basic Disney World ticket, whose price has risen at an annual average rate of 5.9 percent since 1985, more than double the 2.6 percent rate of inflation.

As stratified as these experiences may be, the truth is Disney could erect many more Velvet Ropes at its parks if it wanted to. In fact, the company is leaving a fair amount of money on the table by refusing to charge outright for front-of-the-line access at its parks like Universal does. Keeping FastPass free also enables the company to live out Walt Disney's ideal, said Scott Hudgins, chief commercial official for Walt Disney World. "If it's included for everyone, there's less of a Velvet Rope," Hudgins said. "When people can lock in three tent-pole experiences per day during their visit, it takes the stress out of it." At the same time, according to Hudgins, "something for everyone is not a static concept."

Secreted away near the Pirates of the Caribbean attraction in Disneyland in Anaheim, above the stores that dot New Orleans Square, is a semisecret spot called Club 33. Inspired by the corporate entertainment suites that Walt Disney visited at the 1964 World's Fair in New York, Club 33 was intended to be a place where the founder could host fellow CEOs, business partners, and vendors. It only opened after Disney's death in 1966, but Club 33 has evolved into a hideaway for celebrities and other members who must pay a rumored $25,000 initiation fee plus $10,000 per year to belong. It's also one of the only places at Disneyland where alcohol is served.

Disney keeps all of the details of Club 33 secret to enhance the allure, but this much is known: for the first time in 2018, Disney opened up a discrete Club 33 in each of its four Orlando parks. One is designed to resemble the interior of the SS *Normandie,* the ocean liner Walt Disney and his wife took for their first transatlantic trip, complete with mirrors that resemble portholes. Another re-creates the atmosphere at the Academy Awards where Disney received an Oscar for *Snow White and the Seven Dwarfs* in 1939, with gold walls symbolizing the statuette.

The new Club 33s, as well as Enchanting Extras, are part of an attempt to reach out to elite consumers without explicitly creating haves and have-nots in the park itself. Stratification, in other words, need not be a dirty word. "The more we can stratify our experiences, the more we can meet our customers' unmet needs," Hudgins said. "And we don't always need a rope that is visibly bifurcated. When the rope is overt, people on both sides don't feel as comfortable as we want them to be."

Disney-style discomfort about elite privileges evaporates when I arrive at archrival Universal's mammoth park down the road in Orlando the next day. Actually, I didn't even have to set foot in the park to see that—it's obvious from Universal's website. "Get To The Fun Faster," Universal promises, with a Universal Express Pass that lets visitors "skip the regular lines at most of your favorite rides and attractions." Nor is Universal shy about its version of the VIP Tour. "Get the Red Carpet Treatment," Universal announces in bold type. "You don't have to be a celebrity to experience Universal Orlando Resort like a star. . . . You'll get exclusive backstage access, learn fun insider information and enjoy the parks' most amazing rides and attractions without waiting in line." There's even a helpful chart laying out which packages include extras like valet parking, free meals, and reserved seating at shows.

"It's not a childlike fantasy land that Universal is pushing like Disney," said *Theme Park Insider*'s Robert Niles. "They don't have to be quite as soft. They've got a lot of price points and they want to sell them. They're saying, 'We're Hollywood, it doesn't have to be free.'" Indeed, as I tour the park, each ride features the same hierarchy—a mass of sweaty people on the regular line, a much smaller group of cool and collected families moving swiftly on the Universal Express queue, and a handful of people flying through with their VIP Tour guides. The latter also escort their charges to areas off-limits to everyone else, revealing hidden nooks others can't see under the roller coasters and letting VIPs pose with the extraterrestrials at Men In Black Alien Attack.

Universal's corporate culture is very different from Disney's, according to Duncan R. Dickson, a former Disney World director who now teaches at the University of Central Florida's Rosen College of Hospitality Management. Under both its former corporate parent, General Electric, and present owner, Comcast, Dickson said, "Universal's theme parks were considered to be cash cows. There was always huge pressure from the parent company to boost cash flow. They really put the screws to these guys."

While Universal visitors are divided into haves and have-nots by Express Pass, Six Flags' Flash Pass has divided its park into have-nots, haves, have-mores—and have-it-alls. If you're willing to pay to jump the line, the regional theme park operator has three options, each one more expensive than the next. With the plain vanilla version, riders simply book the next available time and return then, using what's known as a virtual queue. Flash Pass Gold buyers also book a time, except the wait is 50 percent less. And Fast Pass Platinum cuts the wait by up to 90 percent. A simple ticket to Six Flags Great Adventure that doesn't include any line-cutting costs $59.99. The simple Flash Pass adds $45, while the charge for Gold is $75, and Platinum runs an additional $115. So to enjoy a fully hassle-free day without lines, a family of four must spend $700.

The shameless hierarchy at Universal and Six Flags dates back to a trip a British engineer named Leonard Sim and his wife, Henrieheta, took to Disney World in the summer of 1992. The couple had been in line for an hour for Voyage of the Little Mermaid, when a Disney worker told them the ride had broken down and it would be another twenty minutes—at least. "Quite a few people left the queue and we moved up," Sim recalled in his thick Scottish brogue. More time passed, however, and the line didn't move. "By then all the smart people had left but we waited. Finally a guy came out, and said, 'Sorry, folks, it's broken.' By then we'd spent two and a half hours waiting. My wife was frustrated, and she told me that if you can reserve a ticket for a show, you should be able to reserve one for a ride. 'You're an engineer,' she said, 'you can figure something out.'"

Sim, a radio engineer who specialized in selling microchips for Rockwell, decided to take up his wife's challenge full-time. By the summer of 1998, he'd come up with a prototype, a handheld device he called a Q-bot that allowed visitors to make bookings for rides at Thorpe Park in Surrey, south of London. The concept drew interest from local media, and soon Sim was raising money from family, friends, and acqauintances to take Q-bots beyond the testing stage. Later that year, Sim traveled to a theme park trade show in Dallas to show off the Q-bot's potential. The Q-bot allowed users to book specific times on rides, and notified them when it was time to go. Sim and his partners couldn't yet afford a booth so they set up a demo in the fair's international lounge. "I'm not really a cocky guy, but this was a technical solution to a problem and that gave me confidence," Sim said. "Everyone I spoke to from the parks said this was a brilliant idea, and this is the future."

It was experimental but park operators were game and by 2000, Sim had secured an order for the prototype from Six Flags for their park in Georgia. Like other Velvet Rope products that offer ease, the Q-bot was a hit, and Six Flags was ready to install it in additional parks when the September 11 terrorist attacks threatened to push travel and theme park attendance into a tailspin. Six Flags stepped in and helped Sim's company, by then called Lo-Q, with a half-million-dollar loan. "They could see the revenue potential and by 2005, it was fairly clear this system could make a lot of money."

For clients like Universal, Legoland, and Six Flags, Sim's front-of-the-line technology has proven to be a bonanza, according to Steve Brown. He should know—in 2012, Lo-Q bought the ticketing technology company he founded in 2007, Accesso, for $22 million and took its name. Since then, Accesso's shares have tripled. "It's been a good ten years," Brown told me. "This was revolutionary—the one thing people hate are lines, and you could increase revenue by providing this service."

The financial incentive was primary in Sim's marketing pitch to theme park companies. "Guests have a wide spread of disposable income," said one slide. "Many will pay for freedom from queue line imprisonment." Another slide, citing the company's success at Legoland, was forthright about the target audience—parents: "Very low tolerance of queue lines." Like Laval and the father of the personal seat license, Max Muhleman, Sim didn't expect that his invention would lead to the veritable caste system that's on display at Six Flags and Universal. "Q-bots were conceived so everyone could be on the system," he said. "The concept was for everybody and I was a wee bit sad about it. While I'm certainly happy about how well the business is doing it would be nice to see everyone avoid queueing."

Lines won't be replaced by virtual queues anytime soon—there is too much money to be made charging patrons for the privilege of skipping them. But the ubiquity of lines has given rise to an academic discipline known as queue theory. Besides academia, queue theory has adherents throughout the hospitality industry, from restaurants and hotels to casinos, and of course, amusement parks. Queue theory is a staple of Professor Duncan Dickson's classes at the University of Central Florida and to help his students, many of whom are destined for careers in the theme park industry, he's boiled the subject down into eight rules:

1) Unoccupied time feels longer than occupied time.
2) Pre-process waits feel longer than in-process waits.
3) Anxiety makes waits seem longer.
4) Uncertain waits are longer than known, finite waits.
5) Unexplained waits are longer than explained waits.

6) Unfair waits are longer than equitable waits.

7) The more value perceived in the service, the longer I will wait.

8) Solo waits feel longer than group waits.

As Dickson's rules suggest, the goal of queue theory isn't to eliminate lines—it's to make them less painful. Rule No. 1 is why you'll notice Disney is featuring more characters walking among the crowds waiting for the Frozen Ever After ride or Enchanted Tales with Belle. Universal is doing the same at Race Through New York Starring Jimmy Fallon, providing tabletop electronic games for kids and a barbershop quartet performing rap songs, a Jimmy Fallon hallmark. Keeping people occupied while they wait is also why hotels place mirrors next to elevators on each floor, as well as why there is recorded music to distract callers on hold. Rule No. 2 explains why check-in often precedes the snakelike formation of the queue. To allay anxiety (Rule No. 3), airlines will provide gate information for fliers trying to make tight connections, just as doctors' offices often feature videos and pamphlets about unfamiliar procedures. Whether it's on the New York subway system or in the Magic Kingdom, the reason for the sign stating the wait time is Rule No. 4. When takeoff is delayed, gate agents will explain that a late arrival of an inbound flight is to blame (Rule No. 5).

What about Rule No. 6, unfair waits, like watching Express Pass holders speed by? That's trickier but Dickson has an answer, according to a 2005 paper he coauthored. "When situations like these occur, attempts should be made to disguise this two-priority system or explain it in a way that seems reasonable to those not getting the priority," he wrote. Keeping up the illusion is especially critical in the theme park business, which is why the "perceived value entrances" for VIP Tour guests are unmarked, as are the new Club 33s. To be sure, none of this makes the merge point, where the likes of Universal Express or FastPass holders and everyone else come together, any less awkward, as Dickson noted. "Among my students, no one wants to work merge," he said.

. . .

With VIP Tours priced at several thousand dollars a day, and products like Express Pass at Universal costing several hundred, there's plenty of room left in between. Enter Adam Borgos, the general manager of Michael's VIPs, one of a handful of private companies that's sprung up to make life easier for families who can't face a day at Disney or Universal on their own but lack the dough for the real-deal VIP experience. Unlike Kelly, Borgos doesn't deliver front-of-the-line access or unlimited FastPasses and instant intros to Mickey and Minnie. But in the Velvet Rope Economy, sometimes just a little ease is enough, and that in-between space is drawing entrepreneurs looking for crumbs left over by corporate giants like Disney in the race to service the rich.

For a minimum of $900 per day, Michael's VIPs will design schedules for first-time visitors, quickly zipping them between parks. "They don't want to have to go to a new town and have to read a map or prioritize," Borgos said. "Every day, they make decisions for hundreds of people. They're CEOs, movie producers, hedge funders, lawyers, and wide receivers and they want to feel comfortable giving up the reins. The big dogs expect quite a bit." Borgos identifies the most popular rides, and makes sure his clients get an early start so they can beat the lines that build up by midday. While he can't use Kelly's employee-only shortcuts to dash between parks, he knows the layout well enough to make sure his charges make the most of their time.

Michael's VIPs was founded by a former VIP Tour guide at Disney, and several veterans of Michael's have gone on to start their own independent tour companies. Borgos went to work for Michael's twelve years ago, after serving as an assistant cruise director at Celebrity Cruises, and he's grown accustomed to making sure everything flows smoothly, without even a hint of friction for his clients. With a staff of twenty, Borgos oversees guides in Los Angeles and Las Vegas as well as Orlando. The setting may be an amusement park but in the Velvet Rope Economy delivering ease is serious business, he told me. "I'm the front line, I've got thirty seconds to figure out what they want and how to give it to them," Borgos said. "You're like a frog. When they say, 'Hey Frog,' you jump."

Over the years, Borgos has seen his clientele evolve. Before the financial crisis of 2008 and the Great Recession, self-made entrepreneurs like builders, contractors, and real estate salesmen were as common as white-collar professionals like lawyers and bankers. The latter have become more prevalent in recent years, as they have throughout the Velvet Rope Economy. "They want what they want and they don't want to wait for anything," he said. "With blue-collar people, they're more concerned with how much things cost and are more realistic. With white-collar clients, the value of each dollar they spend isn't so important. If it weren't for their kids, they'd be in Spain or British Columbia or the Hamptons."

Disney tolerates Borgos's firm, but some of his less scrupulous competitors ran afoul of Disney a few years ago when they began to deploy disabled guides in wheelchairs to get their perfectly ambulatory clients front-of-the-line access. "If Disney catches people doing this, they can hit them with lifetime bans," said *Theme Park Insider*'s Robert Niles. "They were gaming the system and trying to use a disabled person to get the ultimate FastPass."

Exploiting the disabled to jump the line is appalling—it was halted after NBC's *Today* show spotlighted the scam in an investigative report, complete with undercover video. Disney termed the act "deplorable" but one of the phony guides had a ready answer for *Today*'s correspondent. "We live in a capitalist country," she said.

And to some observers, the whole practice of selling the ability to jump the line isn't much better. In a 2012 *Esquire* article, essayist Tom Junod told the story of Leonard Sim and recounted how his invention had shaped the experience of visiting a Georgia water park with his daughter. Junod noted that with the rise of FastPass and its ilk, ordinary ticket holders find themselves waiting longer, and end up taking fewer rides than they did in the past, even as wealthier park goers cruise by. "The experience of the line becomes an infernal humiliation," he wrote, "and the experience of avoiding the line becomes the only way to enjoy the water park." He mourns the passing of the small-d democratic experience of waiting in a wet bathing suit with people of all sizes, shapes, and colors, and sees the stratification that has replaced it as signifying much more than merely jumping a line:

> It sounds like an innovative answer to the problem that everybody faces at an amusement park, and one perfectly in keeping with the approaches currently in place at airports and even on some crowded American highways—perfectly in keeping with the two-tiering of America. You can pay for one level of access, or you can pay for another. If you have the means, you can even pay for freedom. There's only one problem: Cutting the line is cheating, and everyone knows it. Children know it most acutely, know it in their bones, and so when they've been waiting on a line for a half-hour and a family sporting yellow plastic Flash Passes on their wrists walks up and steps in front of them, they can't help asking why that family has been permitted the privilege of perpetrating what looks like an obvious injustice. And then you have to explain not just that they paid for it but that you haven't paid enough—that the $100 or so that you've ponied up was just enough to teach your children that they are second- or third-class citizens.

The end result, Junod concluded, is that "your experience—what you've paid full price for—has been devalued." That was Dick Kinzel's worry made flesh.

But according to one prominent theme park executive who worked at Disney and Six Flags, the country and the economy have moved on. Kinzel's autoworkers and Junod's misgivings, in his view, belong to the past and the Velvet Rope Economy is the future. "You have to understand," he said. "For people buying the Platinum Flash Pass, $100 is the same as $1,000. They're beyond that. It's like a burger for people staying on the club floor of one of Disney's hotels. They don't care if it's $8 or $40. For the upper tier, there is essentially no ceiling."

Although he lives next door to the park in Sandusky, Kinzel rarely visits Cedar Point these days. He did give his son, daughter-in-law, and grandkids tickets to the park a few years ago, and they came back raving about Fast Lane. "I said, 'I can't believe you spent $250 on Fast Lane when those tickets were free,'" Kinzel recalled. "My son said, 'I'm only here for a day. My time is more valuable than having to wait on a line for a ride.'" Kinzel still doesn't like Fast Lane in theory, but in practice, he knows it's here to stay. "I'd have a difficult time paying $80 to jump the line," he said. "It's a different culture and I'm not in that culture. But if you're seeking an elite crowd, it works. And unless people stop buying it, I don't see it going away."

Rudd Davis couldn't figure out what was the matter with his pitch.

The thirty-seven-year-old entrepreneur was in a conference room with Vinod Khosla, a top venture capitalist in Silicon Valley, making the case for why Khosla should invest in his new private jet start-up, BlackBird Air. A cross between Uber and Airbnb, Black-Bird connects fliers with available space on private jets, filling up seats on short-haul flights for less than the cost of a traditional charter or even many business class fares. BlackBird uses local airfields in places like Santa Monica and Palo Alto, sparing passengers the endless delays and long lines that are now a fact of life at big airports like LAX and San Francisco International (SFO). Palo Alto airport is just a twenty-minute drive from Khosla's office in Menlo Park, and Davis described how much easier it is for busy tech types like Khosla to get in and out of there. At rush hour, getting to SFO from Silicon Valley or downtown San Francisco can easily turn into an hours-long slog. BlackBird seemed like an idea that should sell itself, or at least appeal to anyone who travels regularly.

But Khosla, who made more than $2 billion from his prescient technology investments and counts Bill Gates as a limited partner in his firm, definitely wasn't getting it. "He looked at me blankly and there was an awkward silence," Davis recalled over drinks at The Battery, an exclusive San Francisco club. "I explained that traffic was terrible and was only going to get worse because we hadn't maintained our infrastructure." Finally, one of Khosla's associates cleared his throat and spoke up. It turned out that Khosla had a bypass of his own. "Vinod has no idea what you are talking about," he told Davis. "He hasn't driven for years, he flies over the traffic in his helicopter." Everyone in the room laughed, and Khosla just shrugged his shoulders, according to Davis.

Khosla told me he doesn't recall the meeting with Davis, and that he uses a private jet rather than a helicopter. But his reaction, at least in Davis's telling, underscores a dirty little secret about the very rich in America. Not only does their wealth enable them to avoid the routine friction everyone else has to contend with on an almost daily basis, increasingly they are so out of touch they barely know that friction exists. And when that ignorance infects corporate decision makers or the donor class in politics, it dulls the impetus of our political leaders to address it.

"There's a danger when affluent people use the market to opt out of shared public places," said Eric Klinenberg, author of *Palaces for the People,* which looks at how public spaces like libraries and parks shape social interactions and civic life. "The risk is that they'll lose their interest in the common good or making sure public places work well." At the same time, he said, when the only people using public infrastructure are those who can't afford better, "public places become stigmatized and they lose their popularity."

In Washington and most state capitals, politicians have failed to agree on how to fix the country's overburdened infrastructure so things continue to worsen. Conservatives have opposed tax hikes and greater public spending on principle, while many Democrats have been similarly unwilling to support tax increases because their wealthy contributors don't want to foot the bill. The rich would rather pay private companies for ease than fork over more in taxes so everyone's commute or trip to the airport improves.

Unlike politics, economics abhors gridlock. So entrepreneurs like Davis have discovered there are riches to be earned in providing an escape from jammed highways, decrepit public transit, and congested airports. Rob Wiesenthal, co-founder of Blade Urban Air Mobility, is one. While BlackBird uses fixed-wing aircraft on most of its routes, Wiesenthal has his eye on even shorter hops. His fleet of helicopters already gets travelers from heliports on the East and West Sides of Manhattan to airports like John F. Kennedy International, Newark Liberty, and LaGuardia in minutes instead of hours. In March 2018, Blade closed a $38 million round of investment from venture fund and hedge fund backers to expand, a sign the big money types know how desperate they and their counterparts are to find an easier way to get to the airport.

Fractional jet ownership, in which individuals or companies buy a share of a private jet to obtain a certain number of flights, became more common in the 1990s and 2000s, and is still dominated by NetJets and Flexjet. But it remains the province of a small fraction of the top one percent. A new breed of companies is betting that a combination of lower prices and the ability to book a private jet flight online as easily as a commercial one will appeal to a much broader market. And there's certainly plenty of reasons to avoid the biggest airports in favor of their smaller brethren. In early 2019, 22 percent of all flights leaving SFO were delayed, according to Department of Transportation data, up from 14 percent in 2013. Nor is it a problem limited to California: in early 2019, more than a quarter of all flights from New York's LaGuardia Airport departed late, nearly double the proportion in 2013.

Like Q-bot, BlackBird's creation was spurred by a spouse, this time in the form of an ultimatum. A serial entrepreneur, Davis had sold his first start-up in the media business to Gannett in 2008. Next he founded a software company called Swarm, which was bought by Groupon in 2014. In San Francisco parlance, these are what are called liquidity events and Davis decided to reward himself with a house on Lake Tahoe. But as Bay Area traffic worsened amid the tech boom, what was supposed to be a four-hour drive sometimes took six hours or more. Davis's then-one-year-old son would get carsick, and his wife was fed up with the weekly trek out of the city and back. "She said to me, 'We either sell the house or find a better way to get out there.'"

At the time, Davis was taking flying lessons and would frequently drive by the seaplane base in Sausalito, not far from his home in Marin County, which is just across the Golden Gate Bridge from San Francisco. "I began to think, Why can't you fly to Tahoe on a seaplane?" One day he stepped inside the charter company based there and asked if they could fly him to Lake Tahoe. They were happy to—for $1,500 each way, much more than he could afford to spend on a regular basis, even after selling the two companies. But the conversation germinated an idea in Davis's head. He didn't want to own or operate aircraft—or fly them. In fact, he gave up the flying lessons, explaining, "I like risk a lot. That doesn't jibe with being the best pilot."

Rather than start an airline, Davis decided to use his knowledge of software to create a digital platform that would match fliers with privately owned aircraft that sit empty on the runway much of the time. Although Khosla didn't bite, investors like Social Capital and veterans of Airbnb did, providing the early funding to hire engineers and operations specialists. This "asset-light" approach appealed to the venture capital crowd: Airbnb leaves the cleaning and upkeep of its apartments to independent owners, and simply takes a piece of each rental. BlackBird guarantees standards for the planes it relies on, as well as the airport facilities it utilizes, but lets others worry about maintenance and overhead. Owners like it because it generates revenue from an asset that would otherwise sit unused.

From initial flights between Palo Alto and Truckee, the nearest airport to Lake Tahoe, Blackbird has branched out, with scheduled flights linking the Bay Area to L.A., Reno, and Santa Barbara. The Palo Alto to Santa Monica route is especially popular with employees of several tech giants, who frequently travel to Los Angeles from their companies' San Francisco headquarters. It costs $375 each way vs. $120 for a flight at the same time from SFO to LAX on commercial airlines.

But BlackBird and Davis aren't competing on price—they're selling ease. Each BlackBird reservation comes with the option of Lyft or Uber, so all transport is taken care of, door-to-door. Entered into each BlackBird client's profile are small details like their preference of coffee and other personal tastes so they feel special, not unlike passengers in a Royal Caribbean suite or an elite box at Levi's Stadium in Silicon Valley. "We can have the black car sitting on the runway next to the plane when they land," said Davis.

Like many other architects of the Velvet Rope Economy, Davis wasn't raised in a world of private jets or vacation homes on Lake Tahoe. His father managed ski camps in New England and his mother was a teacher. Growing up in Vermont, "there was never a lack of food but there were times when it was pretty tight," he said. "We drove everywhere, we never had money to fly. I think that drove me into aviation, and made me want to free myself from the car."

Despite his tech jackpot, Davis remains hesitant to spend too freely. When he's not flying BlackBird, he takes Economy Plus on United, not business class, let alone first class. Davis did splurge on a personal stylist and, dressed in his white shirt, skinny black jeans, and brown Dior sneakers plus aviator sunglasses, he now looks like he belongs on a private plane. Like BlackBird's customers, he's willing to spend to avoid the hassle of shopping and find an easier, if more expensive, solution. "I want to recapture the time I'd spend in a store to do other things like spend it with family," he said.

"The new form of luxury isn't about things," he added. "It's about the experience, not material goods. What's better than first class or even private? A seamless experience." As big airports get ever more crowded, and congestion worsens, Davis is sure Black-

Bird's appeal will only grow. Vinod Khosla might not have needed to, but anyone who can afford to make life easier for themselves will jump at the chance, Davis feels. "We haven't progressed beyond the car," he said. "What are they going to do, expand the roads?"

The headquarters of Blade isn't much to look at—located next to the West 30th Street Heliport on a Manhattan stretch of the Hudson River, Blade's digs resemble a cross between a Silicon Valley start-up and the cramped office of a taxi dispatcher. Its lounges are a different story. Fliers—Blade never calls them passengers, only fliers—wait to board their choppers in a living homage to Rat Pack cool. Pictures of President Kennedy and Frank Sinatra hang on the walls, there are shag rugs on the floor, and curated cocktails featuring Blade partners like Casa Dragones tequila are on the house. If there's any doubt about the ring-a-ding-ding vibe here, the vintage *Playboy*s and early 1960s *Life* magazines should remove all doubt.

The goal, said Blade cofounder Rob Wiesenthal, "is to create an emotional connection with fliers." So while Rudd Davis sells ease in a nonflashy Bay Area kind of way, Wiesenthal sells it with an extra-large dollop of style. Blade's ads feature modern Gatsbys traveling from their Wall Street offices to the latter-day equivalent of East Egg—the Hamptons—surrounded by leggy girlfriends and stewardesses. Cheesy, to be sure, but nobody ever said the Golden Age of Air Travel was politically correct.

Blade was launched in 2014 as a helicopter service between the Hamptons and Manhattan. Since then, it has broadened its offerings with a keen sense of what rich, demanding New Yorkers and Los Angelenos will pay top dollar for when they want ease in the air. On certain summer weekends, Blade offers longer hops by helicopter and plane from the tri-state area to elite summer camps in New England and Pennsylvania, designed for parents who want to be there for visiting day but are too busy to take a long road trip. "We just can't subject you to the Seven Hour Camp Visiting Day

Drive," Blade's marketing material tells prospective customers. "We promise you won't land on the camp soccer field and embarrass your kids."

One of Blade's most successful charter offerings is helicopter service from Los Angeles to Coachella. A former media and entertainment executive, Wiesenthal turned the service into a hit with entertainment industry types, and the company even hosted invite-only parties at the music festival. In the winter, there's service to Miami on Blade One, a CRJ-200 jet that accommodates seventy passengers but which Blade has reconfigured to seat just sixteen fliers in the lap of luxury. Blade One lands at Opa Locka Executive Airport, so travelers don't have to contend with the masses at Miami International and can still get to South Beach in minutes. For someone headed off to a weekend in the Hamptons, Wiesenthal said, "We can change the architecture of someone's lifestyle and make a two-day trip into a three-day weekend."

He has banned the words "exclusive" and "luxury" from Blade's offices and marketing material, calling them clichés. "Those words mean nothing today," Wiesenthal said. "Unique" is verboten, as is "premium" and, wait for it, "VIP." A former top executive at Sony, Wiesenthal cites ease as the key competitive advantage in keeping Blade aloft. The epitome of that is the Special Ops list, Blade's semi-secret equivalent of United Global Services or Delta 360°. Out of 180,000 travelers who've flown with the company, Blade selects its 500 best customers along with a sprinkling of celebrities, and makes travel especially easy for them. When Special Ops fliers arrive at the heliport, a luxury car is waiting next to the chopper with the air-conditioning on, the front seat moved up for maximum legroom in the back, and the trunk open.

"We operate like an advance team," Wiesenthal said. "That's the way these people are used to traveling." Special Ops passengers receive special luggage tags, which frequently prompt other customers to inquire about how they can join the program. "We tell the staff to say they don't know," Wiesenthal crowed, amused at how little pieces of plastic can spark such longing. "We don't really talk about it."

What Wiesenthal does like to talk about are why ease and convenience have become so sought after. Blade's online blog is full of items detailing how it now often takes two hours to get to the airport, and how much worse traffic has become in New York City because there are now over 100,000 car service and rideshare vehicles on the streets. That's more than twice the number in 2013.

The solution is Blade Bounce, a helicopter service that soars above the traffic. For $195 per person, from 7 a.m. to 7 p.m., Blade's choppers ferry travelers to JFK and Newark from the West Side of Manhattan in less than ten minutes. The price is high enough to earn a profit for Blade and just low enough to lure bankers, lawyers, real estate execs, and other denizens of the Velvet Rope Economy out of their Ubers and limos. Delivering ease isn't necessarily easy, however. An electronic ticker in the Blade offices runs inspirational messages from Wiesenthal to his team, and it suggests just how hard it can be to break through the traffic congestion in New York, even with tens of millions in venture capital support. "Our number one customer service priority is Blade Bounce," it reads. "It is a difficult product that we, through brute force, make seamless."

Blade has struck up a partnership with American, so passengers can be screened before they board the helicopter. After the short flight, these travelers are deposited close to American's gates. Blade Bounce passengers are treated like ConciergeKey members and are ferried in a waiting car from the helicopter directly planeside. "You get out of the chopper and into your Porsche," said Wiesenthal. "You don't even have to wait with other people at the gate, let alone deal with security." Wiesenthal's chutzpah earned him a shout-out from his friend Ivanka Trump in her book, *The Trump Card: Playing to Win in Work and Life*. She recounts how Wiesenthal, then an investment banker in his twenties, walked past security into the office of the CEO to persuade Dime Savings Bank to loan him the money to build a home in the Hamptons.

A couple of decades later, the bread and butter of Blade's business, or perhaps artisanal jam and baguette, are flights to the Hamptons. Business is so good that in the summer of 2018, BlackBird ventured to the East Coast for the first time and went into direct competition with Blade with service to the Hamptons, Nantucket, and Martha's Vineyard. "Tell Rob I'm going to eat his lunch," Davis boasted after I told him I would also be writing about Blade.

Rising competition for these super-elite fliers is a stark contrast to commercial aviation. A wave of mergers has whittled down the number of major airlines from nine to just four—Delta, United, American, and Southwest—over the last fifteen years. At ninety-three of the top one hundred airports in the country, one or two carriers control a majority of gates, up from seventy-eight a decade ago. Not surprisingly, prices on the least competitive routes tend to be the steepest. In 2005, USAir accounted for 66 percent of the traffic in Philadelphia and fares were 4 percent below the national average. By the end of the following decade, USAir had merged with American Airlines and the combined airline controlled 77 percent of the seats, with fares now 10 percent higher than the national average.

Packed airports served by near-monopoly airlines are a world away from the Blade experience. Just up from the Water Club along the gray-green waters of the East River is Blade's lounge at the East 34th Street Heliport. On summer Fridays, it resembles a bar in the Hamptons, with customers already dressed for their destination in white slacks and blazers, Louis Vuitton luggage in hand. Evan Licht, the company's general manager, tells me that before Blade came along, what's now the lounge was a construction trailer laid waste by Hurricane Sandy. Blade did a deal with ABC Carpet & Home, and the dilapidated trailer was turned into the chic anteroom for the Hamptons. "People can walk in here in the most foul mood and everybody walks out to the helicopter, smiling and ready to go," said Licht. "It's a fifteen-minute morph."

The flight to the Hamptons isn't much longer—about thirty-five minutes, compared with a three- to five-hour drive at rush hour, or a three-hour train ride. The price is steep—$365 to $1,425 each way vs. $33 for the Hampton Jitney bus, or $35 for the train. But it's an easy call for Harley Saftler, a young advertising exec. "My family's been going to the Hamptons my whole life and there are more beautiful places to be than the Long Island Expressway," he said. "The bus stops a million times and there's no guarantee of a seat on the train. I've done both way too much."

Saftler's girlfriend, Janet Sousa, chimed in: "Blade is the only way to get there that doesn't detract from the experience." But is an extra $600 or more *each way* really worth it? "Sometimes," Saftler said, "you got to splurge and not give a shit."

In Houston, rush hour lasts a lot longer than an hour. Highways get jammed starting at 6 a.m. as commuters head downtown, and the jams don't ease till almost 9 a.m. The congestion returns at 3:30 p.m. and goes on until around 7 p.m. as drivers head home to the suburbs after work. "The roads are at capacity," said Rob Benz, a research engineer at the Texas A&M Transportation Institute. With the tech and energy industries booming in Texas over the last fifteen years, as many as 1,000 people a week move to the Lone Star State. "That's 50,000 people a year and they're going to do what they do, namely drive," he said.

But even in Houston, which is known for horrendous traffic, the Katy Freeway stands apart. It's among the world's widest expressways, with six lanes in each direction, and it links downtown Houston with the prosperous suburbs to the west of the city. Only four of those lanes move at a snail's pace during rush hour each morning and afternoon, however. Vehicles on the innermost two lanes whizz by but they aren't necessarily carpoolers or other drivers taking advantage of the HOV (high-occupancy vehicle) lane. In many cars, a single occupant is at the wheel, pedal to the metal. They're not breaking the law or risking a fine, though. Here in Houston, as in an increasing number of American cities, solo drivers can pay a toll and drive in what critics have dubbed the Lexus Lane. Like visitors to Universal, they are simply trading money for time and ease, in this case $7 to $9 each way, each day, to beat the daily traffic jams.

No one truly needs to visit Universal, or get to the Hamptons, but just about everyone in Houston has to take the highway to get where they're going. There's no mass rail transit to speak of, and the bus system is limited, especially when it comes to traveling between suburbs in the sprawling metropolis. So while the rich—or those running late—pay up, everyone else is stuck in the slow lane. Officially, the fast lanes are known as the Katy Freeway Managed Lanes, or high-occupancy toll lanes (HOT), but cars with an occupancy of one now make up the bulk of the vehicles there. That's true even though vehicles with more than one passenger can still use the fast lanes for free, as in a more conventional HOV arrangement.

If speedy highways for the rich and bumper-to-bumper traffic for everyone else sounds like something out of the world of Ayn Rand, the free market fundamentalist philosopher, well, that's because it is. The Lexus Lanes that are now a feature of the daily commute in more than forty American cities are the brainchild of Robert Poole, a cofounder of the libertarian Reason Foundation, a think tank dedicated to pursuing free market solutions to any and all problems. After the foundation moved to L.A. from Santa Barbara in 1986, Poole found himself frustrated by his commute. When he heard about a company in Dallas that was installing a new type of toll system on a highway there, he decided to pay a visit in 1988.

The Dallas project was the ancestor of today's E-ZPass and Fas-Trak, where drivers put a transponder on the windshield of their car and the toll is automatically collected as they pass through a toll plaza. It was designed to speed up toll collection and ease traffic since drivers would no longer have to stop and pay, but could drive right through. "I spent the whole day with the company as they installed it," recalled Poole, an MIT-trained engineer. "I asked if they'd tested it at highway speed and the answer was yes. Then a light bulb went off in my head—with transponders and automated tolls, you could adjust the price depending on traffic."

Letting solo drivers have the option of paying to use the HOV lanes was in keeping with the market-oriented philosophy propounded by Rand and the Reason Foundation. The Reagan revolution had made free-market solutions fashionable and Poole wrote a Reason Foundation paper calling for putting tolls on conventional carpool lanes. Letting drivers trade time for money seemed like a classic laissez-faire solution to an otherwise intractable problem—traffic.

The problem was only solved for those who could afford the fast lane, of course, but the idea found support among conservatives. One of them was Robert K. Best, the director of the California Department of Transportation at the time. He was a past president of the Pacific Legal Foundation, then and now a force on the right that promotes free enterprise, limited government, and a business-friendly approach to regulation.

With Best's support, Poole's paper was soon on the desk of California's Republican governor, George Deukmejian. Government approval in hand, a private company financed, developed, and operated a new toll road on a crowded stretch of highway east of Los Angeles in Orange County. Like Leonard Sim, Poole became an evangelist of allowing people to pay to jump the line, or in this case the traffic jam. He went on to advise state transportation officials in Texas, Florida, and Washington State, all of which now have HOT lanes. More private companies are getting in the act, developing multibillion-dollar private toll roads in Texas and other states. "Some people will feel resentful, no doubt," he said, noting that in Florida even the HOT lanes sometimes get crowded. The toll there is capped at $10.50, which is the problem in Poole's opinion. "They've been slow to raise it," he said. "The cap should be raised or eliminated."

Heidi Stamm, a Seattle marketer and product development specialist, coined the term Lexus Lane during a successful fight against putting tolls on carpool lanes for solo drivers in her city in the 1990s.

She had first promoted van pools for the city of Seattle in the 1970s and didn't think people who played by the rules and shared a ride should make way for people who simply paid to go faster.

But Stamm's victory was temporary. By the last decade, HOT lanes were in place on major highways in Seattle and more are on their way. What changed between the 1990s and now? The deterioration of the nation's government-funded infrastructure and the ever-present hunger for new revenues at cash-strapped state governments are big factors. But another is that citizens have been conditioned by the Velvet Rope Economy. Faster lines for those who can pay more at the airport or for a ride at the amusement park—both strictly optional ways to spend your time and money—have paved the way for public goods to be auctioned off at the highest price.

As Seattle has boomed and tech workers flock to suburban campuses like Microsoft's headquarters in Redmond, a new elite has proven more than willing to pay up for ease on their morning commute. In fact, a 2014 study by Mark Burris of Texas A&M found "a pattern of substantial decreases in carpools on many of the HOT lanes." The reason for the decline, Burris suspects, is "that you've given people another option. They can now use that lane without carpooling." Other academic studies have reported a correlation between use of the HOT lanes and household income, with richer drivers naturally using them more frequently than poorer ones. No wonder—on I-66 in Virginia near Washington, D.C., prices are updated every six minutes and a solo trip on the ten-mile route peaked at $40 during the morning rush hour after the HOT tolls debuted in late 2017. Heidi Stamm has watched these phenomena play out as traditional HOV lanes are converted into toll roads in the Seattle area. "We get hit twice," she said. "Fewer people carpool and then those lanes get slower, as do the regular ones. I think people just say, 'Fuck it, I'm just going to take my car.' Everyone else is on their own."

.   .   .

Transportation engineers like Rob Benz and Robert Poole tend to speak dispassionately about the subject of HOT lanes. They use terms like traffic flow and shear speed, the difference between the speed in the whizzing toll lane and the others where traffic is crawling.

David Hablewitz is an engineer, but calling him passionate on the subject doesn't do him justice. He hung a banner for an hour from an overpass at rush hour near Seattle, a few miles from Microsoft's sprawling offices, with the address of a website he set up, *http://stop405tolls.org*. He gathered tens of thousands of signatures for petitions opposing the tolls and as he sits in an hour's worth of traffic each way each day, he resists the urge to ante up and speed to work.

"How does this help things?" he asked. "The social inequity it creates is horrendous. When you think of the rights given to Americans, mobility is one of them." There are other, more tangible hardships—in the months after the HOT lanes opened, the number of accidents on the road jumped 55 percent. Since then, Hablewitz's activism and testimony before the state legislature has brought results—he helped force the state to drop the tolls after 7 p.m. and on weekends and to open the HOT lanes to everyone during those times.

But in a few years the HOT tolls will be extended to a new stretch of road south of Bellevue, a crowded tech hub where many of his fellow software engineers work and will happily spend what it takes to make life easier in the fast lane. Already, Hablewitz said, some companies are reimbursing employees who can pay the solo toll and arrive at the office earlier. For the cost of a month of tolls, a law firm can add several more billable hours to a partner's monthly schedule, a very profitable arrangement that would no doubt make Ayn Rand smile. "I fear this is where we are going as a society," he said. "It shouldn't be a matter of being able to go faster because I have more money."

Robert D. Putnam, a professor of public policy at Harvard, sees a broader significance in paying to skip the queue. Putnam is the author of *Bowling Alone: The Collapse and Revival of American Communities,* a landmark book on the erosion of social capital and civic engagement, and he links those trends to the increasing prevalence of jumping the line. "It's part of the movement away from being a We society to more of an I society," he said. "Jumping the line erodes trust in other people and makes [those watching] less likely to obey shared rules. They think, 'Why should I obey the rules, if nobody else is?'"

4.

Access

Dr. Ethan Weiss is an exceptional cardiologist, whose specialty, preventive cardiac care, can mean helping people who've already suffered one heart attack avoid a second, fatal one. Dr. Weiss only devotes 20 percent of his time to treating patients at the University of California, San Francisco Medical Center; the rest of his schedule is reserved for cutting-edge research into metabolism, obesity, and blood clotting in a high-tech lab in Mission Bay. As a result, new patients can wait six months before Dr. Weiss sees them for the first time.

But when they are referred by Dr. Jordan Shlain it's a different story. This select group is ushered into Dr. Weiss's office in a matter of weeks, not months—and sometimes there's no wait at all. "If you come in through the front door or the hospital website or call, it'll be next year," said Dr. Weiss, a lean, youthful fifty-year-old who followed his father into cardiology after aspiring to a career as a jazz musician. "When Jordan calls, I do pick up the phone. So if they're from him, I'll try to see these patients sooner. If they're really sick, I'll see them tomorrow."

Jordan Shlain is what most of us would call a concierge doctor, although he himself doesn't like the term. And his practice actually has little in common with more conventional concierge medicine, where patients typically pay $500 per month or so for their internist's cell phone number and guaranteed same-day service. For starters, Dr. Shlain charges at least ten times that amount per month, and his bill to care for a multigenerational family over the course of a year can run into the six figures. He makes house calls in the middle of the night as a matter of course, and provides his patients with detailed semiannual health reports that resemble a brokerage statement with their charts and goals, and supplies tailored, kimono-like robes to don during exams. But those are just the bells and whistles, like a sunroof or a satellite radio on a high-end Mercedes. At Private Medical, as Dr. Shlain's medical group is called, the real engine that drives demand is access.

Having money has always made a difference in a patient's medical experience: a private room on the high floor of a hospital, better food, and more attention from doctors and nurses who are advised when a benefactor is admitted to their ward. But in the Velvet Rope Economy, there's always a race to provide new and pricier benefits. And the cutting edge of these is access.

Until recently, ostensibly nonprofit spheres that provide intangibles like health and social mobility, medicine and education were somewhat insulated from the Velvet Rope effect by prevailing social norms. It's one thing to pay up for more legroom in the air or a porthole on board ship but access to the upper realms of the meritocracy—such as admission to Harvard—isn't supposed to be for sale. (That's why it's called a meritocracy in the first place.) The same goes for access to specialized medical care that can mean the difference between life and death. But whatever inhibitions tempered the urge to segment this market in the past have diminished over the last couple of decades. The explosion of wealth at the very top end of American society, combined with increased global competition for scarce resources like admission to the Ivy League or experimental treatments for cancer, have made health care and education the new frontier of the Velvet Rope Economy. And access is the calling card.

Just as it's tougher than ever to get into Harvard or Stanford, it's also harder to get a doctor's appointment, with the wait to see a specialist becoming worse in recent years. On average, it takes twenty-one days to secure an appointment with a cardiologist in the United States, according to an annual survey by Merritt Hawkins, a Texas health care research firm. That can be a nerve-wracking, even dangerous delay. And in a few places, the holdup is more extreme. In Boston, a city that boasts some of the best heart surgeons and hospitals in the world, cardiac patients must wait forty-five days on average for an appointment. That's twice as long as in 2009. The reason is simple: there aren't enough doctors to go around in many parts of the country, and specialist physicians frequently find their schedule booked solid for weeks or months in advance. Even lining up an appointment with the family doctor is taking longer. Nationally, patients waited twenty-nine days to get an appointment with a primary care physician in 2017, up from twenty in 2009.

The Affordable Care Act has made medical treatment available to millions of Americans who used to go without routine care. That's created an upsurge in demand for primary care appointments and the number of family doctors hasn't been keeping pace. Similarly, as the baby boom generation ages and requires more health care, the strain is being felt throughout the medical system. The number of annual office visits is expected to hit 565 million by 2025, according to a 2012 study in the *Annals of Family Medicine,* up from 462 million in 2008. The authors of this paper estimate that the country will need an additional 52,000 primary care physicians to cope with this increase, but the supply of new doctors isn't growing anywhere near that quickly.

Paralleling this trend, and quite possibly worsening it, has been the rise of concierge medicine, especially the super-elite version. Founded in 2002 in San Francisco, Private Medical opened offices in Menlo Park, the heart of Silicon Valley, in 2011 and in Beverly Hills in 2015. By mid-2019, Dr. Shlain was planning to open an office on Park Avenue in New York and looking at locations in Boston, Washington, D.C., and Miami. A slightly less expensive rival, MD Squared, has grown even more quickly. From a single practice he established in Seattle in 1996, founder Howard Maron has taken

MD Squared nationwide, with clinics in ten cities, including Boston, Chicago, New York, and Dallas. The onetime doctor for the Seattle SuperSonics and a private internist before that, Dr. Maron, sixty-five, said his inspiration was to deliver care to all of his patients the way he treated members of the basketball team.

"In my old waiting room in Seattle, the CEO of a company might be sitting next to a custodian from that company," he told me. "While I admired that egalitarian aspect of medicine, it started to appear somewhat odd. Why would people who have all their other affairs in order—legal, financial, even groundskeepers—settle for a fifteen-minute slot?"

Dr. Maron's epiphany enabled him and his fellow MD Squared concierge docs to achieve the kind of outsized financial success few physicians enjoy in the era of managed care. There are other rewards, too, namely time. Each MD Squared doctor treats a maximum of fifty families, whose $25,000 annual fee allows him or her to carry a caseload that's a fraction of most normal practices. Dr. Harlan Matles joined MD Squared's Menlo Park practice after working as an internal medicine specialist at Stanford, where he treated twenty to twenty-five patients a day and barely had time to talk to them.

That workload took a toll on his marriage and his health, Dr. Matles said, adding that he never made it to an event at his children's school until he joined MD Squared. Like all doctors who join MD Squared, he had to jettison the vast majority of the patients he had gotten to know at Stanford. "I wish I could have offered this to everyone in my old practice, but it just wasn't feasible," he said. "I am able to give the time and energy each patient deserves." In addition to time, Dr. Matles is up front about his ability to provide something just as valuable—access. "If you need to go to Mass General, we can get you in," Dr. Matles said. "We are connected. I don't know if I can get you to the front of the line, but I can make it smoother. Doctors like to help other doctors."

John Battelle, a healthy San Francisco media entrepreneur with a wife and two teenagers, initially had his doubts about whether it made sense to pay thousands of dollars per month to Dr. Shlain to treat his generally healthy family. But then Battelle's teenage son broke his leg during a suburban soccer game after school. Naturally the first call his parents made was to 911. The second was to Dr. Shlain. "They're taking him to a local hospital," Battelle's wife, Michelle, told Dr. Shlain as the boy rode in an ambulance to a nearby emergency room in Marin County. "No, they're not," Dr. Shlain instructed them. "You don't want that leg fracture set by an ER doc at a local medical center. You want it set by the head of orthopedics at a hospital in the city." Within minutes, the ambulance was on the Golden Gate Bridge, bound for California Pacific Medical Center, one of San Francisco's top hospitals. Dr. Shlain was there to meet the Battelles when they arrived, and their son was seen almost immediately by an orthopedist with decades of experience.

Despite his guilt over what he admits is very special treatment, the experience dispelled any doubts Battelle had about the benefits of paying for access. "I feel badly that I have the means to jump the line," recalled Battelle, a Berkeley graduate and self-described liberal Democrat and Trump-hater. "But when you have kids, you jump the line. You just do. If you have the money, would you not spend it for that?"

The combination of younger, generally healthy millionaires and billionaires who are pressed for time but expect top service and elite access has made San Francisco and Silicon Valley a mecca for Velvet Rope medicine. For doctors, the sight of friends and former classmates in tech making millions overnight while they're still paying off loans for medical school is an additional incentive to join a concierge practice.

"You have no idea how much money there is here," said Dr. Matles, who worked one day a week as a doctor on call at Google, in addition to his regular practice, before joining MD Squared. "Doctors are poor here by comparison." Concierge medicine may not bring the riches that an IPO does on Wall Street or the buyout of a start-up on Sand Hill Road, but it does represent a big step up even from the most elite traditional practices. An internist who takes insurance in New York or San Francisco might earn $200,000 to $300,000 per year, according to Dr. Shlain, but Private Medical pays $500,000 to $700,000 annually for the right practitioner. Besides the money, many doctors are drawn to concierge practices in search of a better lifestyle. Instead of facing a blizzard of paperwork from insurers and hectic schedules, physicians can spend more time with fewer people.

"It's more like a family office for medicine," Dr. Shlain said, referring to how very wealthy families can hire a team of financial professionals to manage their fortunes and assure the transmission of wealth from generation to generation. Only in this case, they are managing health, on behalf of clients more than equipped to pay out of pocket—those for whom, as Dr. Shlain put it, "this is less expensive than the annual gardener's bill at your mansion."

"When I'm at a country club or a party and people ask me what I do, I say I'm an asset manager," Dr. Shlain explained. "When they ask what asset, I point to their body." The son of a San Francisco surgeon, Dr. Shlain learned Swahili and taught science to high schoolers in rural Kenya after graduating from Berkeley. Following medical school at Georgetown University and residency at a top San Francisco hospital, Dr. Shlain joined a practice with an aging doctor downtown, with a promise that he'd inherit it before long. He quit when his older partner decided not to retire after all, and found himself having tea one afternoon at the Mandarin Oriental. It was there that he stumbled upon his true vocation in medicine—providing white-glove service to wealthy, demanding patients.

"I saw all these fancy people coming and going, and I thought, 'What's going on here?'" he recalled. Dr. Shlain walked up to the Mandarin's concierge and asked who the hotel doctor was there. "Who are you?" was the answer. When he explained he was a physician himself, and was offering his services, the concierge was skeptical, although the previous hotel doctor had left not long before. "I may be one-star smart but I deliver five-star service," she told him. "You guys are five-star smart but deliver one-star service. You've got to learn what separates four-star from three-star and three-star from two-star." Intrigued, and willing to assume the humble stance of an acolyte, Dr. Shlain asked her to teach him how to be the Mandarin's hotel doctor.

Twenty years later, that concierge, Charisse Fazzari, works for Dr. Shlain as director of patient experience for Private Medical. "He earned my trust by being earnest," she said. "And he's a great talker." He was a good listener, too, acquiring an understanding from Ms. Fazzari that with elite customers, "Above and beyond has to be the standard." After serving as the hotel doctor at the Mandarin for four years, Dr. Shlain founded Private Medical in 2002. It's no longer a one-man show—Private Medical has twenty-six doctors on staff—but his experience at the Mandarin with Ms. Fazzari still informs how he interacts with patients every day.

So when Dr. Shlain opens doors and obtains an appointment with a specialist, Fazzari makes sure that doctor has all the information he needs and that the logistics are nailed down long before the Private Medical patient walks into his office. "Our families often have one point person who works for them, so Charisse will do all the coordination with them and the nurses and specialists' staff first," Dr. Shlain said. "It has to be seamless. All the heavy lifting has to be in the background. The patient, like the guest at a top hotel, should never see it." That also means small touches like learning what kind of music a patient likes and playing it when she comes in for a checkup. Or instead of saying "I have to go" at the end of an exam, he closes with "Is there anything else you wanted to ask about?"

"The Mandarin Oriental's secret was understated elegance," Dr. Shlain said. But it didn't come cheap, and working as a doctor there helped him overcome the reticence he noticed many physicians have when it comes to talking about money. After treating a top lawyer for an attack of appendicitis, overseeing his transfer from the hotel to the hospital and the recovery from surgery, Dr. Shlain added up how much time he'd spent on the case. It was about ten hours. So when the guest had recovered and returned to his room in fine fettle, and offered to pay him for his time, Dr. Shlain had a question ready: How much do you charge per hour? $785 was the lawyer's answer and Dr. Shlain had his response ready. "That's so funny," he said. "So do I."

"He couldn't say his time was more valuable when I'd just saved his ass," Dr. Shlain said. "He was post-op, on the mend, and in a gigantic suite! And if he could get into the Mandarin, he could afford my fee." Trim, with a goatee and funky square glasses, Dr. Shlain looks younger than his fifty years. That, plus his caffeinated manner and TED-talk-like ability to pontificate on how technology will change the world, fits in well with the techies who make up a considerable portion of his patients. He's still a long way from amassing Silicon Valley–style super-wealth, but Dr. Shlain spends weekends with his wife and four children at their spacious Marin County home when he's not at conferences sponsored by Harvard and other institutions. In a drawer in his office, he keeps framed copies of two reimbursement checks from insurers in his old career as a traditional doctor to remember just why he left the world of co-payments, managed care, and prior approvals far behind. "I billed $350 and got 70 cents. Another time I billed $55 and got $10.12. I framed them so I don't forget it's a broken system."

Even today, Dr. Shlain finds that some very wealthy patients think they are entitled to discounts. "One guy who came in had just torn down a house and built a new one for $20 million," Dr. Shlain said. "When I said it would be $100,000 a year to treat him and his family, he said it's crazy to pay that for health care and left in a huff. A few hours later he called back and apologized—he admitted he pays his estate manager half a million a year."

The annual fee covers the cost of visits, all tests and procedures in the office, house calls, and just about anything else other than hospitalization, as well as personalized annual health plans and detailed quarterly goals for each patient. "You can lie to me but nothing screws up a good story like data," Dr. Shlain said. The data-centric approach, complete with PowerPoint-like charts, is especially appealing to executives from Silicon Valley.

"We organize health care for the entire family," he said, sitting in Private Medical's hip-but-not-too-fancy clinic in a nondescript

building in upscale Presidio Heights. Old-school record album covers decorate the waiting area, while his own office features a guitar
on the wall—in addition to being a foodie, he's a musician in his
spare time. He doesn't display pictures of his kids on his desk or
his degrees on the wall. "When a patient comes into my office, the
focus should be on them, not me. And if someone is going through
a divorce or an illness, they don't want to see me and my kids walking on the beach."

For families, Dr. Shlain and his team will coordinate treatment
for grandparents in a nursing home and routine care for their middle-
aged children, as well as provide adolescent or pediatric medicine
for the grandchildren. For example, when a teenage patient with a
history of depression or anxiety moves across the country to Boston
for college, Private Medical will make sure they have access to a top
psychiatrist near the school before freshman year begins. Or if a
middle-aged patient is diagnosed with cancer, Dr. Shlain will secure
an appointment in days, not weeks or months, with an oncologist
in Houston or New York. "It's not because we pay them," he said, a
practice which would be illegal. It has more to do with the fact that
elite medicine is a small, clubby world. "It's because we have relationships with doctors all over the country," Dr. Shlain said. "We
do the heavy lifting and do a complete workup and treat them with
the respect they deserve."

In the event of an uncommon diagnosis, Private Medical will locate the top specialists nationally, book an appointment immediately,
and accompany the patient to the exam, even if it is on the opposite
coast. Wealthy, powerful people can find themselves flummoxed by
a health care system that can seem all but opaque to outsiders and
nonmedical professionals. "I don't cut the line, I eliminate it," Dr.
Shlain likes to boast.

Despite Dr. Shlain's confidence about the advantages of his particular brand of concierge medicine, he admits he struggles with the
ethical issues of providing elite treatment for a wealthy few, even as
tens of millions of Americans struggle to afford basic care. Dr. Shlain
founded a software start-up, HealthLoop, which raised $10 million

in venture capital funding and aims to "democratize" his boutique approach by allowing patients to communicate directly with their doctors through daily digital checklists and texts. He also argues that innovations are often initially available only to the very wealthy then gradually become more widespread. A few decades ago, he noted, airbags were only available as a pricey option from Mercedes and other elite carmakers. Now all cars are required to carry airbags.

But he believes there is no reason that the medical world should not respond to consumer demand like any other player in the service economy. "Whenever I bump into a bleeding-heart liberal, which I am, I mention that schools, housing, and food are all tiered systems," he said. "But is health care an island of socialism in a system of tiered capitalism? Tell me how that works."

For many, it doesn't. And after showing patients what Private Medical has to offer, Dr. Shlain discovered something else. There's practically no limit to what his clientele—he describes them as a combination of old money and suddenly rich tech types—will pay for access to top-tier specialists and personalized medical service whenever they want it. Initially, he worried "who's going to pay $10,000 per year? That's crazy," he recalled thinking. "But they value their time so much, there's almost no amount of money you couldn't charge. They have much more money than time." Despite now charging some multigenerational families more than $100,000 annually for bespoke care, there's a waiting list to join his practice. Recently, a hedge fund manager approached Dr. Shlain about hiring Private Medical for nearly $1 million to treat the firm's top partners, their spouses, and children. He took them on. "It's worth it," Dr. Shlain said. "He said to me, 'I run a multibillion-dollar hedge fund but if one of my employee's kids is sick and they're worried, they're not at work.'"

For hospitals, providing special treatment can be a way of rewarding donors. At Stanford, some donors receive a red blanket when they check in as patients. For doctors and nurses, it is a quiet sign of these benefactors' elite status, which is also noted in their medical records. "You don't get better care," said Dr. Henry Jones III, one of Silicon Valley's original concierge doctors. "But maybe the dean comes by, and if it's done well, it's done invisibly. It's an acknowledgment of a contribution to the organization."

Not far from Dr. Jones's office in Palo Alto, Stanford's new hospital building just opened in the fall of 2019. Designed by the star architect Rafael Viñoly, it features a rooftop garden and a glass-paneled atrium topped with a sixty-five-foot dome. And unlike the old hospital, all of the new building's 368 rooms are single occupancy, a crucial amenity for hospitals competing to attract elite patients from across the United States and overseas.

Stanford raised a portion of the project's more than $2 billion price tag by cultivating those red blanket patients. Stanford's appeals have been especially effective among the gazillionaires of Silicon Valley, though other wealthy enclaves are out to match or even exceed Stanford's efforts to serve the high end of the market. Not to be outdone, Lenox Hill Hospital in New York hired Joe Leggio, a veteran of Louis Vuitton and Nordstrom, to create an atmosphere that would remind VIP patients of visiting a luxury boutique or hotel, not a hospital. "This is something that all patients asked for, and we want to go from three-star service to five-star service for everyone," said Mr. Leggio, associate executive director of patient and customer service.

In its maternity ward, the Park Avenue Suite costs $2,000 per night, twice what a deluxe suite at the Carlyle Hotel down the street commands, but that's not a problem for well-heeled new parents. Beyoncé and Jay-Z welcomed their baby, Blue Ivy, into the world at Lenox Hill, as did Chelsea Clinton and her husband. So did Simon Cowell and his girlfriend. With a separate sitting room for family members, a kitchenette, and a full wardrobe closet, what's come to be known as the "Beyoncé suite" is quite a bit different from the semiprivate experience upstairs at the hospital, where families share an old-fashioned room divided by a curtain. Less exalted but private rooms in Lenox Hill's maternity ward start at $630 per night.

As the parade of celebrity couples suggests, there is plenty of demand for these upscale options, which are crowding out traditional maternity wards. Lenox Hill is exploring a major revitalization effort that would replace shared maternity rooms with private rooms, a far more profitable offering for hospitals since patients typically pay the higher cost for them out of pocket, not through insurers or HMOs that can bargain down rates.

Giving wealthy people special access isn't always about money or getting other favors in return. Sometimes, the gatekeepers behind the Velvet Rope get a frisson from providing access. Dr. Weiss, for example, receives no payment from Dr. Shlain or anyone else to carve out time when the latter refers a patient to him. "My wife asks me all the time, 'What do you get out of this?' Part of it is that we're all star-fuckers at some level," Dr. Weiss confided to me. "It's fun to see some of these people, you get an ego boost. I'm sure the maître d' at a restaurant is willing to take that call from Beyoncé." Dr. Weiss told me he also squeezes in other patients who get in touch with him directly via email, or by another route, whether they drive a bus or run a hedge fund. "If they can find their way to me, I will make time," he said.

But to paraphrase F. Scott Fitzgerald, the very rich are different from you and me—even when they are sick. "We are surrounded in San Francisco by a lot of money," Dr. Weiss said. "A lot of these people got where they got because they are magnetic and fun to be around. I've taken care of actors, politicians, sports stars, and tech people. There are a handful that are a pain in the ass, but in many cases I didn't want to leave the room." Access also means more than just the ability to book an appointment in days or weeks, not months. "I can spend an hour and a half or two hours with these patients," he said. "There's a lot of psychiatry involved, and maybe a little rabbi and a little bartender. It's important to them to spend that amount of time and it does a lot to build rapport. That's what's missing from medicine."

.   .   .

In some ways, the Velvet Rope Economy is self-reinforcing: as more resources are earmarked for elite fliers on separate security lines at the airport or shifted to patients who can pay more at the hospital or make a sizable donation, the need for special access only becomes more pressing.

And when it comes to health care, access can mean the difference between life and death. For newly diagnosed cancer patients, nothing is more precious than time—every day counts, and a delay of weeks or months to see an oncologist at cancer centers like MD Anderson in Houston or New York's Memorial Sloan Kettering can limit treatment options and shorten life expectancy. Even when the stakes aren't quite that high, as in cases of chronic pain or debilitating but not life-threatening diseases, a similar calculus comes into play, with few people willing to wait if they can pay to jump the line. So when patients with deep pockets face a medical emergency, the demand for access becomes another case of what economists call price inelasticity. Translation: higher prices have no effect on consumer behavior. No one who can afford it balks at the price.

Take David Sager. He joined CNN when it was just getting off the ground in 1981, and eventually served as an executive producer. Later he worked as a writer and show runner for television programs in Hollywood, picking up an Emmy for a special in 1994. He was well connected—with a couple of phone calls, he could reach anyone that mattered in the media and entertainment worlds.

The medical arena was different. After being diagnosed with esophageal cancer in 2011, Sager initially went to Cedars Sinai, one of Los Angeles's top hospitals, where he was seen by a prominent oncologist. The treatment was grueling—hours-long surgery to remove his esophagus and part of his stomach, thirty straight days of radiotherapy plus chemotherapy—but he achieved a hard-won remission. Then, in 2014, the cancer turned up again in one of the scans he underwent every three months.

"They kept finding little specks," he said. "The scan showed all kinds of spots, in my liver, my lungs, my this and that." Sager's doctor, who had been positive at the start of his treatment, turned pessimistic. Sager began to research the condition, spending sleepless nights looking up the latest research on the Web, but his oncologist wasn't interested. "My doctor gave up on me," Sager recalled. "He told me I was going to die in six months because the cancer had spread to other organs. I'd bring him stuff from the internet. He wasn't interested. He said there was nothing they could do." Sager's brother Bobby, a wealthy entrepreneur and philanthropist, had already arranged for a genetic analysis of Sager's tumor but now he had another idea. "Let's get Leslie on the phone," he said. Bobby Sager knew Leslie Michelson from the Young Presidents Organization, a networking group for chief executives, and it turned out that Michelson had built a business around cases like that of David Sager.

Called Private Health Management, Michelson's firm enters the picture when patients facing the most serious medical issues have run out of options or doctors have given up hope. For people diagnosed with cancer, who make up about half of Private Health's caseload, that often means obtaining recommendations from multiple experts and getting into a clinical trial. And even for patients at top cancer centers, like MD Anderson or Memorial Sloan Kettering in New York, the process of getting into a clinical trial is byzantine.

In many cases, doctors are only aware of trials that are connected to their institution. Although all information on clinical trials is public via the website of the Food and Drug Administration, there is no equivalent of Expedia or even Google to sift through all that data and locate the right experimental program. Some trials are open only to patients who have already been treated with certain types of chemotherapy, others exclude patients who've been dosed with specific drugs. And when it comes to oncology, which has become a burgeoning field for Big Pharma and the biotech industry in recent years, the newest treatments target specific forms of cancer with particular genetic patterns, reducing the eligible patient population still further.

As it happens, Leslie Michelson is not a doctor or scientist but is expertly acquainted with how to work the system. A Yale Law

School graduate, Michelson worked for the Department of Health and Human Services early in his career and later started a business that set up and ran clinical trials for the pharmaceutical industry. Another company he founded recruited doctors and patients for trials on behalf of the drugmakers. And as the chief executive of the Prostate Cancer Foundation in the early 2000s, Michelson frequently found himself connecting friends and acquaintances with doctors or advising them on the best place to go for treatment. "Everybody who got sick started to call me to bump the queue," Michelson recalled. "I wasn't doing it to bump the queue, but I would coach patients, who became generous donors and funded research. It was a virtuous cycle."

A serial entrepreneur, Michelson, then fifty-six, decided he "needed to build one more business. I wanted to take what I was doing for a few dozen people, and do it for hundreds or thousands of people." Private Health Management was born in 2007, and with no shortage of desperate patients out there, not to mention an explosion of new treatments and clinical trials for cancer and other serious diseases, it has grown rapidly since then. With offices in Century City in Los Angeles and on Park Avenue in Manhattan, the staff of Private Health Management has tripled in the last four years.

Although Michelson has lived in Beverly Hills for years and has sold three companies, the hint of a New York accent in his otherwise polished style betrays his roots growing up in Union, New Jersey, a middle-class suburb of Newark. Throughout his high school years, Michelson's mother suffered from severe bipolar disorder so when his father was diagnosed with a heart condition and a local cardiologist recommended open heart surgery, then a risky new procedure, the seventeen-year-old Michelson sprang into action. He phoned Lenox Hill Hospital, the only medical center in Manhattan he'd heard of, and set up an appointment for his father, a wholesaler. The cardiologist ruled out a risky procedure, and diagnosed the problem as a benign heart murmur.

"He lived for nearly forty more years and died at eighty-three," Michelson recalls with a catch in his voice. "He never had heart disease. If my father had undergone surgery, he might have died right there on the table." It was an early lesson in the difference the right doctor and treatment could make, and while Michelson didn't join the pre-med track as an undergraduate at Johns Hopkins, he was drawn to the world of health care. "The best medical care isn't reserved for the wealthiest people," he said. "It goes to the savviest consumers."

Of course, in the Venn diagram of American life, there's plenty of overlap between those two groups. "We've been retained by people with net worths ranging from several hundred thousand dollars to tens of billions of dollars, but we are not VIP MDs," Michelson said, referring to concierge medical practices. "They're generally primary care physicians who take care of their patients. We are care navigators, we are managers, and while we don't provide care, we know how to find the best care." In practice, that means searching through medical journals for articles on the latest trials, clinical developments, and other innovations, while maintaining relationships with fifteen thousand physicians in more than 350 subspecialties. When new clients sign up, Private Health Management's research team, which includes physicians, PhD scientists, nurse practitioners, and pharmaceutical experts, does a "work-up" of the case from scratch. They comb through the entire medical history and all patient records, and analyze test results and exam notes.

The goal, Michelson said, is to look at everything with fresh eyes. Once the facts are established, Private Health will locate the top specialists for that condition, run the details of the case by them, and ask them for recommendations. "That's how you find the real experts," Michelson said. "If you have breast cancer, you don't see a general oncologist. You need a breast cancer specialist. And if it's the triple negative form of breast cancer, which is rare and very aggressive, you need a breast cancer specialist who just does that. But you have to know who they are and how to have access to them. When you get to somebody who's an inch wide and a mile deep on exactly what you've got, that's when things can change."

Even the best specialists don't have a dedicated research department, however, nor do they have time to go through the sixty thousand articles that appear in medical journals each month. But that's where the opportunity is—scientific discoveries and clinical innovations show up in the medical literature first, long before most doctors become aware of them.

For cancer patients, Michelson's team spends twenty to forty hours or more just going through medical journals and other literature to understand the latest research and identify the most promising clinical trials. Then they focus on the particular genetic makeup of the tumor to determine which trials the patient has the best chance of getting into and offer the most potential for a cure, or at least a better prognosis.

Private Health Management maintains close relationships with the doctors and scientists at hospitals and universities who oversee trials in conjunction with pharmaceutical makers. Known as principal investigators, they are essentially the gatekeepers who stand between desperate patients and potentially lifesaving experimental treatments. While the prerequisites for admission to clinical trials are ambiguous, Michelson says an introduction from Private Health can move a candidate who qualifies to the top of the list. "They won't reverse a decision for us, but they know we bring a lot of information to the table," he said. "We do the homework."

Armed with a genetic analysis of Sager's tumor, Private Health researched the case and discovered that a doctor at the University of Southern California was overseeing a clinical trial into an experimental treatment for Sager's form of esophageal cancer. Sager went to meet Dr. Anthony El-Khoueiry, a professor at USC's Keck School of Medicine, accompanied by a nurse from Private Health carrying a thick file detailing Sager's case and prior treatment. "I told him I'd completely lost hope and faith in my old oncologist," Sager recalled. "I said I have to be assured you're going to tell me the truth and do the best you can to keep me alive. He said he could do those two things, but his eyes lit up when he looked at the file. He said he had a trial under way into that form of cancer and it could work. I turned white as a ghost, and was crying. The nurse was crying, and Dr. El-Khoueiry was emotional, too."

A week later, Sager went for his first treatment, which consisted of a five-hour infusion. "I was told this is either going to save your life or kill you," said Sager. He had no side effects, unlike with previous rounds of chemotherapy. The following week, he went back and gradually the sessions got shorter, with infusions eventually lasting just two hours. Within three weeks, Sager began to notice he had more energy and his appetite began to return. Tests showed a 75 percent drop in cancer cells, which dropped to zero five months later. Five years on, Sager remains in remission and, as he puts it, "I have my life back. I was told my chances of survival were 10 to 20 percent. It's an absolute miracle and if it wasn't for Private Health who pushed this, I would never have found Dr. El-Khoueiry or be alive today."

Just about any cancer patient would want that level of service but only a very few can afford it. Private Health Management charges $50,000 for an initial four-month term. "We literally save people's lives," Michelson said. "If you want to start reaching for the tissues, we have people who are alive today because of what we do. The sadness is that it takes an enormous amount of time and effort, and even the top centers and most dedicated physicians don't have the time and resources to do it." While access to top doctors and clinical trials is the reason desperate families are willing to pay Private Health's price, Michelson insisted he's not in the business of enabling wealthy cancer victims to bypass the queue.

"This isn't jumping the line," he said, with a hint of defensiveness. It's true that Michelson provides access through knowledge and introductions and relationships—but he can't and doesn't buy it. Private Health Management does not pay the doctors it connects to its clients, nor is any money exchanged in the process of finding and enrolling patients in trials. "There are clinical trials looking for people," he explained. "You can't find a clinical trial. With five or ten clicks of a mouse, you can find every airplane seat or hotel room or the mid-century coffee table you are looking for. There is no vehicle remotely like that in terms of clinical trial sites. It's public information but the sheer volume makes it enormously confusing and frustrating."

Michelson has taken his evangelism for savvy consumer health choices on the road with a book, *The Patient's Playbook,* a television special on PBS, and frequent media appearances and speeches. But even the sharpest patient can't begin to duplicate the experience of one of Michelson's clients. Meanwhile, a growing number of companies and hedge funds are contracting with Private Health Management to provide support for employees facing critical illnesses, with unlimited help navigating the health care system as part of their benefit packages.

While Private Health's base of elite customers is growing, for everyone else the trend is moving in the opposite direction. The Affordable Care Act and other efforts to broaden access to medical treatment face an uncertain future. What's more, as the wait to see a specialist grows, the newest breakthroughs in cancer treatment, like targeted therapies for particular genetic forms of the disease, are most likely to go to patients with deep pockets and connections to top doctors.

Access to the latest drugs and the most sought-after doctors is no guarantee of survival, of course. Many clinical trials end in failure, with experimental drugs showing little or no additional clinical benefit. Sager is one of the lucky ones, but he said that without his brother's generosity, his story would have had a different ending. "Everything has a cost, everything has a price," said Sager, who estimates that his brother paid Michelson and his firm $150,000 over his course of treatment. "Private Health is not inexpensive but if you have the wherewithal, it's worth saving your life. Even if you have to spend every penny, I'd rather be alive."

Access to elite colleges isn't a matter of life and death. But for many parents in the American elite, giving their children a shot at

getting into Harvard or Stanford is a rite of passage that will determine the course of their lives. Moreover, the nation's top universities
are much more selective than they were even twenty years ago, making the hurdles that much steeper. In the 1980s, Harvard admitted
16 percent of applicants. By the mid-1990s, that figure had drifted
lower to an intimidating but still hope-permitting 11.8 percent. In
2017, the ratio stood at an all-but-impenetrable 5.2 percent. Stanford poses daunting odds for aspiring high school seniors, too, with
a huge surge in students from overseas who see the university—
correctly—as a stepping-stone to Silicon Valley riches. Stanford
took 16 percent of college applicants in the mid-1990s compared
with 4.7 percent now.

The odds of admission have lengthened dramatically at other
elite schools, as well as at somewhat less choosy colleges that were
once considered safety schools, not reaches. Bucknell, a liberal arts
college in Pennsylvania, receives more than 10,000 applications, but
only can offer admission to 3,200 students. At Bucknell, the crush
of submissions has forced the admissions team there to allocate six
to eight minutes to eyeball each application, down from twelve to
fifteen minutes.

Top public universities are no exception, either—the University of Michigan in Ann Arbor accepts fewer than one in four. In
the mid-1990s, it took nearly 70 percent of applicants. At Georgia
Tech, which received 35,600 applications for 3,000 slots in its freshman class in 2019, admissions officers decide whether to take, reject, or wait list students in less than ten minutes, and rarely revisit
their initial decision. What is more, the deluge of applications has
made the waiting list itself something of a mirage in many cases. In
2017, Dartmouth put 1,345 applicants in the Ivy League equivalent
of purgatory, according to National Public Radio. Of these, exactly
zero were ultimately admitted. The numbers were only slightly better at the University of Michigan—of the 4,124 on the list, 470 were
eventually accepted, according to NPR.

The spread of the Common Application, which permits students
to apply to multiple colleges with a minimum of tailoring, has en-

couraged more students to roll the dice with more universities than in the past. In 2016, according to the annual survey of college freshmen by UCLA's Higher Education Research Institute, more than one third of students applied to six or more colleges. In 1996, only 7.9 percent applied to that many. Whether due to grade inflation or a more accomplished pool of students, the same survey showed admission has also become more competitive in terms of high school academic performance. In 1996, 31.5 percent of college freshmen said their average high school grade was an A- or better. By 2016, the proportion that reported grades that high stood at 55.1 percent.

All these factors have made the ability to influence the deliberations within the admissions office infinitely more valuable. An annual donation to the college fund or attendance at cocktails with alumni and prominent professors is not enough. For the very, very rich, a pledge big enough to put their name on a building will do the trick, as will a seven- or eight-figure gift. Jared Kushner's father famously donated $2.5 million to Harvard in the 1990s, and lo and behold, his son was admitted, despite middling grades in high school.

When emails from Sony Pictures Entertainment were leaked in 2015, one of the more curious revelations was how Michael M. Lynton, the company's chief executive at the time, acted as a bridge between Harvard's admissions office and well-connected parents. Lynton, an alum who is a member of Harvard's powerful Board of Overseers, was there to help when the children of friends applied. "Your magic worked," a prominent New York lawyer, Stephen Warnke, said in an email to Lynton after his daughter got into Harvard in March 2014. This was "something she genuinely did not expect and was thus all the more thrilling—an acceptance from Harvard," Warnke wrote. "The hard-copy letter just arrived in the mail, with a hand-written post-script from Dean [William] Fitzsimmons, short but personal and sweet. Clearly, a fat thumb was pressed on her application." Some parents and others are willing to go much further. In March 2019, federal prosecutors charged dozens of parents in a scheme to pay out bribes in exchange for help getting their children into the colleges of their choice. Among those ensnared in the case were actresses Lori

Loughlin and Felicity Huffman. Coaches were also accused of taking millions of dollars and vouching for the athletic prowess of applicants to colleges like Wake Forest and Georgetown, even though the students in question were not candidates for the schools' teams.

For families who are wealthy but lack the Kushner fortune or ties to the likes of Michael Lynton, and want to stay on the right side of the law, there's Kat Cohen, the chief executive and founder of IvyWise in Manhattan. Technically, Cohen is a private college counselor. There are private college counselors throughout the country but they have about as much in common with Cohen as Jordan Shlain does with a twenty-four-hour urgent care clinic. Cohen's Manhattan-based firm, IvyWise, is more akin to a high-powered lobbying or public relations firm in Washington than a traditional college advisor.

IvyWise does do the things that regular college counselors are known for, like editing personal statements, providing feedback in mock interviews, and identifying the schools that will become the reaches, targets, and likelies for each student. But as is true throughout the Velvet Rope Economy, IvyWise's offerings are tiered, and these traditional services represent only the bottom rung. Not that they come cheap: $1,350 is the starting fee the firm charges a family that approaches them at the beginning of their child's senior year in high school. And that's late in the admissions process for students and parents hoping to jump the college line with IvyWise's help.

The real appeal of IvyWise, and the reason some families pay up to $150,000 to shepherd their kids through the applications process over four years or more, is for access to the admissions departments at Harvard, Yale, Georgetown, and the like. Not directly—that would violate the firm's policy barring contact with current admissions staff on behalf of individual clients. Instead, IvyWise hires admissions officers from these schools who might have decided it's time to cash in or want to do something different, much as top military brass go to work for defense contractors after serving in the Pentagon, or when major pharmaceutical companies hire former Food and Drug Administration officials to lobby their former agency. Like those private sector employers, IvyWise can afford to pay significantly more than what the academic sector offers.

Some of the people on IvyWise's payroll served in junior roles in the admissions office, reading over essays, watching audition videos from aspiring music majors, or evaluating scouting reports for athletes. A few have decades of experience in senior roles. Others fall somewhere in between, like a former senior interviewer at Wesleyan. "These are the people who are in the room where it happens," said Merrily Bodell, IvyWise's chief operating officer, citing an oft-quoted line from the musical *Hamilton*.

Premier counselors, the top echelon, can have twenty years or more experience in the top jobs at the most exclusive universities, like the one who formerly worked as the director of selection at MIT. Another premier counselor joined after serving as associate dean of admissions at Amherst, then Princeton. A standard program with a premier counselor runs about $20,000 per year. Master counselors, whose services average a slightly more reasonable $12,000 a year, typically have about eleven years of experience, and come from highly selective institutions like the University of Chicago and Swarthmore. Principal-level counselors have at least three years experience at still exclusive schools with just a little less cachet, like Boston College and Colgate. Their rate is about $9,000 a year, or less than half what the Ivy-oriented premier counselors charge.

Nevertheless, all of IvyWise's clients draw on the insights of the most experienced admissions game veterans. Each student works with a single counselor from one of the three tiers, but all applications are reviewed by IvyWise's twenty-one-member team, known as the IvyWise Roundtable. Working as a group, they replicate the thumbs-up, thumbs-down ritual that takes place around the table at the most selective schools, and offer tips to students who seem destined for the latter fate. They also provide the same "fresh eyes" approach to personal statements that the experts at Private Health apply to medical histories. During crunch time at IvyWise, from August to December, as seniors prepare to submit their applications, the advisors may check in with their students almost daily.

The counselors themselves hold firm-wide weekly conference calls to review the progress of IvyWise's entire caseload of more than one hundred high school seniors and determine exactly where they stand.

"We are very direct about our students' chances," said Bodell, and that frankness extends to the comments and suggestions offered as their clients rework drafts of their personal statements and other writing samples. When Stanford asked applicants to write a supplementary 100- to 250-word letter to a potential future roommate, the counselors from IvyWise's Roundtable understood it was more than a getting-to-know-you exercise, even if the student didn't. "She comes across as sweet and likeable; however, I don't learn much about her of substance through these tidbits," one IvyWise counselor with experience at Yale and Georgetown commented diplomatically. "The way she talks about music, emphasizing her modest ability, won't help her stand out at Stanford. I'm not seeing evidence of the adventures she wants to have."

That feedback was softened slightly when it came time to relay it to the student herself, but the message was clear. "I think we need to look at revamping the letter the most of all the supplements," she was told. "General things to change: Focus on revealing more depth here of your character and personality—so instead of 10 smaller quirks about you focus on some of the larger, big ticket items. Can have some fun things in here, but balance that with specifics of your maturity as well."

For overseas students, who make up 30 to 50 percent of IvyWise's clientele in a given year, the firm has counselors fluent in languages ranging from Spanish and Portuguese to Thai and Mandarin. More than merely essay editors and application polishers, these counselors also translate the cultural politics and nuances of class that animate discussions on many American campuses these days, and head off potential missteps by students who might not know better. Asked to provide an example of how he overcame a failure or setback, a Latin American applicant to NYU told of the time he crashed his Porsche 911 while pursuing his hobby, race car driving. "He writes vividly about racing," IvyWise counselor Christine Chu commented diplomatically, "but part of me wonders if some admissions readers might be put off by such a topic, which suggests privilege."

The Roundtable provides insights about a wider range of schools than a single counselor can. When the essay of an applicant to NYU's Tisch School of the Arts needed work, one advisor didn't hold back. "This isn't an essay that will be favorably read by admissions officers," said the IvyWise advisor, an NYU graduate who served in the school's admissions office before joining IvyWise, implying it would be screened out by admissions officers. The feedback on essays and transcripts is no doubt valuable, and it is what the firm highlights on its website and in marketing material. But it doesn't really explain why parents from all over the world are forking over six figures for IvyWise's services.

Among the reasons IvyWise is worth that kind of money is access to specialized and highly valuable information. And in a process as convoluted and competitive as getting into an Ivy League university, possessing information that others don't have can make all the difference. "Let's say we have a student who plays the cello and the top cellist at a school on her list is graduating," Cohen said. "In some cases we can find that out. We don't directly advocate for our student with the university, but we may be able to find out what their institutional needs are."

Cohen and her team can sometimes learn which schools are short of poetry majors, need a goalie on their hockey team, or don't want yet another aspiring Wall Streeter at their business school. "Our counselors are still very connected to their network and have their ear to the ground in terms of the admissions world," said Bodell. "They know what specific schools are looking for and how they assess these applications. They can say 'This is not necessarily a Yale kid, but he or she might be a good fit at Dartmouth.' They have the experience and ability to be able to sniff this out."

No one has better olfactory abilities than Cohen herself. She personally takes on only five of the firm's three hundred clients per year, and charges a minimum of $100,000 to each family. Cohen founded IvyWise more than twenty years ago in her Manhattan apartment after graduating from Brown and earning a PhD in Spanish literature from Yale. While in New Haven she worked as a reader in Yale's admissions department, and later taught SAT prep at the Princeton Review, where Bodell also worked before joining IvyWise in 2013.

What also sets Cohen apart is an unusual ability to hold the hands of wealthy students and parents during a process that's famously stressful, without sugarcoating the odds, or the inequities of today's admissions landscape. "The American middle class is getting squeezed out," she told me matter-of-factly in her office on Madison Avenue, where she spends about half her time. The rest is spent on the road, with families willing to fly Cohen to Los Angeles, São Paulo, or Dubai, and pay her handsomely per day for one-on-one help.

For those who can afford it, the admission rates for IvyWise's clients suggest the money is well spent. More than one third of Ivy-Wise students who applied to Harvard between 2014 and 2018 were admitted, compared with 4.7 percent of all other applicants. At Yale, Brown, and Columbia, 40 percent or more of clients were admitted, again dwarfing the overall pool's chances.

IvyWise encapsulates how changing social norms enable the Velvet Rope Economy to expand. The age-old advantages bestowed by family connections and legacies are now for sale like anything else. Reflecting on her experience at the Princeton Review, Bodell said that bespoke admissions advice "is a decade or two behind where test prep is. The SAT used to be seen as a test of the intellect, and people thought we were doing something dirty, like giving out secrets or cheating. Virtually everyone does some sort of test prep now.

"The admissions process is a lot more opaque than testing but as more people take advantage of what we have to offer, the more socially acceptable it becomes," Bodell added. If parents are becoming more open to the idea of hiring a high-priced counseling service like IvyWise, the firm still has to tread gently when they recruit new counselors. "It's a little bit verboten to make money in education," she admitted. "It's seen as crossing over to the dark side, which works against us. IvyWise may be the poster child for making money in education but we're proud of what we do." Senior admissions officers earn between $100,000 to $200,000 at top universities and IvyWise can top that, while sparing them the travel and the need to read thousands of applications like they would face in a university role. What's more, nearly all of IvyWise's counselors work remotely and communicate with students and colleagues via Skype, providing an appealing work-life balance.

These days, many colleges like Harvard and Princeton profess they are doing everything in their power to overcome the inherent advantages of wealth and privilege in their admissions process. They are scouring the country for more minority applicants and increasing economic diversity by providing scholarships for students whose parents earn less than roughly $160,000. But helping to cover the cost of that largesse are rising numbers of foreign students from wealthy families in Asia, the Middle East, and Europe. They generally pay full freight and totaled 1.09 million in the United States in 2018, double the number twenty years earlier. Students from families in the middle of the economic barbell, neither rich nor poor, have a harder time, as do even upper-middle-class students whose demographics and interests are already overrepresented in the applicant pool. The latter make prime candidates for IvyWise's services, roughly half of whom come from elite private schools.

"If you are a white girl from the Northeast who is interested in the humanities and is only in regular history class, the odds aren't in your favor," said Cohen, with an air of finality. "The same goes for an Indian American boy aspiring to be an engineer with high math and science grades but who doesn't have anything else that helps him stand out. Fair or not, that's the way it is."

Kat Cohen can't alter those facts, or guarantee the doors to a particular college will swing wide open—points she makes clear to all of her clients at the outset. But she can improve the odds markedly with an insider's knowledge. When the daughter of a Penn graduate had her heart set on early admission to Yale but wasn't a shoo-in there, Cohen told her to apply immediately to Penn instead in order to make the most of her edge there. "Legacy counts for much more in the early rounds," Cohen explains. "At Penn, early legacy applicants have a 25 percent admission rate. We know it from the admissions office. But in the regular process, legacies don't do much better than everyone else." That's true at many schools, but as Cohen notes, "Penn has a unique policy that grandparents and aunts and uncles also count toward legacy admissions. There are lots of idiosyncrasies like that."

Then there's the spadework that IvyWise does ahead of time for its students, especially if they know which college major they are likely to pursue once they arrive on campus. "We can call departments and find out which research projects professors are working on or look up their latest articles and books for students," Cohen said. IvyWise also sends more than two dozen representatives to the annual National Association for College Admission Counseling conference, where they glean info from fellow private advisors and the university admissions officers who also attend. "Our counselors will run into deans of admission and ex-colleagues, and they'll learn what's going on," Cohen said.

Citing a particular professor or research project in an application not only makes IvyWise's students stand out—it also helps convince admissions officers that the applicant is serious about their particular school. "Colleges want to admit people who want to attend," said Bodell, noting that for universities, estimating the proportion of accepted students who will actually enroll is notoriously difficult. In a bit of ju-jitsu, IvyWise can turn this percentage, known as yield, to their students' advantage by advising them to seed their applications with specific insights into the school. For the same reason, when students visit prospective colleges, IvyWise encourages them to audit a class, eat in a dining hall, or meet with particular professors to demonstrate to admissions staff their heightened level of interest.

For the true high-rollers who seek out Cohen's help, and get the most her firm has to offer in terms of access, the real work begins years before the essay-writing torment or the campus tours are arranged. Some parents approach IvyWise when their kids are still in junior high school to strategize about the kind of course load elite colleges will want to see down the road, as well as to get to the front of the line for the most impressive summer jobs or the most beneficial extracurricular activities. "You might still be a preteen but here are some ways to pursue your interests throughout high school," said Bodell. "As soon as you hit ninth grade, everything counts. And you pick ninth grade classes in eighth grade." For the parents who can afford it, that's a valuable advantage, even if their children attend elite boarding schools in New England or tony private schools in New York like Dalton.

"If you didn't start preparing for the admissions process until junior year, then we're making lemons into lemonade," said Bodell. "Even at most elite private schools, guidance counselors don't really get involved until junior year. And in public schools, the advisors have huge caseloads so there isn't time for so much individual attention."

Based on what a client's particular school offers, IvyWise designs a schedule emphasizing honors and AP classes for its clients, with an eye toward developing two to three areas of expertise. An aspiring engineer is told to take the most rigorous science and math classes the school has to offer. For others, IvyWise suggests online programs in economics or spending the summer at the Stanford University Math Camp (SUMaC), a four-week residential program in Palo Alto that costs $7,000. That's a small expense compared to the tutoring services IvyWise arranges, which is separate from the college counselors but works in conjunction with them. IvyWise's stable of tutors communicate with students via Zoom, a videoconferencing service, for up to ten hours each week so clients don't fall behind in those rigorous courses and can ace the SAT and ACT exams. The virtual instruction may run an additional $20,000 or so per year, and tutors will occasionally spend school breaks in places like Southampton and Zermatt cramming with their charges for standardized tests or playing catch-up after a weak semester.

For a high school freshman interested in history, IvyWise might suggest doing an independent research project on ancient Rome, using a reading list of classics like Edward Gibbon's *Decline and Fall of the Roman Empire*. The student would then write a paper on how different historians explain the course of Roman history. Finally, he would submit the paper to *The Concord Review*, a journal featuring the work of high schoolers.

Pursuing interests early in high school can throw off the scent for college administrators who are wary of highly coached kids, which of course is exactly what IvyWise students are. "Schools are savvy," said Meghan Riley, director of client relations at IvyWise. "We don't want kids just doing something for an application."

Parents tend to think colleges are looking for well-rounded students—strong in all the usual subjects, with high test scores, participation in a team sport and an extracurricular activity or volunteer effort. But in today's hyper-competitive college admissions game, that's necessary but hardly sufficient. "They want pointy kids," said Bodell, admissions-office-speak for students whose unusual interests or experiences stand out. "They want a well-rounded class, but in terms of individual students, they want to see passion, leadership, and defined interests. Building a house for a week in Latin America junior year to check a community service box—that doesn't do it."

What does do it? What qualifies as a "pointy" experience, rather than just résumé-padding? How about shadowing a Hollywood movie director for the summer on a set for a student interested in film? Or doing medical research in the lab of a top medical center? Or even an internship at a hip tech company, an experience usually reserved for older students already in college?

IvyWise's clients have done all of the above, thanks to a partnership with a special coordinator who opens doors and enables students to secure these kinds of opportunities at elite companies and other institutions. Like most things in the Velvet Rope Economy, this level of access isn't included in the standard package. The cost of placement, as it's known, varies in price depending on the nature and scope of the project, but can run $8,000 for a summer. "This is concierge-level service," said Riley, the client relations director. "We can secure internships, find social entrepreneurship opportunities, or create tailored programs. It's optional, but we can do all the heavy lifting." That might mean extra help in coding so an internship developing apps in Silicon Valley goes more smoothly. "It's not running after coffee," Riley adds. For work on a movie set, tutoring isn't necessary, but IvyWise can also arrange a mentor to guide students through what may be their first time in a work environment.

Students are encouraged to come away with something concrete. For a high schooler interested in public health, an internship was arranged at a federal agency researching infectious diseases. Afterward, she published an article about her experience in a newsletter. For students interested in volunteering overseas, IvyWise knows what seems like a cliché and what seems, well, pointy. A teenager interested in Latin America, for example, wouldn't go on a one-week junket shortly before senior year starts. Instead, IvyWise would recommend reading Latin American authors throughout high school, connecting with a Hispanic student association, and then doing volunteer work that lasts four weeks or more over multiple summers. "Those experiences that can be very differentiating," said Bodell.

Employers like the arrangement with IvyWise, too, according to Riley. "These kids are vetted and the mentors make sure the kids can handle it," she said. The irony of IvyWise's success is that even as it guides its young charges through the stations of the cross of the modern meritocracy, the way it functions is a throwback to the age of aristocracy. Indeed, in exchange for tens of thousands of dollars, IvyWise is replicating the connections and access the old WASP elite once used to dominate admissions to Ivy League schools during the Gilded Age of the late nineteenth and early twentieth centuries.

Naturally, Kat Cohen is aware of the optics, which is one reason she emphasizes that one in ten students at IvyWise is helped pro bono, including many from minority communities. At the same time, she notes that even without IvyWise, the playing field is hardly level for students seeking admission to the most selective universities. "Is it fair if your parents went to the school you want to go to and you are a legacy?" she said. "Or that someone's older brother has a PhD and can help them in math and science? It's in everything."

Fair or unfair, the rise of the Velvet Rope in college admissions has broad implications. Over the last few years, a team of economists led by Harvard's Raj Chetty has detailed the links between declining social mobility in America and access to elite education for the very rich. At what they call the "Ivy Plus" universities (the eight Ivy League colleges plus Stanford, the University of Chicago, Duke, and MIT), more students came from the top one percent of American households than from the entire bottom 50 percent of households in terms of income. At Yale, a top choice of IvyWise students, the median household income of parents was nearly $193,000 with 69 percent of the student body hailing from the country's richest 20 percent of households. Students in the least affluent 20 percent of households account for just 2.1 percent of Yale's class. To put it another way, a child born into the one percent is 77 times more likely to attend an Ivy League college than a child born into the bottom fifth of American households.

Increasingly, elite college campuses look like gilded palaces for the children of the one percent. Flush with donations from wealthy parents and alumni and a rising stock market that's bulked up endowments, schools like the University of Pennsylvania have gone on a building boom. Whether it's cutting-edge labs and academic facilities or country-club-like dorms and dining halls, elite American universities are harder to get into and much more lavish for the small number of applicants who do attend.

As we shall see, even as the top schools have become more exclusive, opportunities on the other side of the Velvet Rope have narrowed. State schools and community colleges, which have long operated as engines for moving Americans from the underclass or working class into the middle class, have seen state funding drop. One surprise is that the Ivy League can be an engine of upward mobility, too, though primarily for the minuscule group of poorer Americans who are fortunate enough to go. Over half of Ivy Plus students from families in the lowest quintile of income eventually earn enough to make it into the top quintile, according to Chetty's research.

More than in other countries, though, Americans have long looked to the educational system, especially higher education, as the passport to a better life. Without the high-priced handling and careful positioning high-paid counselors provide, talented students who lack access have a harder time standing out in the win-or-lose admissions game. As other, wealthier applicants pay to jump the line, the odds for even the smartest middle-class students lengthen.

This isn't just a case of individuals losing out—there are societal implications, too. The most selective colleges are more than just places to get a great education. They create lifelong networks that put graduates in a prime position to eventually run corporate America, government, the media, and other industries. With the wealthiest and most connected applicants making up the lion's share of those admitted, a new aristocracy is forming. Indeed, the rise of firms like IvyWise or concierge medical practices speaks to how a small sliver of the population can essentially live a different life in the same country. Real obstacles that everyone else has to contend with—gaining admission to a selective college or securing an appointment with a specialist—melt away for a privileged few. The end result is an elite whose special access leaves them more and more out of touch with their fellow Americans.

For Richard Reeves, author of *Dream Hoarders,* which looks at how upper-middle-class parents pass on their status to their children through the likes of college counseling and intense tutoring, something more pernicious is at work in education than in spheres like travel and leisure. "What's being bought is opportunity for life," he said. "It's not just a better seat, a better view, or a glass of champagne on takeoff. If you get into a college you wouldn't have otherwise gotten into, it has real consequences." For those outside the Velvet Rope, Reeves said, "queue skipping goes from being an inconvenience to something that puts you at a disadvantage in terms of your chances in life."

5.

Security

Calls that come long after bedtime rarely bring good news.

So it was for Dick Fredericks, a San Francisco money manager and former ambassador to Switzerland and Liechtenstein, one Sunday night in October 2017. Fredericks was at his home in the city, not at his sprawling vineyard and estate to the north in Sonoma County. Before going to sleep he had smelled smoke, prompting him to check the stove to make sure it was off, but thought nothing of it and went to sleep. At 1 a.m. the phone rang. It was a friend and neighbor from Sonoma telling Fredericks that wildfires had broken out overnight and were threatening his property in the hills above Glen Ellen. Fredericks realized that had been the source of the smoke in the air earlier that evening—and if he could detect it fifty miles to the south in San Francisco, that meant some big fires were spreading. That autumn marked one of the most destructive wildfire seasons in California history. Fires in northern California alone consumed about 8,400 structures over nearly four hundred square miles of land, killing more than forty people.

The acres of vines under threat at his place were special—old-growth Zinfandel with rootstocks dating back nearly a century—but the house was a gem. Fredericks and his wife had designed their home a decade earlier and oversaw every aspect of construction. Made nearly entirely of wood in a farmhouse style, it had been used as a backdrop in photo shoots for Pottery Barn, Williams Sonoma, and others. Surrounded by grape vines on three sides and a grove of olive trees on the other, the house looked out onto rolling Sonoma hills, densely forested with stands of oak trees as far as the eye could see. Fredericks knew the place wouldn't stand a chance in a wildfire, so he did the only thing he could think of: he got into his Mini Cooper and sped across the Golden Gate Bridge in the middle of the night, desperate to save what he could. On his way to Glen Ellen, a wall of acrid smoke descended. And as he crawled up narrow country roads toward the house, his fear mounted.

"On the way up I was wondering, what do I take out of the house?" Fredericks said. "I don't know what I was thinking, to be honest. The computers were backed up. But I wanted to save my Native American blankets and art." By the time he got within a mile and a half of the house, embers filled the air and an orange glow lit up the sky. At that point, he ran into a roadblock. A hook and ladder truck blocked both lanes and firemen weren't letting vehicles go any further—it was simply too dangerous. "I said, 'My house is just up there,'" he recalled. "The fireman said, 'You don't have a house.' When I told him it was surrounded by vineyards, he said I had a shot." In some cases, the long rows of grape vines can serve as a barrier and block encroaching flames, depending on the winds and ferocity of the wildfire.

Fearing the worst, Fredericks turned around and headed back to San Francisco determined to do something. "It's my house, I'll do anything," he said. He wondered about the possibility of dropping fire retardant on the house from the air, so the following day he called a friend with a plane, only to be told it wasn't safe to fly because of the smoke. "Do you know anyone with a helicopter?" he asked, but the answer was the same—too risky to go up in the air in a chopper.

The next morning Fredericks dug out his insurance policy and called his agent, Steve Leveroni. "He reminded me I had Chubb Wildfire Defense Services," Fredericks said. "I couldn't remember if I'd paid extra for it, but I immediately called Chubb." The company's response surprised him. "They said they were watching my house and referred me to Wildfire Defense Systems," he told me. It turned out that help was on the way, but not from the local fire department or any of the other public agencies Fredericks assumed would be on the front lines in Sonoma County.

Based in Bozeman, Montana, Wildfire Defense Systems (WDS) fights fires—but they don't work for the taxpayers. They're hired by some of the country's biggest insurers to protect the property of individual policyholders like Fredericks. "They get called in kind of like Blackwater in Iraq," said Fredericks, referring to one of the private contractors who took on combat responsibilities for the Pentagon in the Middle East. "They said, 'We're watching it and when it's within two miles, we'll move,'" Fredericks remembered. "I said it's within two hundred yards, you better go. I was trying to impress on them that it was a whole lot closer than they were saying."

When the private firefighters arrived on Wednesday, the fire had already consumed one house up the road and was bearing down on Fredericks's place and others in the area. First, the private team went about securing the structure itself, clearing leaves from the gutters, raking mulch away from the house and removing cushions, mats, and other flammable material that could be set alight by flying embers. When they returned later that week, what Chubb calls an "active fire" had reached the property.

Each time the flames got near, the private firefighters fought it off, using a huge water truck and long hoses. They sprayed down hot spots to prevent the flames from reigniting, always a danger in dry areas with plenty of combustible material on the ground. By the next day, the fire was attacking from another direction near the pool house, so the team pumped water from the pool to beat it back and wet down a large area to create a barrier between the house and the flames.

Like a World War I battle, every inch of ground mattered—the fire crept as close as twenty feet at one point—but WDS spent nearly a week in the area and managed to hold it off. Most important for Fredericks's state of mind, WDS called to reassure him that the place was safe and even emailed pictures of the house, still standing. To Fredericks, private firefighters were a godsend but for Chubb they are a smart financial bet. As Fredericks put it, "Would the insurance company rather pay for a few guys on my property for a few days or for a new house?" All that was lost on his property were a handful of hundred-year-old olive trees that burned to the ground. In the end, it cost several hundred thousand dollars to field the team that saved Fredericks's home—far less than the millions Chubb would have had to spend to replace it.

Dick Fredericks is the definition of well connected: he went to college at Georgetown with Bill Clinton, which is how he ended up as ambassador to Switzerland from 1999 to 2001. As a securities analyst who followed the banking industry, and later as an investment banker and money manager, he was on a first name basis with many of the top financial executives in the country. Connections didn't matter when his home was threatened. What mattered was money. And in the Velvet Rope Economy, money doesn't just buy happiness, it frequently buys security. Even as life becomes more precarious and unpredictable for those without financial resources, cash doesn't just provide ease or access or exclusivity—it provides peace of mind.

On sunny California afternoons, when the mercury tops 90 degrees and the humidity drops, Mark Heine starts to worry. As fire chief of the Sonoma County fire district, he watched in 2017 as the conflagration that nearly claimed Fredericks's house in Glen Ellen swept over the Sonoma hills and devastated his district. Known as the Tubbs fire, the blaze destroyed a fifth of the homes and businesses in Rincon Valley. "God forbid we should experience another fire like that," he said.

The fire department itself was not spared. Along with the structures that burned to the ground, a fifth of Rincon Valley's tax base also went up in smoke. As a result, Heine is confronting a shortfall of $500,000 in his $4 million annual budget. It will be years before those properties are rebuilt and that deficit is closed, he said. In the wake of the fire, state officials had talked about supplementing the budgets of towns that were on the front line of the wildfires, like Rincon. But little additional money has been made available by the state.

Even before the Tubbs fire, Rincon Valley's resources had been thin on the ground. If they'd had more engines and firefighters, Heine said, the force might have been able to attack the fire itself during the first hours, rather than concentrate on rescuing people in the path of the flames. Guidelines call for one engine per 10,000 people, but the department serves 35,000 residents with two engines. There's no chance of buying an additional engine now. New fire stations, another necessity, will also have to wait for years, if not decades. "It's fascinating that a large wildfire could destroy the very fire department that responded to it," he noted.

Heine's territory in Sonoma is dotted with multimillion-dollar homes and residents who fall in the top one percent of U.S. earners, if not the top one tenth of one percent. You'd think they'd be willing to contribute more for a government service as essential as firefighting. But Heine finds himself scrambling for additional funds. "We're competing with all the other city services—law enforcement, parks and recreation, sanitation and water," he said. So as wildfires worsen, and public efforts prove inadequate, the private sector is coming to the aid of those who can afford to ante up. "When we roll into a street, our job is to save every property there," Heine said. "The insurance company wants someone parked at the house because their mission is different. They're protecting what they've insured, not what's most threatened."

That's prompted concern among California lawmakers like Assembly member Cecilia Aguiar-Curry. Her district includes much of Napa and Sonoma counties but after reports of seventy-five different firefighting firms with forty-one engines showing up during one wildfire in 2017, she proposed legislation that would require the state to develop standards and regulations for any privately contracted fire prevention teams operating during an active fire.

Private contractors would be required to check in with the public firefighting agency that is in command, and heed warnings to evacuate if ordered to do so. In addition, private vehicles couldn't use lights or sirens and would have to be labeled as nonemergency to prevent confusion with public first responders. "We have to have a clear chain of command and know who's on first," Ms. Aguiar-Curry said. "These homes are very expensive and owners pay a lot of money to make sure they are well taken care of. But I want to make sure everyone is taken care of."

Years of budget pressure have made that impossible, however. The Great Recession took a toll on local fire departments that was never rectified, according to Carroll Wills of the California Professional Firefighters union. "Municipal fire departments saw their ranks contract," he said. "When the recession hit, local agencies started closing fire stations or left positions unfilled." That attrition has undermined the mutual aid system in which fire departments share resources like fire engines and water trucks in the event of a wildfire outbreak. During the first twelve hours of the wildfires in northern California in 2017, local fire departments requested 305 engines from their counterparts further away. Only 130 arrived.

For homeowners like Fredericks, the security provided by Chubb's private firefighters is well worth the cost of going with a more expensive insurer. "Local jurisdictions and counties approve building in high-risk areas without providing for adequate fire protection," according to Dave Jones, the state insurance commissioner. "Because of the desire to have a bigger tax base, or allow more people to move in, or provide more amenities, the costs get shifted to the state or individual homeowners."

In 2011, the state imposed a fee of up to $152 per structure in heavily wooded or brushy areas, with the funds earmarked for the state fire department. However, after several years of complaints from the 800,000 or so property owners subject to the charge and opposition in the state legislature, the fire prevention fee was repealed in 2017. "The state was trying to rationalize this crazy system where local government put more people in harm's way but bore none of the costs," Jones said. "There was a hue and cry from residents of those areas who didn't want to pay."

Steve Leveroni, Fredericks's insurance agent, has deep roots in San Francisco—his great-grandparents arrived in northern California before the Gold Rush of 1848. Four generations of his family have lived in a house in North Beach that his grandfather rebuilt after the 1906 earthquake and fire that devastated the city. Even so, he wasn't prepared for the ferocity of the wildfires that nearly consumed Fredericks's home. "When you have something as catastrophic as happened here, resources get stretched," he said.

As Fredericks was heading to bed that fateful Sunday night, Leveroni was already in front of his computer. A client had phoned Leveroni at 10:30 p.m. after getting the call from the sheriff's department that everyone fears—his house had just burned down. "I put in all the zip codes of where we insure homes and up popped all my clients," Leveroni said. He started phoning insurers to make sure they were aware of the situation and had alerted private firefighting contractors like WDS.

Consumers tend to think of insurance as a commodity, with companies like Geico, Allstate, Chubb, and AIG basically offering the same product at nearly the same prices. The reality is different, said Leveroni. "Chubb specializes in high-value homes," he said. "They'd rather pay for private firefighters than pay out a $5 million or $10 million claim for a house destroyed in a fire." Not all the homes Chubb and Wildfire Defense Services saves are multimillion-dollar spreads in high-priced areas like Napa or Sonoma. Some are ordinary homes in other parts of the country ravaged by wildfire, as WDS's chief executive, David Torgerson, points out.

There are more than 250 private firefighting firms in the United States, and the largest, WDS, has resources rivaling public agencies. Founded in 2001, WDS began offering what Torgerson calls "loss prevention" to insurance companies in 2008. "In the past, it's been an all-government operation," Torgerson said. "But wildfire conditions are changing."

With more than one hundred full-time employees, WDS maintains an operations center in Bozeman, Montana, that is a private version of the federal government's National Interagency Fire Center in Boise, Idaho. Staffed 365 days a year, "it's unique to have such an operation in the private sector," Torgerson said. Working with ten major insurance companies, WDS's operations center tracks fires, gathers intelligence about their speed and direction, and determines which ones pose a threat to properties insured by the insurance companies it contracts with. The firm monitors tens of thousands of fire starts a year, Torgerson said, although only about 3 percent of them "threaten structures and go big."

Actually turning back fires or hosing down hotspots, like the firm did to save Dick Fredericks's home, is the exception rather than the rule for WDS. Most of their time is spent on preventing fire-related damage before properties are in danger. Professionals visit homeowners in the off-season to show them how to move combustibles away from the house and lower the risk in wildfire season. When fires are raging but still a safe distance away, the private firefighters can return and set up sprinklers with temporary water tanks on the lawn, close vents to prevent embers from lodging in vulnerable spots, and spray down houses with fire retardant gel. "We know the locations of these properties," said Torgerson. "Once they get to a certain threat level, it's about being prepared in advance. We know where the fires are, where the houses are, and when to dispatch our professionals."

It's a great service for those, like Fredericks, whose home would have gone up in smoke otherwise. But Amy Bach of United Policyholders, a San Francisco advocacy group for consumers, is uneasy with the rise of private firefighters who work at the behest of insurance companies. "You can't protect the few at the expense of the many," she said. "I would like those fire suppression and prevention techniques to be used for the benefit of everyone, not just people wealthy enough to patronize an insurance company that provides this service." But the reality, she acknowledged, "is that insurance is a for-profit industry. And innovation often happens in the private sector through entrepreneurial investment." And as each wildfire season proves worse than the last, private firefighters are drawing more notice.

In many ways, the erosion of public sector firefighting and the rise of private services for those who can afford them is a return to what prevailed in the United States in the eighteenth and nineteenth centuries. Back then, the economy was more laissez-faire and citizens couldn't rely on the government for basic services. Before the Civil War, private groups of volunteers would form firefighting companies and collect fees for saving homes or businesses in the event of a disaster. In a few cases, different groups of private firefighters would arrive at a conflagration at the same time and battle each other instead of the fire. There is a scene showing just that in the movie *Gangs of New York*. The tensions in California today between private firefighters and public ones are a contemporary echo of such nineteenth-century conflicts.

Even earlier, insurance companies employed their own firefighters to protect the properties they had underwritten, said Fran O'Brien, a senior vice president at Chubb. In fact, in the late 1700s, one of the predecessor firms that formed Chubb, the Insurance Company of North America, hired firefighters to work on their behalf in Philadelphia. In some cities, buildings had what were called fire marks, iron plates showing the logo of the insurer who protected the house. Chubb is today the world's largest publicly traded property and casualty insurer but its homeowners' coverage is focused on affluent property holders. "We do offer broader coverage than the mass market carriers," said O'Brien. "We're aimed at clients who want a different experience. In every market, there's an insurance company that could be cheaper but we have a more service-oriented approach."

Chubb began offering the private fire protection in thirteen states in 2008, and has since extended it to eighteen states. Chubb doesn't charge extra for the coverage—instead, it's built into the cost of the premium, which is why Dick Fredericks only vaguely remembered having it as part of his policy. Chubb doesn't pick which properties are rescued by private firefighters—that's in the hands of WDS, and it depends on the exigencies on the ground, not the value of the home.

Nevertheless, said O'Brien, "we do look for a return on the value of the program and we have to cover the cost in the premium. Over the course of ten years, given all the money we've put in, we've saved enough properties that it pays for itself." In 2017 alone, Chubb's service through WDS served one thousand homes and saved sixty-one properties that the company believes would otherwise have burned to the ground. Given that the 2017 California wildfires struck some of the most expensive real estate markets in the country—Santa Barbara, Bel Air, Napa, and Sonoma—that's a potential savings of hundreds of millions of dollars.

Besides the private fire protection, Chubb offers its well-heeled customer base other benefits in the event of a disaster that run-of-the-mill insurers don't provide. Before a hurricane, Chubb will move art or other valuables to a safe place for policyholders. In the event of an evacuation, Chubb representatives will visit properties within forty-eight hours of the storm's passage to alert homeowners about the condition of their house and expedite the response to a claim.

If Chubb is oriented toward wealthier consumers, then a specialty insurer called PURE is focused on them like a laser beam. Indeed, the name alone makes clear its target market is the one percent—PURE stands for Privilege Underwriters Reciprocal Exchange. The wealthy hardly lack for options when it comes to choosing from different insurers. But PURE chief executive Ross Buchmueller said that when he started the company in 2006, "we felt this was a large, growing market that was underserved. We felt we could do things better." Buchmueller knew the space well—he had previously created the private client business at insurer AIG, where he once hired a diver to retrieve a watch lost at sea. AIG helped pioneer private fire protection well before Chubb. But PURE goes beyond what its bigger competitors offer, delivering a whole different level of hand-holding and peace of mind to its elite clients.

PURE won't insure homes worth less than $1 million, but that's really only the starting point. Many of its clients are people whose personal compass points from Fifth Avenue in Manhattan to the Hamptons in the east, Palm Beach to the south, and Aspen out west. "This is a fairly common picture and the puzzle of their life comes together with us," Buchmueller told me.

When a Chicago family's prized collection of rare African American Christmas ornaments was destroyed in a fire, PURE replaced all of the pieces, which had been assembled over thirty years. "We could have written them a check but money was not the issue," Buchmueller said. "They had spent a lifetime putting that collection together. Over the course of a year, we visited shops and craftsmen and hung out on eBay and re-created the entire collection." PURE also helps homeowners secure and install their own private generators, another example of how in an age when public utility service is eroding, the wealthy take matters into their own hands to safeguard their homes and assets. To reduce damage from burst pipes, PURE covered repairs and contributed to the cost of installing digital monitors for Long Island homeowners who winter in Palm Beach and other warm weather locales. If temperatures plunge again, or the heat fails and no one is home, the team members visit the house to make sure the pipes don't freeze.

PURE works with the likes of WDS but sometimes even that's not enough to hold the flames back. When a PURE member lost his house in the same fire that nearly claimed Fredericks's vineyard, a claims adjuster used floor plans to locate the family's safe. When it turned out not to contain the jewelry the family was looking for, the adjuster returned to the site with a family member and dug through the charred rubble. Eventually, they managed to recover a handful of prized rings. "I don't know whether she will ever wear the jewelry again, but she got it back," said Buchmueller.

The security and second chances enjoyed by the likes of PURE's clients is a world away from the sense of precariousness that envelops the lives of many Americans, especially since the Great Recession. In a 2017 Federal Reserve survey, a quarter of Americans said they skipped medical treatments because of the cost in the prior year, while 23 percent said they did not expect to be able to pay the current month's bills in full.

The white-glove treatment at PURE and other high-end insurance companies also stands in sharp contrast to what people who file claims at less expensive carriers often run into, according to Amy Bach of United Policyholders. "If you file a big claim, to some degree insurance is like everything else: You get what you pay for," she said. And as the claims process becomes more arduous at mass-market insurers, those who can opt out turn to specialized insurers like Chubb and PURE. Buchmueller, it turns out, was right about the demand from the rich being there—PURE's business has been growing by more than 20 percent a year, far above the single-digit growth registered by more conventional insurers.

Gavin de Becker was barely out of his teens when he saw how Hollywood royalty traveled. It was a world apart, where any and all needs were attended to, every courtesy extended, and all the details taken care of ahead of time. "Never wait a second for a car, or a table at a restaurant, and every elevator door held open," de Becker recalled of his days working as an assistant to Elizabeth Taylor and her then husband, Richard Burton. Later, as Hollywood's go-to security consultant, he advised stars and studio heads on what he terms threat assessment, analyzing the danger an obsessed fan or stalker might pose, and recommending how to respond.

His L.A.-based firm, Gavin de Becker and Associates, employs 840 people and operates in nine countries, guarding international executives, politicians, members of wealthy families as well as figures from the Hollywood milieu where he got his start. He even found time to write a best-selling book, *The Gift of Fear,* which became a favorite of Oprah's. It told readers how to recognize real threats and not be distracted or troubled by imaginary dangers. "My main work is anti-assassination services," he said. "I'm in the business of preventing tissue damage."

It's an unusual résumé—physical security, logistics, psychology, and celebrity all come into play. But de Becker had an unusual insight. "What movie stars experienced forty years ago can be simulated, even nearly replicated, for a fee," he explained. Out of that was born the Private Suite at LAX, which opened in 2017. A separate, stand-alone terminal at the airport, it serves commercial airlines but mimics the privacy and protection available to those who can afford bodyguards and private jets. Far from the prying paparazzi with their telephoto lenses or the iPhones of selfie-seeking fans, the Private Suite is an island of serenity and privacy in a place where both are in very short supply.

As my American Airlines flight pulls up to the gate at LAX, I spy a silver 7 Series BMW idling on the tarmac during a tryout in spring 2018. It's for me. And when the cabin door opens, not one but two people are there to greet me as I step off the plane. The black-suited Private Suite employee barely says a word as an uncharacteristically friendly American Airlines agent greets me and then punches in a code to open a locked door by the jetway. After she walks me down the stairs to the car and the handover is complete, the Private Suite representative introduces himself and a man behind the wheel. "My name is Chris and this is Ryan, who will be driving," he says. Ryan and Chris are equipped with earpieces to stay in touch with the other members of the eight-person team assigned to me. Why does a single traveler need a staff of eight? Well, one is responsible for admitting the guest to the secure building, and another escorts him or her to the suites. A third and fourth assist with any special service requests like meals or scheduling a medical visit in the suite, while the fifth takes them through TSA and Customs. The sixth drives clients to and from the plane, while the seventh serves as an advance person on the jet bridge. An unseen eighth employee deals with luggage.

Ryan opens the door for me and I take a seat in the back of the BMW, where the windows are shaded for maximum privacy. The silent treatment is standard protocol for members of professional security teams, who are trained not to disturb the high-value targets they protect, and it is the model for the Private Suite's employees. As we make our way past jumbo jets taxiing for takeoff and a cluster of parked private jets, Chris speaks up. "It might seem like we are going slowly," he says, "but there is a twenty-mile-an-hour speed limit on the runway." Amid the sheer pleasure of not having to fight my way through the crowded terminal or search for my luggage at the carousel, I hadn't even noticed.

When I arrive at the Suite, the additional staffers are there to greet me. At every stage of transfer, there are always "eyes on" the client, and I am walked to a tastefully designed room. Here, I can relax, sample snacks like raw dark chocolate with Himalayan pink salt and mini bottles of tequila and bourbon and take a hot shower. Like the rest of the Private Suite, the aesthetic is minimalist modern, with a palette of grays and beiges to soothe weary travelers. There's a garden as well, with a tent for kids to camp out in while families wait for flights, and an area for pets to stretch their legs. I'm just in for the day, so I lie down on a banquette and watch planes take off and land until it's time to chat with de Becker himself. If I were staying in Los Angeles, I'd zip out of the gate and onto the freeway—the Private Suite is accessed through a different entrance than the rest of the airport, so there's no need to deal with the traffic snarl that is an ever-present feature of driving in or out of LAX.

The Private Suite, de Becker explains, is the antidote to what modern travel has become. "Airports are an environment of suffering and misery," he says. "It's a real cattle call. They shout at you if you don't know to take off your shoes." The atmosphere at the Private Suite is just the opposite. TSA and customs agents are a few steps from my room—the Private Suite pays the government for the equipment and personnel—enabling clients to skip another of what de Becker terms "pain points" for fliers. Frequent fliers and elite credit card holders may have access to club lounges at the airport but they don't provide the space the Private Suite does. "Clubs are beautiful at 6 a.m.," he said. "At 6 p.m. there's a butt in every seat."

Unlike those spots, there aren't many communal areas at the Private Suite. The emphasis here is definitely on privacy, as the name suggests. "Some younger people said we should have a bar," he told me with a shake of his head. "It's not a pickup joint. There is no shortage of opportunities for travelers at the regular airport to experience other people. This place is providing the one thing that's unavailable in modern travel and that is calm." Los Angeles is a gateway for travelers from Asia and other distant places, and the goal is to provide them with the sense of finally arriving at their destination and being able to relax and decompress, even if they're just waiting for a flight. "If your plane is delayed when you are at the gate, that extends your suffering," de Becker said. "If it's delayed and you're at the Private Suite, that extends your comfort."

For decades at his security firm, de Becker had toyed with the idea of creating what would eventually become the Private Suite. "Since 1980, I'd wanted to find a way to make LAX not a nightmare or a potential security breach for my clients," he said. But as time passed, the obstacles seemed too great, especially after airport security was tightened dramatically following the terrorist attacks of September 11, 2001. "Before then, a few of my clients could drive up to a plane," he said. "That became impossible after September 11th." Travel was turning into something arduous—even for people who normally had the resources to clear the brush in other spheres—and de Becker doubted whether he could get the proper approvals to create a separate, secure environment for fliers.

Then one day, about ten years ago, de Becker received a text from a friend in London. It was a photo of what was then called the Windsor Suite, a semisecret oasis at Heathrow that was funded by the British government and catered to royalty (hence the name), visiting foreign leaders, and the occasional A-list actor or celebrity. "I flew over immediately and checked it out," he said. Besides its own terminal, the Windsor Suite had its own security screening, rendering any contact with the main terminal unnecessary in many cases.

Elite passengers could walk into the Windsor Suite and be driven directly to the plane. "You didn't have to think about which gate to go to, what time to line up, boarding passes, baggage, or customs and immigration," said de Becker. "All of that was taken care of and the logistics were smooth."

Now called Heathrow VIP, it features certain quintessentially British touches—travelers are greeted by a doorman in top hat and tails and there are butlers to help guests—but it became the inspiration for de Becker. He actually hired two veterans of Heathrow VIP to help him create and run the Private Suite.

Private equity giant TPG, which owns a slice of his security firm, is now a part-owner of the Private Suite as well. A constellation of forces aligned to help turn de Becker's vision into a rarefied reality. TSA and customs staff were delighted at the prospect of moving people off the sidewalks and out of the lines at the main terminal, where celebrity sightings frequently brought things to a halt. "There was a daily drama with celebrities and paparazzi at LAX," de Becker said. "Tens of thousands of regular passengers were affected."

Government agencies now also use the Private Suite as a testing site for new technologies and processes, like more advanced X-rays and other screening equipment. The perpetually cash-hungry city authority that oversees the airports was happy to have an additional $350,000 each month in fees from the Private Suite. But above all, the commercial airlines were eager to see it succeed as a way of clawing back market share from private jets, according to de Becker. "Every airline is trying to beat the pain point on the ground," he said. "You can make the airplane as nice as possible but you still have the airport. Luxury is predictability—when passengers typically drive to the main terminal at LAX, you might spend ninety minutes trying to get through traffic."

Getting in and out of LAX didn't always resemble the time-bending obstacle course that now confronts anyone who can't afford the Private Suite. But LAX's evolution, or perhaps devolution would be a more appropriate term, is part and parcel of why the rich are flocking to solutions like the Private Suite in the Velvet Rope Economy. Jack Keady, a West Coast manager for American Airlines from 1976 to 1993 who now consults for airports and airlines, remembers when it actually was a pleasant place to catch a flight. "It used to be far easier," he said. "No traffic jams, and dropping passengers off or going through security was a piece of cake."

But the last complete makeover of the airport was in the early 1980s, in advance of the 1984 Olympic Games in Los Angeles. At that time, LAX was designed to accommodate up to 40 million people annually. Nearly 87 million people used it in 2018 and traffic is growing by 4.5 percent annually. "It's just a natural mathematical progression and more people need more space," Keady said. Although the public agency that oversees the airport has spent billions on new terminals, he explained, "they haven't added a square foot of new roadway in decades, nor have they added curb space." A massive $14 billion renovation has been under way since 2009 and is expected to be finished in 2023. But with traffic steadily rising, it's an open question whether it will do enough to relieve the congestion. Transportation industry advocates say 100 million people could use the airport annually within a few years.

The arrival of carriers with direct service to Los Angeles from Asia, like China Southern and Hainan Airlines, and fast-growing domestic budget airlines, like Spirit, has only added to the crowds on the ground. The end result is more congestion. The Private Suite is good news for those who can afford it, Keady said, "but the airport and the government and the airlines have gradually conditioned people to a worsening situation. Does a public airport really want to cater to the ultrarich?"

The answer is yes. And the Private Suite shows how far public entities like LAX will go to relieve the hassles and headaches faced by their most wealthy and influential customers, said Michael DiGirolamo, former deputy executive director of operations at LAX. "I've spoken to people who use it and they love it," he said. "But the fact that they're willing to pay that kind of money is a reflection of how bad the congestion is." With travel on the rise in the 1990s, Los Angeles airport officials began planning an expansion that would have centered an additional new terminal to the west of the current terminal complex and spread traffic more evenly through the area. But the alternate site never got off the ground.

"It was handled very poorly and the community was very vociferous about not expanding the airport," said DiGirolamo. An urban studies major by training, DiGirolamo worked at LAX from 1975 to 2010 and watched as more and more passengers gradually overwhelmed the airport. "They can't get the planes in and out of the gates in a timely manner," he said.

Flying in and out of LAX would still be a reasonable experience even if 65 million passengers a year used it. At 87 million, "everyone is looking for a way out," DiGirolamo said. Getting the Private Suite itself through the public oversight process wasn't simple but it had political support from entertainment industry executives and other L.A. movers and shakers. "LAX moves a lot of Hollywood types and high-end travel companies wanted to see it work out," he said. What's more, the Private Suite hired former Customs and TSA officials to advise it, helping clear the way to have officers from those agencies on site.

So at the Private Suite, it's just a few steps from the private airport entrance to the compound. A few steps more and you're through TSA security and into the waiting BMW when it's time to fly. From a control room equipped with satellite and video technology, staff members communicate with the airlines so they can take guests directly to the plane when it is time to board, avoiding side trips through jammed departure lounges. The average number of steps from car seat to plane seat at LAX is 2,200, according to de Becker. At the Private Suite, it's just 60.

About half of the Private Suite's members are based in L.A., but de Becker is seeing more travelers from the Middle East, Russia, and Europe sign up. In many cases, Hollywood stars expect studios to cover the cost of the Private Suite in their movie deals. "It's becoming a standard contract term, like first class travel or luxury hotels," de Becker said. For paying customers, the price might seem ridiculously high, but it's a bargain compared with the cost of a charter, de Becker pointed out. Instead of spending $200,000 to charter a flight to London, a studio can use the Private Suite and spend a fraction of that getting stars and their assistants to London on a commercial flight. Members of the Private Suite pay $4,500 to join—service for each flight costs $2,700. It's possible to use the service à la carte if you're not a member for $4,000 per trip.

Encouraged by the success of his project at LAX, de Becker launched the Private Suite at Century City for elite shoppers at the Westfield mall there. Members drive in via a special ramp gate and put their car into a private parking area for extra security and privacy. From there, it's a short walk to the suite where personal shoppers from the likes of Bloomingdale's, Nordstrom, and Tiffany can display their wares. If a client wants to take a walk and check out the Tesla dealership or have a bite at Eataly, there's a private elevator and security guards from Gavin de Becker and Associates are there to escort them. "My company can bring Rodeo Drive to them," he said. "We go in the back door of most of the shops. We can even arrange to have a movie theater give private screenings for our clients."

Like several other architects of the Velvet Rope Economy, de Becker followed an unusual path before becoming a gatekeeper to the elite world of security and comfort. He attended Beverly Hills High School, where he made the initial Hollywood connections that helped determine his idiosyncratic path in life. But that was only because his grandfather rented a one-bedroom apartment in Beverly Hills so de Becker could attend school in the ritzy district. It was a troubled upbringing. "We lived in ten places before I was ten and I was poor through high school, on welfare and food stamps," de Becker said in a matter-of-fact way. "We got a color TV once but it was repossessed."

He witnessed violence at home, including when his mother, who was a heroin addict, shot his stepfather. He survived, but de Becker's mother ultimately committed suicide at age thirty-nine, when de Becker was sixteen. By high school, he had already learned not to react with surprise to the extreme wealth he saw around him. A friend would come to school in one of two Rolls-Royces his family owned, either a powder blue model or a burgundy one. "I pretended not to notice," de Becker said. "I acted like it was normal."

Carrie Fisher was a friend in high school and they remained close friends until her death, when he delivered a eulogy at her memorial service. Another key player in de Becker's life was Rosemary Clooney, the singer and actress, who looked after him following his mother's death. After becoming Clooney's road manager at eighteen, he worked for Dean Martin's family. He was soon hired as an assistant by Elizabeth Taylor, and the rest, as they say in Hollywood, is history. "I had moxie," he said. "I was Elizabeth Taylor's only traveling staff member and I developed an expertise from having to hire guards, pilots, doctors, and other staff whenever we traveled."

While still in high school, de Becker also became obsessed with security and the ever-present threat of violence. "From the Kennedy assassination onward, I was fascinated by strategies for keeping people safe," he said. Self-trained, de Becker wrote a report on protecting public figures for a trade journal in the mid-1970s, which was eventually picked up by the U.S. Department of Justice. Soon, de Becker was working with agencies like the Secret Service, the State Department, and the Justice Department. He launched his private security firm in 1979, and more recently created MOSAIC, an online tool that helps potential victims of domestic violence assess the dangers abusive partners or other family members pose.

At sixty-five, de Becker realizes that he owes some of his success to the extreme segregation of the rich from everyone else in society, even as he finds it bizarre at times. Indeed, given his background and sensitivity to the needs of others, he's deeply aware of America's growing social divisions. Many others in his orbit—he lives in Maui and visits L.A. and the Private Suite about once a month—are oblivious. "It's like something out of Ayn Rand," he said. "I don't know what the solution is but the folks in Silicon Valley aren't even talking about the problem. San Francisco is like the Roman Empire. They assure their dinner guests that everything is all right while people are gathering outside the palace walls." There were huge incongruities between how he lived as a child and what he saw in classmates' homes in Beverly Hills, but thanks to social media everyone now lives with the awareness of these social gaps. "Johnny Carson was quiet about being rich," he said. "He wouldn't mention his tennis court. Now it is for everyone to see. No intelligent culture would make that choice."

Paradoxically, until de Becker created the Private Suite, LAX and other airports were a glaring exception in the otherwise tiered Velvet Rope Economy. "The airport was a democratic environment," he said. "It was shitty for everyone. The only place where VIPs were treated badly was the airport."

Now, anyone with enough money can travel like a Hollywood star, with money subbing for talent. And de Becker has plans to open versions of the Private Suite at other airports, starting with John F. Kennedy International in New York. The Private Suite is already partnering with American Express and the Four Seasons hotel chain. Some deep-pocketed travelers on their way to Las Vegas from Asia and the Middle East are also ferried through, courtesy of the casinos. A faster connection, and less stress at the airport, means gamblers will have more time at the gaming tables and be willing to place bigger bets. "Casinos want to treat high rollers well," he said. "We can help with customs and immigration and quickly have them in a private jet on their way."

Caryn Seidman-Becker is creating a similarly frictionless experience for a much larger but still privileged group. Her company, Clear, uses biometric markers like fingerprints and the irises of a person's eyes to speed paying customers through security lines at thirty airports and more than a dozen sports stadiums.

A former Wall Street analyst and asset manager, Seidman-Becker envisions a world where everything from presenting an ID to swiping credit cards and signing in as a visitor to an office building is replaced by biometric data. Members join Clear for $15 a month or $179 a year and their information is recorded, encrypted, and stored. Verification at Clear stations requires seconds, so at the airport Clear members can make it to the X-ray machines well before the poor souls who are forced to wait in the regular security line and need to show a driver's license. Delta, which owns a 5 percent minority stake in Clear, allows members to check in to its elite lounges using fingerprints. The company is now working with sports teams so fans can use fingerprints to enter the ballpark, pay at concession stands, and prove their age when purchasing alcohol.

"A customer doesn't buy security, you buy a frictionless experience," Seidman-Becker said. "But we can't offer that unless we are a company focused on security. Security is the oxygen we breathe." It sounds slightly dystopian—Clear customers serenely shop, fly, and check in with their biometrics (giving up a little privacy to facilitate the process) while ordinary folks are relegated to slow-moving lines. But that division is Clear's business model. "So much of the world is bottlenecks," she said. "People spend years of their lives waiting in line."

Clear might seem like more evidence that as the experience for the majority of consumers deteriorates, it improves for a select few. Naturally, Seidman-Becker sees it differently. "There are different levels of the Velvet Rope," she told me. "Can the Velvet Rope be more mass?" It's hardly mass at this point, but Clear is growing rapidly, with more than 3.5 million members. "It took six and a half years to get to the first million and less than a year to get the next million," she said. By 2020, Clear aims to have 10 million members.

For a company that specializes in speed at the airport, Clear had trouble getting airborne. First launched in airports in 2005, Clear signed up 200,000 users before running out of money in 2009 and filing for bankruptcy. Seidman-Becker and her team bought what was left of Clear at a bankruptcy auction. They slowly rebuilt the company, retooling its procedures to win over wary airport managers who had watched it collapse the first time around.

Orlando International Airport, which handles 47 million passengers each year on their way to and from the lines at amusement parks like Disney and Universal, gave the company a second chance and helped get it back on its feet. Since then, Seidman-Becker has been able to convince outside investors to put money into Clear. Besides Delta, investment firm T. Rowe Price is a backer, as is Jeffrey Boyd, the former chief executive of Priceline.

Like the Private Suite, Clear was helped by the fact that airports are always looking for additional funds. Clear pays a percentage of its revenues as rent but there are other advantages for the airports in moving travelers through rapidly. "If someone gets through security more quickly, they are more likely to spend at Starbucks or Hudson News on the other side," she said.

Seidman-Becker has long been drawn to turnaround stories. A political science major at the University of Michigan, she dreamed of a career as a sports reporter but took a more conventional path and got a job on Wall Street soon after college. After working as a research analyst, she joined an asset management firm, searching for companies that seemed like promising investments. Although Wall Street is famously male-dominated, Seidman-Becker said she "never thought of herself as a woman, only a passionate team member" until she was eight months pregnant and raising money for a new hedge fund. After finishing her pitch, the potential investor had a question. "What makes you think you are going to come back after you have a child?" he asked. "I was dumbfounded. I said, 'I'm sitting here, aren't I?' I was always the one who wanted the ball."

She watched the turnaround of Apple and later Priceline, and was fascinated by the difference smart management could make at a troubled company. "I had great experiences buying flops, so I'm happy with a low bar," she said with a laugh. She scooped up stock of Activision Blizzard in the early 2000s for a few dollars a share when the videogame maker was struggling; it now trades for nearly $50 per share. So when Clear was put up for auction following its bankruptcy filing, she saw an opportunity that was too good to pass up. "It was out of business but consumers missed it and I wanted to build something," she said. "I didn't want to die and have someone say she picked good stocks. I had invested in biometrics before and believed it could change the way people live, work, and travel."

At airports, her goal is to get fliers through the Clear line to the X-ray machines in five minutes or less. Every morning at 5:30, Seidman-Becker gets a report showing the volume of passengers at each Clear location, including verifications per hour. It used to take 3 seconds to verify each Clear member but the company has cut that to 1.5 seconds, with half a second as the goal. Once every two weeks, Seidman-Becker goes out into the field, visiting Clear checkpoints, and observing traffic flow. As of 2019, Clear had more than 1,700 employees, and is hiring several hundred new staffers per year.

Clear's technology—using human features to verify identity—has the potential to go far beyond airports or stadiums. "Why do you have to pull out your health insurance card and have it Xeroxed at the doctor's office?" she asked. "Or whip out your Sam's Club card? You can do all of that with biometrics. Clear can put wallets out of business." It can also deliver instant gratification, she said. For example, a restaurant chain or airport lounge could record your preference in coffee or taste in wine, matching it with your iris, fingerprints, face, or voice, so drinks can instantly be served up without even having to ask.

What will happen to people who can't afford to be members of Clear or partake of similar fast-track services in the Velvet Rope Economy? In past historical epochs, when the gap between the privileged and the hoi polloi grew too wide, the result was a revolution from below. In France, aristocrats faced the guillotine, while in Russia, the bourgeoisie were violently stripped of their homes and fortunes.

It's a bleak vision but one Gary Lynch, general manager of Rising S, deals with on a daily basis. Lynch is in the business of building bunkers and bomb shelters for Americans who believe war, civil unrest, or an economic collapse threatens the country and want to protect themselves when the government can't or won't. Lynch's customers are often depicted as eccentrics holed up in country hollows awaiting the end of the world. Survivalists like those got star treatment in the hit National Geographic channel show *Doomsday Preppers.*

Rising S, a Texas-based company, does build bare-bones underground shelters for that crowd. But since 2012, Lynch has been catering to a different group—wealthy citizens who want all the comforts and amenities of home if and when catastrophe strikes. "We've revolutionized the bomb shelter," he told me. "Everybody was building cold and clammy structures, with no color, no nothing, just a storm shelter with some shelves. You could drive to work in a Kia but what if you want a Mercedes and can afford it? Our clients are like that."

Lynch's upscale clients share the view that society is splintering and fear the consequences for the privileged in a world where the collective trust in public institutions has weakened. It's a dark take on American society, but one that keeps Rising S's nearly 100,000-square-foot factory humming with new orders. "We are one unjustified police shooting away from having riots across the United States," Lynch said. "A lot of people are worried about war, social and civil unrest." So far, that's meant building an underground swimming pool for one client, while another ordered a hidden stable to keep his valuable stud horses safe.

Even people whose views aren't that pessimistic are taking matters into their own hands. And as basic municipal services like firefighting become unreliable, maybe deluxe bunkers aren't so crazy. It's a view that's gaining popularity in the wealthier tiers of society where the Velvet Rope Economy is thriving.

Six years ago, Roman Zrazhevskiy founded a company that provides personalized emergency kits. "We're the REI of the survival business, with a little bit of Stitch Fix," he said, referring to the online styling and personal shopping service. Zrazhevskiy assumed his customers would be what he called "the doom and gloom crowd, people who spend their lives thinking about the worst case scenario each day." In fact, his clientele is shockingly normal. "Ninety percent are regular people with regular jobs, upper-middle-class families with income above $100,000," he said. His customers would need that kind of income to afford his kits, which average $2,200 for a family, although much cheaper options are available for as little as $200. The basic kit includes food rations to last seventy-two hours, pepper spray, heat packs, and glow sticks. Other popular additions include gas masks and decontamination gear in the event of a chemical, biological, radiological, or nuclear attack. Recently, he's seen an uptick in demand for bulletproof backpacks for children in the wake of mass school shootings and active shooter situations.

For the very rich, physical risk is no different from financial risk—it's something to be managed, said Tom Gaffney, a competitor of Lynch's who has carved out a niche building hundreds of bunkers and safe rooms in the tonier precincts of Manhattan. "They look at the numbers," he said. "High-end townhouses on the Upper East Side are a big market for us. TriBeCa and SoHo, too." A native of County Sligo, Ireland, Gaffney got his start in the 1980s, building check-cashing stations in the South Bronx. "Ballistic glass, steel walls—they were basically safe rooms," he said.

Because space is at a premium in New York, Gaffney's shelters tend to be dual use, with an underground movie theater or entertainment room frequently doubling as a bunker billed as capable of withstanding nuclear, chemical, or biological attack. A twenty-by-forty-foot underground bunker might cost half a million dollars, while an aboveground safe room just off the bedroom in the form of a walk-in closet is a bit less, about $300,000. "The aesthetics have to match," Gaffney said. He uses high-end veneers and rare woods so visitors never notice the walls in a particular room are bulletproof and resistant to forced entry.

His firm, Gaffco Ballistics, is based in South Londonderry, Vermont, but several times a month Gaffney drives into Manhattan to supervise the installation of one of his high-end shelters. September 11 was an initial catalyst for individuals, but business has picked up in recent years, with orders rising 30 percent annually. "There is a sense of a lack of security in the world," he said. "Every time there is a school shooting or a terrorist attack, that adds to it."

Bunkers underneath townhouses sometimes plunge two stories below ground, and come with a separate air filtration system, radiation detectors, and a generator and battery packs if the generator fails. "Particles from a dirty bomb won't go below concrete," Gaffney explained, citing one particular fear of his clients. In what seems like something out of *Dr. Strangelove,* or perhaps the tomb of a latter-day pharaoh, gourmet chefs prepare freeze-dried meals that can last two years, including treats like pasta with chicken and spaghetti Bolognese. "It's got to be microwavable," he said.

And in a nod to Clear, Gaffney's clients are asking for biometric entry instead of an old-fashioned lock and key, so safe rooms can be accessed with an iris scan or a thumb print. For a wealthy homeowner in Greenwich, Connecticut, Gaffney created a safe room that was also a wine cellar, with four hundred bottles ready for Doomsday. "He said if the worst happens, he wanted to be able to drink his wine," Gaffney remarked. "I'd rather sit in a bar like Rosie O'Grady's pub in Times Square."

These fears and the desire for protection spring from "an awareness the government has limited resources and that people need to be responsible for themselves," said Anna Bounds, a professor of sociology at Queens College who has studied urban preppers in Manhattan. "They know from Hurricanes Katrina and Maria that FEMA isn't reliable." Indeed, Bounds sees a larger pattern in the booming demand for the services that Gary Lynch and Tom Gaffney provide. "This is just one illustration of the wealthy opting out and creating their own world," she said. "Only the rich have the ability to opt out of the system through these mechanisms."

For those who can't afford to opt out, life outside the Velvet Rope hasn't merely become less secure and less predictable. Increasingly, things that were once part and parcel of middle-class life are out of reach for them. That's the focus of this book's second section, Outside the Velvet Rope.

Outside
the
Velvet
Rope

....

6.

Exclusion

....

The bucolic town of New Albany, a thirty-minute drive into the Ohio countryside from the state capitol in downtown Columbus, is a picture of prosperity. Multimillion-dollar homes line Kitzmiller Road. These include the property of the wealthiest man in Ohio, Les Wexner, the founder of L Brands, which owns Victoria's Secret and The Limited. Wexner spearheaded New Albany's development, buying up farmland that he turned into upscale subdivisions. The mayor of New Albany, Sloan Spalding, compares Wexner's strategy to the way Walt Disney quietly assembled the real estate parcels that would become Disney World in Florida.

New Albany has been transformed in the past twenty years from a small town with fewer than five thousand residents into an exurban bedroom community for white-collar professionals who work in Columbus. "It was rural—there were more cows than people," jokes Spalding. And in a Velvet Rope meets *Field of Dreams* way, New Albany is a case of Build It and the Affluent Will Come. "They built a golf course and country club before they built houses," Spalding said. The bet worked—New Albany's population has doubled to roughly ten thousand.

It may be a bit manufactured but residents pride themselves on small-town friendliness, and there's a tidy collection of restaurants and shops in a development called Market Square that doubles as a downtown. Spend a morning at the Starbucks, and you'll see New Albany's leading citizens pass by, along with stay-at-home moms and dads who work locally. "We try to remind our children that we live in a bubble," added Mr. Spalding. "This isn't reality."

But reality has a way of intruding into even the most idyllic places. In New Albany's case, trouble was brewing in the schools. The size of the student body grew along with New Albany's population, even as state funding for the district stayed flat for years. Costs were rising, too, but in the fall of 2014 voters rejected a ballot initiative to raise taxes for the local system. It was a shock—tax levies had routinely passed for years, including in the late 1990s when the town built a new high school and athletic fields.

Something had to give and the school board moved quickly: more than fifty teachers were cut and families were forced to pay $250 a year for their kids to participate in extracurricular activities like Model United Nations and band. Bus service within a few miles of the school was eliminated. And to help cover the cost of high school and junior high athletic programs, New Albany turned to a solution that's becoming more and more common across America—pay-to-play fees. Unless parents handed over $625 per sport per semester, their children couldn't join a school team, whether the game was basketball, soccer, football, or baseball. There was no cap, so parents with two children in school who wanted to play football in the fall and baseball in the spring now faced an annual bill of more than $2,000.

If all of the students in New Albany lived on Kitzmiller Road and the neighborhoods near the country club, the fees wouldn't have been much of a problem. But New Albany includes more modest middle-class pockets as well. And there was an additional wrinkle—the borders of New Albany's school district extend well beyond the town itself, and encompass much less affluent areas in the city of Columbus.

For the most affluent, the decision to reject the tax hike made perfect sense in a bottom-line, dollar-and-cents calculation. Some well-off parents sent their children to private schools or no longer had children at home, so participation surcharges didn't affect them in the slightest, unlike a tax hike. For those who did send their children to public schools, the higher fees often worked out as less costly than having to pay thousands of dollars in additional taxes. "There was a sense of community but when the tax levy failed, it was go to your corners," said Michael Klein, a school board member at the time. The attitude among wealthier residents, he added, was that "if you had money, fine. If not, something had to be sacrificed and if it's the people who don't have money, so be it."

Klein is not among New Albany's wealthiest residents; he's solidly middle-class. When he was young, he dreamed of going to Syracuse University and becoming a broadcast journalist. "My parents sat me down and said we couldn't afford it," he explained. Klein attended Ohio State and graduated with a degree in journalism, but couldn't imagine living on the $13,000 salary that entry level positions in the field afforded. He joined Anheuser-Busch, earning $35,000 to start, and is still there after twenty-eight years, making about $75,000 a year as a quality-assurance analyst, testing Budweiser and other beers as they go through the production process.

With help from grandparents and his ex-wife, Klein scraped together enough money for one sport per semester for his two kids. A divorced father, the fifty-year-old Klein told his children why sacrifices would have to be made, much as Klein's parents had told him when he was applying to college. "Our older one did cross country in the fall and begged us to run track in the spring," he said. Klein also had to explain to them why other kids could play on as many teams as they wanted.

In New Albany and many towns like it throughout the country, sports are about much more than games, Klein said. And teams from New Albany routinely make it into state championships. "It's all-encompassing," he said. "It's a conversation starter and finisher in every interaction." On a more practical level, playing on a team would be very important as his daughters applied to college and sought to build up their applications. "One thing I learned about the college application process is that you want a good résumé," he said. "But the kids that come from wealthy families have a distinct advantage over the kids from less wealthy families. You're from the other side of the tracks."

Klein's fellow school board members were more affluent as well. "They're not people who have to look at their checkbook every Wednesday," he said. As a school board member, Klein voted for the cuts and the imposition of fees, believing there was no other choice. But he had second thoughts and left the board soon afterward, and then led a public campaign to roll back the fees. He launched a petition drive on Change.org and set up Facebook groups to help organize the opposition. With his journalism background, he knew how to write press releases and pitch the story to local media. It became front-page news in *The Columbus Dispatch* and on the local television news. The effort did create tension with his former school board members but they relented only slightly—the fees were lowered to $425 per sport per semester.

Even at that level, Klein said, "people had to decide between going on vacation and having their kids play track." For their part, the school board saw the issue as a matter of priorities. The town may have been sports-mad but ultimately academics came first. If fees weren't imposed, then more teachers would have to go. "School board members would say 'Maybe they shouldn't go on vacation,'" Klein recalled. "Maybe that's true but that's a heck of a thing to say to someone. There was an empathy gap."

The passions have cooled but the wounds from the fight over fees have yet to heal in New Albany. "There was a tremendous amount of division and protest," said Kevin Reed, the athletic director for New Albany schools from 2010 to 2016. "It really hurt a lot of people." Local boosters and community leaders have contributed to a fund to provide aid for students, but it only goes so far. For middle-class families in New Albany, pride made it hard to step forward. "People don't want to ask for handouts," Reed said. "So they went away." Klein ended up catching flak from both sides. After the school board vote, people accosted him and yelled about the participation fees. When he reversed his stand and led the campaign against the fees, "at Starbucks, so many people let me know they didn't like my tactics."

Raising money to help pay for student athletics didn't begin with New Albany. Both school teams and local recreational leagues have long relied on fundraisers and sponsorships by neighborhood restaurants and other small businesses for support. What makes pay-to-play different is that it's not a volunteer effort; it's a mandatory, district-wide policy that doesn't affect students equally—yet exceptions are rarely made. Increasingly popular club teams, which aren't connected to schools, cost thousands of dollars a year to join. So ability no longer determines whether you make the team—money does.

In the first part of this book, most of the examples revealed how consumers face tiering and increased segmentation as they interact with private companies and institutions. But separation is now taking place within public institutions as well, subverting the values that made them public in the first place. "It's disconcerting that parents have to raise money for basic necessities like art or a library," said Kajsa Reaves, whose daughter attends public school in New York City. "Ideally, the public school system should not be based on socioeconomic status the way it is now."

As the Velvet Rope Economy spreads into every corner of our society, public schools and colleges are excluding those who can't afford to pay up. In higher education, cuts in funding from federal, state, or local governments push tuition up even amidst institutional decline. At the high school and elementary level, parental resources tip the balance. Public services begin to resemble the private sector, where money takes priority over citizenship and gives society's most likely to succeed an additional head start.

Even in areas like New Albany, where economic resources are ample, middle-class families find themselves excluded from activities they once took for granted. That's the economic impact—but the emotional impact runs deep, too. In the teenage years, sports are a confidence booster, especially for young women. Team spirit and a sense of belonging are just as important for adolescents, as is the knowledge gained from persevering after losses.

None of this has prevented pay-to-play fees from catching on nationally. A national poll by the C.S. Mott Children's Hospital found that 61 percent of young people in middle or high school sports were charged a pay-to-play fee. "We've privatized school sports," said Sarah Clark, co-director of the Mott poll. Almost 30 percent of parents said school activities were more expensive than they had anticipated, a 2019 Mott poll found. The survey also showed that 18 percent of parents earning less than $50,000 felt participation wasn't worth the cost, compared to 6 percent among parents who earned more than $100,000.

In recent years, pay-to-play fees have soared as school budgets became tighter. Nearly a fifth of the families surveyed by Mott said they paid more than $200 to participate on a team. The fees are now spreading from sports to other extracurricular activities and after-school programs, Clark explained. "Our results signal that a similar trend is happening in music but we don't talk about that as much because it's not as sexy as sports," she said. Bruce Howard of the National Federation of State High School Associations is more blunt. "If schools are charging kids $100 to play on the football team, they're charging $100 to be in the band," he said. "Most schools would rather impose fees than get rid of these programs entirely."

The underlying causes of rising pay-to-play fees go well beyond the school board meeting room or the local polling place and extend to state legislatures and governor's mansions. In Ohio, state aid to local districts was flat between 2009 and 2014 as then-governor John Kasich tried to close a post–Great Recession multibillion-dollar deficit after he was elected in 2010. When the economy began to recover, however, the pressure on schools didn't let up. With the deficit closed, Kasich pushed for deep cuts in the state income tax. As a result, according to Howard Fleeter, an economist and research consultant for the Ohio Education Policy Institute, a nonprofit research group, Ohio gave up at least $1.7 billion in tax revenue between 2013 and 2016.

Years of inadequate support from the state took their toll, said Ryan Gallwitz, the former principal of East Knox High School in Howard, Ohio, a community in farm country an hour's drive from New Albany. Participation fees were make-or-break for many families there. "Kids who couldn't afford it didn't play and we couldn't get quality coaches," he said. In Ohio, parents can switch their children to nearby public school districts. So many East Knox parents decided to move their children to the school system in neighboring Danville, which had better-funded programs and teams that were still winning. "The whole athletic program in East Knox took a nosedive," Gallwitz said. "Pride in the whole school system went down." Music and art were eliminated at the elementary and junior high school level. "Kids picking up a musical instrument for the first time in high school?" he asked. "You know how well that works out."

Across the state, attempts to ratify new property tax levies to raise funds for schools were failing to pass, just like they had in New Albany. Many school districts simply gave up asking voters for money. Between 2013 and 2017, the number of proposed new tax levies in Ohio fell by nearly 75 percent. One critical factor, according to Fleeter, is that for the rich, fees are much less expensive than new property taxes. And the more expensive the house is, the bigger the impact of any tax hike. "The wealthier you are, the better the deal it is," said Fleeter. "When you look at the recent landscape for funding both at the local and state level, school districts have been under enormous pressure to reduce costs any way they can." In Ohio, 124 districts added fees between 2005 and 2015, compared to 55 in the previous decade.

In East Knox, a tax increase was eventually approved, but plenty of scar tissue remains, Gallwitz said. Some students returned to East Knox but resentment lingered between families who had stayed and those who had left. Gallwitz attended East Knox and played football there and is now principal of the high school in Centerburg, a better-off town that's closer to Columbus and where students are more college-oriented. "There was a loss of connection in East Knox," Gallwitz said. "There's something about a kid playing on the field where his father and grandfather played football."

Spending priorities are set by principals, superintendents, and school boards, but the role of gatekeeper falls to teachers and coaches. It was a painful position to be in. "I had kids crying," said Amy Glenn, who has taught in New Albany for twenty-four years and coaches girls' track. Sometimes, young people would show up at practice, even if they couldn't afford the fee, hoping to be allowed to participate. "I'd think to myself, how do I help this child?"

As much as she wanted to let them play, Glenn couldn't bend the rules. Students were eventually allowed to carry a balance, rather than have to pay it all at the beginning of the semester. But the board still meant business—if students owed fees when it came time to graduate from high school, the district would withhold their diplomas. Nor were teachers exempted. "I had to pay $425 to coach my own kids," Glenn said. She applied for a scholarship from a local community foundation. "It was an extremely lengthy process—it was like taking out a mortgage," she said. "In the end, they awarded me $50."

New Albany is considerably wealthier than East Knox, but participation there quickly dropped, too, especially in less popular sports, like track, swimming, and girls' softball. "We barely fielded a softball team for girls this year," said John Townsend, a New Albany parent. Less able players were among the first to bow out, Townsend said, and that's a loss for them and the team. "If they're going to be the seventh or eighth player on the team, it's not worth it," he said. "But there's always a kid who barely made the team in seventh grade and then becomes a star in eleventh grade. Now they may not be there."

Hard as it was on individual coaches like Glenn or parents like Townsend, it was even worse for Kevin Reed, the former athletic director in New Albany. "I was the repo man," he said. "I was spending a lot of time collecting pay-to-play. I'm the one sending reminders and telling coaches that if Johnny hasn't paid by the 15th, he can't come to practice. You have to tell a kid they're done in front of the whole team, while some parents are throwing down $1,800 checks for their kids."

Reed, who worked in education for thirty-four years, retired in 2016, two years after pay-to-play went into effect in New Albany. "My whole premise for doing what I did was to see kids participate," he said. "I'll be honest. The last two years were the most difficult of my career."

Mike Sagas earns nearly $200,000 a year and he could barely afford his daughter's soccer team in Florida. The catch is that her team had nothing to do with school. She was part of a local club team, a parallel world of youth athletics that has overtaken high school sports in many areas and replaced it entirely for the best student athletes. Also known as travel teams, the uniforms alone are more expensive than pay-to-play fees. For soccer moms and dads, the annual cost starts at $2,000 to $3,000 and can quickly rise past $10,000 for clubs that travel frequently to state and national championships. Hockey is considerably more expensive. And taking their cue from the professional sports leagues, club teams are also a big business, with multimillion-dollar facilities to host games and coaches who can earn more than $100,000 a year. All told, with registration, coaching, travel, and facility fees factored in, club teams are a $2.4 billion business, according to Susan Eustis, president of WinterGreen Research, which focuses on the youth sports market.

After-school jobs won't cut it when it's time to come up with that kind of cash. In the end, the opportunity to play—and potentially win a college scholarship—is mostly reserved for kids whose parents' income puts them in the top 10 percent of earners. "It's the gentrification of youth sports," said Jay Coakley, an emeritus professor of sociology at the University of Colorado.

Clubs do provide financial aid so some low-income children can play but the number of these scholarships is limited, and when the cost of travel is factored in, club teams are still out of reach for all but those identified early as super-talented. As for families earning roughly $50,000 to $100,000, they are almost completely shut out. "Everyone is worried about poor kids but there are monies being put in that direction," said Eustis. "There's no talk and no indication that anyone has noticed this is an issue for middle-class kids."

Even more than pay-to-play fees, the rise of club teams marks a profound shift in American society, especially in terms of the lives of young people, both rich and poor. For the latter, athletics were traditionally a way to escape poverty. Think *Hoop Dreams* and inner-city children hoping to make it to the pros in basketball or a Little League phenomenon catching the eyes of a baseball scout. For better-off children, sports has been a great equalizer, uniting kids from both sides of the tracks on one team with one goal— winning. Those days are fading, said Mark Hyman, a professor of sports management at George Washington University. "Sports was a social leveler," he recalled. "My dad was a dentist but the father of the kid who played left field on my team in the 1960s drove a garbage truck." There's a physical toll, too—many club teams practice nearly year-round, leaving young people more vulnerable to getting hurt. Half of youth sports injuries are due to overuse.

Why do parents pour such large sums of money into club teams? The dream of an athletic scholarship for college is a major motivator, said Tom Farrey, executive director of the Sports & Society Program at the Aspen Institute. When a child shows promise in elementary school, Farrey said, parents are willing to write annual checks for $2,000 or $3,000 a few years later in the hope it will get them into the NCAA pipeline. Or even give them a shot at a pro career. "College sports is built on the idea of providing social uplift," Farrey noted. "What's happening and what is new is that the kids who have those opportunities disproportionately come from homes where the parents already went to college and have resources."

Sports scholarship awards for Division I and II teams in the

NCAA have risen from $377 million in 1992 to $3.3 billion, but the odds of winning a free or partial ride as a student athlete are still exceedingly slim. But the bigger pot has helped fuel the club team boom. "That's a lot of chum to throw into the water and the money makes the parents crazy," Farrey said. But just 5.5 percent of high school soccer players make it to the college level. And even among that select few, not all players qualify for scholarships. Division III colleges, the largest group among the NCAA tiers, do not provide sports scholarships at all.

However remote, at least kids on club teams get a crack at athletic scholarships. Or an edge in the admissions game for schools that don't offer sports scholarships. But students who only play on high school teams are increasingly excluded from this process, said Farrey. With the exception of football, he said, "scouts are no longer at high school games. They do all of their scouting through club teams." At club tournaments, dozens of college coaches come to watch the top players on the field on one weekend, rather than having to monitor hundreds of high schools. "The scouts can do all of their shopping in one place," he said. In many cases, club coaches will actively discourage members from playing on their high school squads, making those teams less competitive.

Some talented kids never even try out for club leagues, discouraged by parents who are understandably scared of the cost. Stephanie and Paul Roell's daughter Hailey was a catcher on the recreation league softball team in their Indianapolis suburb when a club league parent saw her play. He called Stephanie and suggested Hailey try out for the team. That was the first sign of trouble—it was $35 for the tryout. Stephanie was still interested even though, on Paul's $70,000 salary, it would be a huge stretch for the couple. "You're looking at $6,000 to $10,000 with travel but I would have worked two or three jobs to do it," she said. "You don't want money to hold your children back." Paul was firmly opposed and there was tension in the house, which Hailey picked up on, Stephanie Roell said. "She's wise beyond her years and she decided against it," she said. "We were happy."

Mike Sagas could afford the club team hustle—barely. And he knew all about how tiny the chances of winning an athletic scholarship are because he's a professor of sports management at the University of Florida. "It's not like I was duped," he said. "I knew the perils and risks." But when his daughter proved talented at soccer in elementary school, he couldn't resist the pull of a club team. He enrolled her at age twelve, paying the standard $2,000 to $3,000 annual fee. Joining early is important—kids who can't afford to sign up immediately fall behind. "If you're not in the club system by eleven or twelve, it's too late," Sagas said. "You don't know the game well enough."

Madison Sagas was gifted and her team quickly outgrew Gainesville to take on club teams from Orlando and Jacksonville. Each of these cities is a two-hour drive from Gainesville, and the gas bills quickly mounted. But that was nothing compared to the charges for hotels and flights as Madison's team competed in one regional tournament after another. Travel expenses for coaches had to be covered as well. By the time she turned fourteen, Madison's team had made it to the national championships in Washington, D.C. "It was the perfect storm," Sagas said. That year, he began tracking every dollar on an app—the annual cost came to $18,311. How did he come up with the money? Other parents put everything on credit cards, and tried to chip away at what they owed later. For Sagas and his wife, Alison, paying for the club team meant no longer going out to dinner and forgoing a new car. "We saved almost nothing," he said. "We were spending everything to keep afloat." Madison did eventually win a scholarship—for $1,000 a year, a fraction of what Sagas had spent on club sports or what he now pays in college tuition for her at the University of North Florida.

Along the way, Sagas occasionally put his professor's hat on and studied the club team phenomenon. The poor were eliminated early on, while middle-class families struggled until they, too, were cut. By the time the travel costs really began to kick in, nearly all the kids who remained had parents whose income was in the six figures. Sagas also discovered that town parks and recreation departments, hungry for extra revenue, would rent out their fields to club teams, even if it meant squeezing out local leagues and residents. "There'd be twelve fields and ten would be reserved and two would be marked public," Sagas said. And the club fields would be better maintained than public ones in many cases. "Your kids are less likely to play on a field with potholes or rocks and dirt," he added. "That's what you pay for."

Tim Schulz needed a job—two of them, actually. He'd retired from playing professional soccer at age thirty-one after his league folded but he wanted to stay in the game somehow. So in addition to a job in construction and another one delivering packages for UPS, Schulz coached two club teams on the side in Littleton, Colorado, outside Denver. He earned $100 a month from coaching—it was 1990 and the club boom was years in the future. "There was a lot of pushback even on that $100," he recalled. "It just wasn't accepted that everything wasn't volunteer." His teams did well, though, and within a few years there were eight hundred children enrolled in what became known as the Colorado Rush. When parents offered Schulz $18,000 to coach full-time, he quit his job at UPS. By the mid-1990s, club soccer was becoming more popular and more kids were signing up. In 1998, the Rush's roster was up to 4,800 players and Schulz was offered $55,000 a year to coach. He quit his construction job.

Soon, club soccer began to catch fire nationally and Schulz started thinking beyond Littleton. "There was a void," he said. National organizations devoted to youth athletics weren't focused on club sports, he said, and many of the new teams didn't know how to handle logistics like budgets, hiring and firing, and fundraising. Although still technically a nonprofit, Schulz transformed the Rush into a franchise operator, licensing out the Rush name and running the back-office functions for teams across the country. Other clubs have emulated Schulz's model but the Rush is the largest soccer club operator in the world, with fifty-four clubs domestically, forty-nine abroad, and 38,000 kids playing in its affiliates.

What began with coaching two teams for $100 is now a sizable operation: when new teams partner with the Rush organization, they pay a one-time initiation fee of $10,000 and then $12 for every player in the club. The Rush's revenues top $2 million per year—a long way from when Schulz was delivering packages and coaching on the side. Indeed, coaches typically earn anywhere from $55,000 to $85,000, with salaries over $100,000 in wealthy areas around big cities like Dallas, Los Angeles, Washington, and New York. When it comes to the advantages club teams possess over their high school rivals, the game is lopsided. "We've got a full-time director of coaching who is a former pro," Schulz said. "A high school coach is probably a chemistry teacher who coaches after school for an extra $3,000. I'm not saying it's right, it's just the reality." Schulz agrees that middle-class kids are frequently excluded from this world. "It's sad," he said. "It's a dilemma."

What accounts for the explosive growth of club teams after decades in which school teams were the main athletic outlet for parents and kids alike? Dev Pathik, who heads up a firm that advises cities and entrepreneurs on how to build facilities for the club market, sees a shrinking public sector as one critical piece of the puzzle. After the No Child Left Behind Act was signed into law in 2002, school districts shifted money out of sports programs to help fulfill testing requirements, Pathik said. The recession further decimated athletic programs, while cuts to parks and recreation budgets limited other once affordable options like lower-cost, rec league teams.

The youth sports world is full of paradoxes—parents chasing will-o'-the wisp scholarships, the best athletes dropping out of their high school teams, and team travel budgets that could qualify coaches for elite frequent-flier status. But the biggest one may be this: even as towns were cutting spending on parks and rec, they've invested in building facilities for private teams, with 70 percent of them now government-owned. They're mostly reserved for paying customers, though, not the general public, said Pathik. "When you have fewer school sports and slots for kids, parents turn to the private sector," he said. "It's become so exclusive, but there's no other outlet for sport."

The city of Westfield in Indiana borrowed $85 million to put up the Grand Park Sports Campus. The four-hundred-acre facility opened in 2014 and features thirty-one fields, twenty-six baseball diamonds, and an events center with three full-size indoor fields with synthetic turf. The latter can be rented for $250 to $525 an hour, depending on the season and time of day. The cheapest option is grass outdoors—for $85 an hour. There certainly is money to be made: club teams practice four or five nights a week and play almost every weekend in season. Local rec leagues pay a quarter of that, but the rent still adds up. "There is nothing in our facility that's free," said T.J. Land, business development manager for Grand Park. "It's kind of weird but we are effectively a business run by the city."

The sports gap between the rich and everyone else is also a matter of health. Participation in team sports is closely correlated to income, according to a 2018 study by the Aspen Institute. Children in households where income exceeded $100,000 were more than twice as likely to play as those where incomes were below $25,000. About 25 percent of children whose parents earned between $25,000 and $50,000 engaged in no athletic activity at all in the previous year, compared with just under 11 percent for the over $100,000 demographic. Tom Farrey, who oversaw the study, summed it up. "We've separated into a nation of sports haves and have-nots."

Sports are only one aspect of the way parental resources make public schools more like their private counterparts, as Kajsa Reaves discovered. By the time her daughter finished second grade, Reaves was ready to switch her to another elementary school in New York City. Geographically speaking, it wasn't such a big move. P.S. 191, which her daughter had attended since pre-K, is separated by fifteen Manhattan blocks from the prospective new school, P.S. 87. (Reaves asked that her daughter not be identified.) Both draw students from the Upper West Side in New York City. One is in the shadow of Lincoln Center, the other is half a block from the American Museum of Natural History. There the similarities end. P.S. 191 draws many of its students—but not all—from public housing. About 85 percent of them are black or Hispanic and 82 percent qualify for free or subsidized lunches. By contrast, nearly two thirds of P.S. 87 students are white, and only 12 percent are classified as economically disadvantaged. Look beyond the data and the contrasts grow larger still. At P.S. 87, school supplies are abundant, as are special enrichment classes. There's no shortage of teacher's assistants in the classrooms. Field trips are free and frequent and there's even money for yoga sessions and chess.

Supporting these kinds of activities is a constant struggle at P.S. 191, or in some cases an outright impossibility. There are no aides in the kindergarten classes and field trips aren't subsidized by the PTA. But unlike New Albany, the problem isn't a question of funding from New York City's Department of Education—on a per student basis, P.S. 191 actually gets 20 percent more money from the city. What makes the difference is the PTA. In each of the last three years for which tax filings are available, P.S. 87's PTA raised more than $1.5 million. It spends the bulk of that each year, but still has $1.5 million set aside for a rainy day. In the best year at P.S. 191, where more than 80 percent of students are economically disadvantaged, the PTA raised about $30,000.

Once restricted to raffles and bake sales, the fundraising and spending power of parent associations at some public schools now rivals that of tony private academies. Indeed, across town at P.S. 6 on the Upper East Side, according to *The New York Times,* the names of the children of top donors are engraved on plaques in the auditorium, a pint-sized version of similar honors at the Metropolitan Opera.

The benefits—or lack thereof—are clear, and, like other aspects of the Velvet Rope Economy, self-reinforcing. After pre-K, more affluent parents pull their children out of P.S. 191 and place them in schools like P.S. 87. Without PTA cash to make up for the gap, P.S. 191 students fall further behind. For Reaves's daughter, the fifteen-block journey meant entering a world of possibilities that were closed off to students at P.S. 191. "She had a nice library and more science labs and art," Kajsa Reaves said. "It felt like there were field trips every week."

Million-dollar PTAs aren't limited to Manhattan, where the gap between the rich and everyone else is a given. They are a national phenomenon, according to a report by the Center for American Progress. "In short, wealthy parents are raising large sums of money to improve their already-advantaged schools," the study concluded. "The situation inevitably contributes to educational inequalities—even though it is completely hidden when looking at public spending."

The highest-grossing PTA in the country was in Highland Park, Texas, one of the wealthiest Dallas suburbs. Districts in California were well represented, and PTAs in North Carolina, Tennessee, and Massachusetts rounded out the list. "We expected there would be more money coming into wealthier PTAs but the amounts were pretty staggering," said Scott Sargrad, vice president of the K–12 Education Policy team at the Center for American Progress and a coauthor of the study. "That buys real things for these schools, like money for staff members to teach art, music, and physical education."

The rise of the Velvet Rope in public schools parallels its development in the private sector over the last two decades. In states like California, public referendums have restricted the ability of school districts to raise taxes. Donating—heavily—to the PTA is a way of getting around public policy, said Ashlyn Aiko Nelson, a professor at Indiana University's O'Neill School of Public and Environmental Affairs. "We'll just innovate to get the funding we want in our district," is how she describes the thinking of PTA parents.

It's a mind-set that's becoming much more common: Nelson found that between 1995 and 2010, revenue for school-supporting nonprofits rose from just under $200 million to more than $880 million, a 347 percent increase. For the vast majority of schools that can't compensate for broader cuts by raising money privately, the options are limited and students suffer. Over the same period in California, where constraints on spending have become a way of life, the state went from ranking in the top 10 states nationally in terms of academic performance to the bottom 10 states, Nelson said. Parents in wealthy towns like Orinda had an out, however, raising nearly $2 million in one year for two elementary schools. "When the government fails to provide the level of services demanded by local citizens, they find a workaround," she said.

Before she transferred her daughter out, Kajsa Reaves did her best to make a difference at P.S. 191. When her daughter started kindergarten, Reaves and two other moms resuscitated the PTA and began raising money. "We were very aggressive, we were pushy," she said. At schools with a preponderance of upper-middle-class parents, PTA presidents suggest annual donations of $1,000 or more. That was out of the question at P.S. 191, and Reaves told parents that if everyone gave $5 or $10, the donations would add up. "We got resistance even for that," she said. Eventually, the PTA did raise roughly $30,000—enough to create a small two-room library at the school with books donated by parents at better-off schools. P.S. 87 held a teacher-appreciation party at a nearby hotel one year but when Reaves was president of the PTA at P.S. 191 they had to settle for a gathering in a classroom. "It didn't measure up to the standards of P.S. 87 but the teachers were very appreciative and grateful," she said. The Education Department bars PTAs from hiring teachers in core subjects like math or English. But hiring extra staff for literacy intervention or math tutoring is fair game, as is creating outdoor space, like a new kindergarten playground at P.S. 87 that was built with PTA money.

Other obstacles besides family income prevent many PTAs from raising significant amounts of money. Many parents in disadvantaged schools don't have the legal and accounting know-how to set up nonprofit foundations, said Dennis Morgan, whose two children attend a school in Harlem. "We had a parent who was an accountant and knew the ropes," said Morgan. "Other schools don't have people who work in those industries and who can draw from those professional experiences." In wealthier schools, he added, better-connected parents can turn to their networks to find auction items like a free week at day camp or a $3,000 discount on sleepaway camp tuition. "That socioeconomic class can create an auction and get very high-ticket items," Morgan said. "They have access."

At P.S. 191, white parents gradually moved their kids to better-performing, wealthier schools as their children advanced, leaving upper grades poorer and more segregated. So with each passing year, the meritocracy moved further out of reach for those left behind. In third grade at P.S. 191, more than half the students were ranked as proficient in English. Two years later in fifth grade at P.S. 191, just 17 percent performed at that level, and none were considered advanced. Meanwhile, at P.S 87, the upward trajectory is practically assured, with 88 percent scoring as proficient in third grade and 75 percent as advanced in fifth grade.

It wasn't easy for Reaves to find a spot for her daughter in another school—zoning rules for public education in New York City are notoriously complicated and parents who want to transfer their children face a thicket of red tape. Some rented small apartments within the catchment zone of P.S. 87 and other top schools in order to have an address that entitled them to entry. Others appealed through the Education Department's byzantine transfer process. "We weren't desperate enough to rent a studio," Reaves said. "But wealthier parents have more ability to work the system."

Because P.S. 191's overall test scores were low for two years in a row, Reaves and other parents were given the option by the New York City Department of Education to move their children into better-performing schools. "As much as I wanted to make things work at P.S. 191, I just couldn't," she said. "They don't have the resources P.S. 87 has. It's like that everywhere in America. It's a class society."

Kristy Sanchez sees both sides of that divide. She took over the

PTA at P.S. 191 after Reaves left but works two blocks from P.S. 87. "If parents can afford the rent in that neighborhood, then paying $800 per child to the PTA doesn't seem like a burden to them," she said. "They're saving on private school. So if you want a better education at public school, you might as well pay for it."

Along with the struggle to raise money for the PTA, Sanchez is frustrated by the exodus of affluent parents after preK. "I had a mom stop me and ask, 'Are you going to keep your son at 191?'" Sanchez recalled. "She said, 'I don't think I'm going to keep my daughter because of socioeconomic issues.' I grew up middle-class but how does she know I'm not poor? Maybe I come from the bottom of the bottom." The PTA does its best to cover the cost of field trips for lower-income parents, Sanchez said, while teachers asked for help in buying basics like hand sanitizer and wipes.

Things have improved at P.S. 191 in the last few years. The school moved into a new building in 2017, with more labs and plenty of natural light that fills hallways and classrooms. P.S. 191 is also known under a new name, the Riverside School for Makers and Artists, and art and design are incorporated into the curriculum, whether it's making paintings or designing a squirrel-proof bird feeder. Still, the school remains a microcosm of the dizzying inequality of present-day Manhattan. The school occupies the first few floors of a new tower where one-bedroom apartments rent for as much as $6,000 a month. While students eat subsidized lunches down below, residents enjoy a dog park, a boxing studio, a wine tasting room, and the services of a twenty-four-hour concierge.

The principal of P.S. 191, Lauren Keville, emphasizes that her school isn't a stereotypical down-on-its-luck, decrepit urban public school, and that's obvious from a quick visit. Children's art projects dot the walls and classrooms are well stocked with instructional material and children's books. Still, as Ms. Keville puts it, "funding isn't holding us back but there are things we'd like to have if we had the resources." Chief among them would be teaching assistants in kindergarten. "The first question prospective parents ask is whether there are aides in kindergarten classes," she said. "We do not have that because it's usually funded by the PTA. But it's a big advantage for students to have that. Early childhood is such an important foundation."

While test scores have improved recently, they remain significantly lower than many other neighborhood schools, and P.S. 191 parents like Sanchez can't help envying P.S. 87's success. "Parents flock to schools like 87 because the test scores are through the roof," Sanchez said. "Their kids are going to make future presidents."

The huge disparities between PTAs in New York recently prompted the City Council to pass legislation that would require the Education Department to track donations annually and make the information public. Mark Treyger, the council member who proposed the bill, told the *New York Daily News* that "there are some schools that have raised more than $1,000,000. But other schools have to start a GoFundMe page just to have basic resources. If a PTA has raised $1,000,000, that's a million opportunities that other kids don't have."

Efforts to remedy the situation by spreading the largesse have been few and far between. The only major city that tries is Portland, Oregon, where a local nonprofit, All Hands Raised, oversees the process. Once local school foundations raise $10,000, one third of each additional dollar of revenue goes into a fund that supports poorer schools. Out of $3.9 million raised in one recent year, about $1 million was redistributed.

Dennis Morgan, the Harlem parent of two, would like to see a similar system in New York. He is a member of the Community Education Council for District 3, which includes P.S. 87 and P.S. 191, and advises the Department of Education. "I have no problem with PTAs raising as much as they want to," he said. "My problem is the inequality and the disparity." When he's raised the subject, some parents respond that their organizations wouldn't be able to raise as much money if some of it were shared. "Others feel, 'Who am I to say how their money should be spent,'" he said. "But we need to start the conversation because right now, the game is rigged." In fact, PTAs from schools with more prosperous families, including P.S. 87, have recently begun partnering with P.S. 191, as have nearby private schools. They provided advice for the auction, and contributed expertise.

It's human nature for parents to want to support their children any way they can, said Dan Ryan, chief executive officer of All Hands Raised, and nothing is going to stop those who can afford it from giving to their schools. Some parents say the split should be more generous, with 50 percent or more going to poorer schools. Others complain the shared donation schemes amount to a tax on those with the means to give. "In Portland, you don't want to be too loud on that," he said. "But this policy reminds people that they are in a public school, not a private school. With that comes a shared responsibility for other kids in the district. It's the right thing to do."

When Michael Bloomberg announced in November 2018 that he would donate $1.8 billion to his alma mater, Johns Hopkins University, the world cheered. And why not? It was part of the single largest donation to an academic institution in American history and boosted the university's endowment by more than 40 percent to over $6 billion. Even better, the money would be earmarked to fund increased financial aid to students from low- and moderate-income families and make Hopkins's admissions policy need-blind forever. As Ronald J. Daniels, the president of the university, put it, Bloomberg's donation was "staggering in its vision and breathtaking in its impact."

Tony Liss should have been among those cheering. He earned a BA in physics from Johns Hopkins in 1979, and it launched him on a thirty-year career as a professor and administrator. But he had mixed feelings about the gift. To be sure, he was proud as a Hopkins alum. But Liss thought about how a donation of that size from

Bloomberg, the former mayor of New York City, would transform the institution where he serves as provost, the City College of New York. At Johns Hopkins, 15 percent of its 6,100 undergraduate students qualify for Pell Grants and other low-income tuition assistance, a share that Bloomberg's gift would push to 20 percent. City College has more than twice as many students pursuing a bachelor's degree, and 63 percent come from low-income households. "Hopkins is already a very wealthy institution," Liss said. "We are a barebones institution. If Bloomberg or somebody else had given us a fraction of that we'd throw the city's biggest party ever."

For generations, City College has stood for a particularly American kind of social mobility. It epitomized the public university that had the power to move its graduates up the social ladder. The children of immigrants, many of them poor Jews from Eastern Europe, flocked to City College in the first half of the twentieth century and their success extended far beyond its gothic campus in Harlem. Ten graduates of City College went on to win Nobel Prizes—more than the total number from Ireland and Brazil combined.

Today, the majority of students at City College and its parent, the City University of New York (CUNY), are immigrants and people of color but the ambition is no less intense. Ranked by their ability to lift students from the bottom quintile of income to the highest quintile, eleven of the top fifteen colleges in the United States were part of the CUNY system. "It's the engine of mobility for poor students and working-class students and it always has been," said Stephen Brier, a professor of urban education at the CUNY Graduate Center. It's also massive—nearly 250,000 students are enrolled at CUNY. That's more than the size of the entire Ivy League.

But there's a major difference between the City College of today and the glory days of the last century, when it was known as the poor man's Harvard. For more than 125 years after its founding in 1847, City College was tuition free. Even during the depths of the Great Depression, when Brooklyn College and Queens College opened, school was free for full-time students. But the policy couldn't survive New York City's fiscal crisis of the mid-1970s, when budget shortfalls forced the city to the edge of bankruptcy. Attitudes toward publicly funded higher education were changing, too, with politicians and the public less willing to cover the costs, according to Brier. When the Ford administration rejected a bid for a bailout of New York in 1975, one of the reasons it cited was the unafford-ability of free tuition at the city's university system.

Tuition costs started off small but gradually rose through the 1980s and 1990s, especially after budget cuts under Democratic and Republican governors alike. Even as private universities saw their endowments rise along with the stock market in the 1990s and 2000s, public institutions endured one lean year after another. More budget pressure followed the Great Recession, which took a toll on New York State's finances. More than half of the classes at CUNY are now taught by adjunct professors who earn $3,500 to $4,000 a course per semester and can't provide as much one-on-one instruc-tion as full-time faculty do. Even if adjuncts teach six classes a year, a full schedule, their pay comes to less than $25,000. "How can you live on that in New York?" said Brier. "You can barely live on that in Columbus, Ohio."

Today, tuition is just under $7,000 per year at CUNY's four-year colleges. Even with the help of scholarships and Pell Grants, that's a heavy burden on campuses where nearly 40 percent of stu-dents come from households earning less than $20,000 a year. At private universities like Johns Hopkins, Brier said, "there's an image of well-scrubbed, well-fed students walking around. Our students look different. They not only have trouble making tuition payments, we've got students who are homeless and food insecure."

Classrooms and hallways look different from private universi-ties, too, according to Liss. When he arrived in 2013, Liss was sur-prised to find pails in some buildings to catch dripping water after it rained. The leaks eventually get fixed but it can take a year or more to get funding to make repairs on the campus, which dates from 1907. "It's difficult to keep up with the problems," he said, especially because the college runs at a perpetual deficit.

As he rides to work on the subway each day, Liss has watched Columbia University's Jerome L. Greene Science Center go up one stop before he exits. Against the backdrop of the Hudson River, giant cranes lower the girders into place. Designed by architect Renzo Piano, the 450,000-square-foot building is the largest Columbia has ever constructed, part of a $6.3 billion extension of the campus into Harlem, and bringing together scientists and scholars from across the university. With donations from the likes of Mortimer Zuckerman and a $10.9 billion endowment, the massive project isn't putting a strain on Columbia's finances. And with a deep pool of applicants to Columbia College, many of whom can afford to pay $77,000 a year to attend, there's always a ready source of additional funds.

City College's endowment totals roughly $264 million, a fraction of what Columbia's new science building alone costs. But what the school lacks in donations, it makes up for in the affections of New Yorkers, said Liss. "If you wear a City College sweatshirt, people stop you," he said. "It's changed so many people's lives. That's why our faculty stays here despite the struggle. Because with almost everything we do, there's a struggle to fund it." Like science labs. When CUNY's medical school replaced microscopes, "we took the hand-me-downs," said Liss. "It was better than what we had."

The college recently had to scramble to find $50,000 to fund a fellowship program that places students from underrepresented groups into PhD programs and eventually into academia. "That's not a lot of money and we will have to figure out how to do it," he said. "But it'll mean not doing something else."

When he studied at Johns Hopkins, tuition was $3,300 a year—a sum Liss covered with student loans as well as a job in a physics lab where he made cables. He got a great education at the university, but never felt connected there the way he does at City College. "I didn't feel like Hopkins needed me," he said. It's true—City College does need him in a way Hopkins did not. But although Liss is dedicated, he's realistic about the limits his institution faces. "We're not waiting around for the state to send us more money because that's not likely to happen," he said. "I don't hold it against wealthy institutions that they have large endowments. What I find upsetting is how people have forgotten what public education does for the country."

For those lucky enough to be in the charmed circle of an elite private institution, it's true that there is considerable financial aid available. One circle further out, at leading public universities like the University of Michigan or the University of Wisconsin, state funding has shrunk and tuition is up, but the situation is not desperate. At the less selective public colleges and universities that enroll the bulk of American students, the picture is bleaker. Here, things have declined precipitously over the past decade, and the sense of exclusion is real. "Inequality is being exacerbated between public and private institutions, and between the flagship and nonflagship public colleges," said Clifton Conrad, a professor of higher education at the University of Wisconsin. "There's an ethos of me over we."

Endowments are growing fastest at the elite institutions that already have the most resources, said Caroline M. Hoxby, a Stanford professor who is one of the country's leading experts on the economics of education. "They have alumni who are richer and can pursue investment strategies that are more aggressive," she said. "Harvard essentially acts as a sovereign wealth fund." The top state universities have other levers to turn to if public funding dries up. Out-of-state students are clamoring to get in, and are willing to pay market rates, which can be used to ease any shortfall. At the University of Michigan, for example, state residents pay about $30,000 a year in tuition and other fees like room and board. Out-of-staters pay $64,000 a year. And like the top private institutions, leading public universities have a large network of alumni who have the means and willingness to donate to their alma mater.

Less prestigious public colleges like Chicago State University (CSU) don't have these options and are much more dependent on the whims of governors and state legislators. And since the Great Recession, they've been increasingly tightfisted. In forty-five states between 2008 and 2018, public spending per university student fell, according to a 2018 study by the Center on Budget and Policy Priorities (CBPP). In states like Arizona, where funding per student fell 56 percent, tuition nearly doubled. That burden fell much harder on minorities, the CBPP report found. In Illinois, for example, tuition equaled 36.6 percent of family household income for African Americans, nearly double the proportion for white families.

Through sheer force of will, some students beat the odds. Nicole Brooks grew up on the South Side of Chicago, not far from CSU. No one in her family had gone to college and she had a son while still in high school. "Some days I didn't have food," she said. "When my mom lost her job or was between jobs, we had ketchup sandwiches and rice every day." But to her, Chicago State was like a beacon. "It's a safe zone," she said. The school, she said, enabled her "to see past what I see every day, the crime and the guys who sell drugs and want to gang bang. I didn't want to get sucked into that life."

Chicago State provided a way out. More than two thirds of its students are African American and an equal proportion are female. The majority are over twenty-five and many have children to support. Brooks had to study by day and work in call centers by night to support herself and her son. Sometimes she dropped out but always came back. "I never had anyone in my family to turn to ask about studying or tell me about college," she said. "I had to figure it out on my own through making mistakes." What made the difference was the support she received from counselors and tutors at the school, as well as from members of her sorority. And after seven years, she earned her bachelor's degree in business. "My mom didn't graduate from high school," she said. "I owed her a graduation." Brooks is now a recruiter, with a tutoring business on the side, and is pursuing a master's degree in psychology.

Her alma mater hasn't fared as well in recent years. Like much of Illinois's higher education system, Chicago State found itself in the middle of a budget fight between a Republican governor and a Democratic state legislature in 2015 and 2016. Appropriations were held up for nearly two years, 20 percent of faculty were laid off, and critical maintenance on campus was delayed. At one point, there was no hot water in the dorms and students had to use showers at the gym. Even before the crisis, Chicago State had been hamstrung by financial mismanagement and a revolving door of administrators. Now it seemed like Chicago State might close its doors.

"There was a sense of doom," said Phillip Beverly, a professor of political science at CSU who also serves as the associate vice provost for the University of Illinois at Chicago. His everyday experiences mirrored how the top state institutions like the University of Illinois were able to weather the state's fiscal crisis, even as less prestigious schools like CSU foundered. "It was night and day," he said, ticking off how quickly CSU's facilities deteriorated. "Where the sidewalk should have been, there was a gravel pit." Other professors describe classrooms infested with vermin and bugs, while offices would flood after storms. "How do you expect to attract students to a university when facilities are like this," said Beverly.

CSU couldn't. Although most—but not all—of state support for CSU was eventually restored, enrollment has plunged, giving fewer students the opportunities Nicole Brooks was able to take advantage of. From more than 7,000 college and graduate students in 2010, when Brooks was studying there, enrollment in the fall of 2018 had sunk to just 2,964 students. "It's very bleak," said Ann Kuzdale, who has taught history there for twenty-four years.

Like City College has Columbia, Chicago State also has a prosperous private neighbor—the University of Chicago. By June 2019, the University of Chicago had nearly completed a $5 billion fundraising campaign, with gifts from more than 125,000 alumni. Gleaming new labs, libraries, and dormitories dot its Hyde Park campus, which is about five miles away from Chicago State on the city's South Side. "We have students who attend Chicago State but who could function at the University of Chicago," Kuzdale added. "By circumstance and because of money, some of them have to come to us. You get so damned frustrated by the lack of resources."

However dilapidated its campus is, professors continue to teach and students continue to learn at Chicago State. "For all the frustration and irritation over the years I can still say we do launch students into the middle class," Kuzdale added. "We have often been tarred as a school of last resort. It is not. I see it as a school of second chances."

For all their individual differences, a common thread links New Albany, the rise of club teams, million-dollar PTAs, and the impoverishment of public institutions like City College and Chicago State. "It's all of a piece," said CUNY's Brier, describing how society and government have shifted money away from public goods and into private entities. Other factors contribute, like changing social norms, but public policy plays an ever bigger role. As taxes are cut or support is cut back, dollars stay in private hands and are redirected into the forums patronized by society's most fortunate members. When those people are parents, they are already inclined to shower more resources into their children's development, furthering their already sizable advantages. In the 1980s, the richest quintile of parents spent $3,000 more annually on education, child care, and goods for their children compared with parents in the middle quintile. By 2015, the gap had grown to $6,000. Poor children's horizons shrink as richer parents worry only about their own families and schools, rather than giving consideration to the broader educational system or society overall.

Jay Coakley, the University of Colorado sociology professor, sees this phenomenon as the culmination of the free market, laissez-faire ideology that's come to the fore in America since the 1980s. In that way, it echoes the transformation of HOV lanes into Lexus Lanes for lone drivers who can afford to pay. "There is no society, only individuals and families," he explained, citing a quote by the late conservative British prime minister Margaret Thatcher. "It's a doctrine that emphasizes economic self-interest, deregulation, privatization, and emphasizes individual and competitive success. Hierarchy and inequality are assumed to be normal."

7.

Division

San Francisco's Mission Bay neighborhood is buzzing with activity. The Golden State Warriors' new stadium, with its multimillion-dollar skyboxes, is there. So is the hospital where some of the city's top specialists see patients who've avoided the usual wait, thanks to a referral from a concierge doctor. At its groundbreaking in 2010, UCSF Mission Bay was billed as the first completely new hospital in San Francisco in thirty years. Five years later it opened, at a cost of $1.5 billion, and today the gleaming, glass-enclosed building showers visitors and medical professionals with light.

Most of the people who find their way to Mission Bay have private insurance. Low-income patients, who depend on Medi-Cal, California's version of Medicaid, or are uninsured, are more rare. Not only do the higher reimbursement rates provided by private insurers help keep the lights on and pay the doctors' salaries, they also enable UCSF to offer the innovative care that draws these well-heeled patients in the first place. Whether you call it a closed loop or a virtuous circle, it works out very well for everyone inside.

Across San Francisco Bay, on the other side of the Velvet Rope, is San Pablo. It's a working-class city in which a fifth of the population lives below the poverty line. Next door is much larger Richmond, where a similar proportion of its 110,000 residents are living in poverty and more than 60 percent are nonwhite. Obesity, high blood pressure, diabetes, and asthma are common. When they were sick, many of these poor people turned to Doctors Medical Center (DMC), just off the expressway in downtown San Pablo. It was certified as a treatment center for strokes and cancer, and more than a hundred patients a day passed through its emergency room.

But even as the new hospital in Mission Bay was going up, DMC was dying. Only 10 percent of its patients were privately insured; 80 percent depended on Medi-Cal or Medicare and the rest were uninsured. This is what health care professionals like Kathy White, the hospital's former chief executive, call a challenging payer mix. At many hospitals in more affluent areas, like San Francisco, the higher reimbursement rates of privately insured patients make up for the low reimbursement rates offered by government plans. As long as a favorable balance is maintained, hospitals can serve a broad swath of the community while remaining solvent.

At DMC, there was nothing to balance out the low reimbursement rates offered by public plans. "This was a safety net hospital," White said. "Our clientele was the poorest of the poor. They were extremely ill because they didn't get preventive care. We would see people with pathologies other community hospitals didn't see— end stage lung cancer, third or fourth stage breast cancer, often at a young age. This would have been caught earlier elsewhere."

Despite the challenges, White said, there were pockets of exceptional care. The heart attack team beat the national average for time to intervention, and DMC's large emergency room made it a magnet for ambulances across western Contra Costa County. And with traffic jams an everyday occurrence throughout the Bay Area, its proximity meant much shorter trips during emergencies in San Pablo, Richmond, El Cerrito, and other nearby towns.

The only other hospital in the immediate area was a much smaller Kaiser Permanente facility in Richmond. Kaiser is both an insurer as well as an operator of nonprofit hospitals. More than 12 million people are covered by Kaiser's plans and it is one of the nation's largest health care providers. The company has deep roots in Richmond dating back to World War II, when shipyards there employed tens of thousands of workers, many of them refugees from the Depression-era Dust Bowl and African Americans from the South in search of better jobs. Henry J. Kaiser, the industrialist who owned the ship-yards, formed what would become Kaiser Permanente to take care of those employees. But today, aside from the emergency room, the Kaiser hospital in Richmond and its fifty beds mostly serve people covered by Kaiser Permanente insurance plans. In its own way, it too is a closed loop.

For thousands of others in the region, especially residents without private insurance, Doctors Medical Center filled the gap. It was a publicly owned hospital, part of the West Contra Costa County Healthcare District; a small tax on real estate in the area was ear-marked to support it. But the money was never enough to make up for insufficient government reimbursement rates, and DMC ran a perennial deficit. Other large hospitals in the county are part of big-ger medical systems with affiliated physicians and outpatient centers that funnel them a stream of patients with private insurance. DMC had none of that. "This was a perfect storm," said John Gioia, a member of the Contra Costa Board of Supervisors who represents the area served by DMC. "The stand-alone, public hospital is a model that's no longer viable."

Even as cutting-edge medical centers like UCSF Mission Bay open in wealthier neighborhoods, traditional urban public hospitals have been closing over the past few decades, said Michelle Ko, a professor at the University of California, Davis. "The public hos-pital serves people who have no other place to go," she said. "Un-fortunately, as poverty goes up in a community, the population that needs the hospital grows but the local tax base also shrinks."

During her training as a medical student in Los Angeles, Dr. Ko did rotations at an inner-city hospital that later shut down. It got her interested in the forces that drive public hospitals to close, so she gave up medicine to study health policy. "A hospital closure is a long process but there is a death spiral first," she said. As the cost of providing treatment increases but public funding stays flat or even drops, the quality of care declines. People who have the option of going to another medical center, primarily insured patients, seek care elsewhere, leaving the public hospital's patient base even poorer and sicker. Doctors and staff, concerned about the hospital's reputation and viability, begin to leave. "There's a growing divide in health care between the safety net and everyone else," said Dr. Ko. "The way health care providers segregate themselves parallels income inequality."

As losses increase, voters and public authorities become less willing to provide additional funds to keep medical centers open. In the case of urban public hospitals, racism plays a role, too, Dr. Ko said. "Support for publicly funded social services declines when it is seen as benefiting minorities," she said. "Closure becomes the inevitable 'solution.'" Add racial segregation to the mix, and the outlook for public hospitals worsens. According to Dr. Ko's research, in neighborhoods where there is a combination of a high poverty rate with a racially segregated black population, public hospitals are 20 percent more likely to close. Dr. Desmond Carson, the former chief of emergency medicine at DMC, watched this process first-hand. "The best way to ensure access to health care is to live in a town that has a Nordstrom," he said.

The division between medical care in San Francisco and the East Bay is replicated within Contra Costa County itself. The East Bay is bisected by the Berkeley Hills. On the west side are lower-income communities like San Pablo and Richmond, while the east side has much wealthier towns like Walnut Creek, Concord, and San Ramon. These three communities each have their own hospital, and as Dr. Carson's telling quip would suggest, Walnut Creek has a Nordstrom as well. West Contra Costa County, by contrast, has come to resemble what health care experts term a medical desert. The end result isn't merely longer ambulance rides or fewer physicians to choose from, serious as those risks are. DMC's closure is part of a larger trend in health disparities driven by income and neighborhood. The life expectancy for Richmond residents is 71 to 74 years; in affluent Walnut Creek it's 85 to 87 years.

．　．　．

For Eric Zell, Doctors Medical Center was a family affair. His father owned a furniture store in downtown Richmond, and by the early 1950s the elder Zell and other local business owners knew that Richmond needed a larger hospital. With the opening of the Kaiser shipyards during World War II, the city's population ballooned from fewer than 25,000 to more than 100,000. The shipyards closed when the war ended but the small Kaiser hospital couldn't accommodate the tens of thousands of residents who stayed and looked for new places to work. "Community leaders decided we needed a full service hospital," Zell explained. They helped pass a tax measure to raise funds and established a public agency to oversee the project. Originally known as Brookside Hospital when it opened in 1954, the hospital served the entire economic strata of western Contra Costa County. "Whether you were someone who had wealth or somebody who didn't, everybody went to that hospital," Zell said.

To supplement tax dollars, the community leaders formed a foundation and sought donations to support Brookside. Businesspeople stepped up to the plate and Zell's father later became president of the foundation. Meanwhile, his mother volunteered as a candy striper and his sister worked as a nurse. It was an era, Zell recalled, when the classes mixed and so did the races, at least in Richmond. Born the same year as the hospital opened, 1954, Zell grew up in El Cerrito, next door to Richmond, and attended Kennedy High School in Richmond. The school was diverse in terms of race and socioeconomic status as well, he recalled. Things began to change in the 1980s. Even as more middle-class and upper-middle-class families began sending their children to private schools in the area, they began seeking medical care at hospitals in better-off Berkeley and Walnut Creek. By the late 1980s and early 1990s, Zell's high school was no longer as diverse. "People with resources left the system," he said.

The same dynamic developed at Brookside, which was renamed

Doctors Medical Center in 1997. Racial factors contributed to these decisions, Zell said, and soon the hospital was mainly serving minority populations in San Pablo and Richmond. "Class became a hidden way for middle- and upper-income people to talk about race," he said. "They wouldn't say 'I'm not going there because they treat blacks and Hispanics' but it wasn't hard to read between the lines."

With fewer middle-class patients seeking care there, voters' willingness to support DMC eroded. Care, in turn, declined. "The rest of the health care district was subsidizing DMC but not using it and the public became more and more reluctant to spend taxpayer dollars to save it," Zell said. A private company, Tenet, was brought in to manage the hospital but they, too, were unable to make a profit and walked away. By the time John Gioia, the county Board of Supervisors member, asked Zell to join the board in 2006, the medical center was falling into the kind of death spiral Ko described. DMC had a good pediatrics department but it wasn't making money and had to close. So did the labor and delivery ward. Maintenance and capital investments were put off, and some areas of the hospital went without air-conditioning.

Zell, who became chairman of the board in 2007, wasn't ready to give up, despite advice that he should. At the very start of the first briefing he attended as chairman, Zell received a blunt message from the county's financial expert.

"Your hospital is going to close," the advisor said. "This is not going to be sustainable."

"What do you mean?" Zell asked. "How come?"

"There's no way to make up for the deficit," he was told. "Too much of the payer mix is Medicare, Medi-Cal, or uninsured."

Despite the warning, Zell resisted pulling the plug and began searching for potential saviors. The state kicked in several million dollars as a one-time subsidy. Meanwhile Zell warned Kaiser that if DMC closed down, their small emergency room would be flooded with new underinsured patients. "They didn't want those patients so they gave us $12 million over a three-year period," Zell recalled.

DMC even signed a contract with San Quentin State Prison to provide medical care, and one floor was essentially turned into a jail staffed by doctors and nurses. The rate of reimbursement to take care of the prisoners was far higher than what was offered by Medi-Cal or Medicare. "We did it only as a means to bring revenue into the hospital but it was a very, very profitable side of the business," Zell said.

Meanwhile, the Kaiser hospital in Richmond drew residents who were covered by Kaiser Permanente insurance, leaving even fewer privately insured patients for DMC. "Kaiser and its hospital became the default system for a lot of middle-class people and employers," said Sharon Drager, a vascular surgeon who practices in San Pablo. And unless they came in through the emergency room, where it was required to treat them by law, Dr. Drager explained, "Kaiser wasn't interested in poor people. It was geared to middle-class, working people, almost all of whom got their insurance through their employer." At DMC, on the other hand, said Dr. Drager, "most of us had some sort of social justice interest in serving everybody. I wanted to take care of people—period."

Across the Bay, the greatest example of wealth creation in modern American history was under way as Silicon Valley boomed and new billionaires were minted. One of them, Facebook's Mark Zuckerberg, and his wife, Priscilla Chan, donated $75 million to San Francisco General Hospital and Trauma Center, which was renamed in their honor and is a safety net hospital that mostly serves patients on Medicare and Medi-Cal. Marc Benioff, the founder of Salesforce.com, and his wife donated $200 million for a children's hospital in the city. It also now bears their name. Zell appealed to both tech titans but never got a response.

The local health care district did manage to persuade voters to approve two small real estate tax increases to help DMC stay open. "We kept doing short-term fixes that kept us open for six months at a time," Zell said. "Every year it was 'We're going to close in six months.' People assumed we were crying wolf." To stabilize the situation, Zell and Gioia pushed for a third real estate tax increase that would be heftier than the first two, equal to 14 cents per square foot, or about $210 for a 1,500-square-foot property. It was aimed at closing DMC's $20 million annual deficit once and for all.

In the 1950s, business owners like Zell's father had spearheaded efforts to approve the tax increases that funded the creation of the hospital. Sixty years later, when the question at hand was whether to pay to keep the hospital open, local business leaders took a different view. Mark Howe, whose real estate company owns about 350,000 square feet of industrial properties and warehouses in the area, polled his tenants about the proposed tax. They were unanimously opposed. "The companies that lease from us were already paying for health insurance for their employees," said Howe. "Why should they get stuck with this?" Howe felt the same way. "Normally I'm pretty charitable," he said. "I try not to be evil greedy. But we have huge taxes already and they're always going up."

In Howe's estimation, DMC was a money-loser that was mainly taking care of the indigent and undocumented immigrants. "It's the hot potato concept," he said. "Who wants to get stuck with that? The thing was losing money and I showed up and pushed it over the edge." Howe and another local developer embarked on a campaign to defeat the tax increase, using direct mail to persuade voters to reject it at the polls. "It was a great deal," he said. The direct mail campaign cost him $10,000 to $20,000 just once but the tax increase would have cost his company $50,000 to $100,000 a year—*every* year. Howe's campaign worked—unlike the two earlier tax increases, the new property assessment was rejected in 2014.

According to Howe, high overhead added to the red ink. "The medical community has nobody to blame but themselves," he said. "Costs were burgeoning for a population that has limited ability to pay." John Gioia, the Contra Costa County Board of Supervisors member, flatly rejects Howe's characterization. "If you're only making money on 10 percent of your patients, due to low Medi-Cal and Medicare reimbursement rates, you're not going to survive, however efficient you are," he said. "It doesn't take a whole lot to defeat a tax measure requiring a two-thirds vote. When the measure went down, it was the end of the road for the hospital."

Still, Gioia had an eleventh-hour idea to save DMC—a county-wide general sales tax of one eighth to one quarter of a cent that would fund health care, with a portion earmarked for DMC. When the board polled residents on the proposal, however, they didn't find much support. Voters in central Contra Costa County, which is considerably wealthier than San Pablo or Richmond, Gioia said, perceived it as a tax to support a hospital in the poorer, western part of the county. Fellow supervisors weren't any more enthusiastic and the idea of a county-wide tax was tabled.

Medical professionals like Maria del Rosario Sahagun, an emergency room nurse, and Sharon Drager, the vascular surgeon, wrote letters to local politicians and created videos in a bid to save the hospital. But the truth is that it was all over but the shouting when the tax vote failed. Zell and Kathy White began laying the groundwork to shutter DMC. "We did everything we could to keep the hospital open for a decade," Zell said. "We were pulling rabbits out of a hat and in 2015 we ran out of rabbits." Two months after UCSF Mission Bay opened its doors in February 2015, Doctors Medical Center shut down, with more than nine hundred employees losing their jobs. For Eric Zell, it was personal. Both of his parents had died at DMC in the years before the closure and now the hospital was gone, too. "It felt like a loss," said Zell. "I lost my parents and then I lost the hospital. I felt like I let my family down."

The parking lot where DMC once stood is full. It's reserved for patrons of the San Pablo Lytton Casino, where gamblers crowd around slot machines and card tables for games of Texas hold'em poker. Like the hospital, it's open 24/7 and there are plenty of customers coming in at all hours.

In late 2018 and early 2019, Dr. Desmond Carson watched as the seven-story white building was torn down. "It's like they pulled your left lung out," he said of the demolition. Carson now practices in a cramped clinic across the street from where he once treated patients in the emergency room. Instead of the old ER's twenty-two beds, the clinic has six examination rooms and is open from 10 a.m. to 8 p.m., not all night.

For Carson, born and raised in Richmond, working as a doctor in the community is about more than treating the sick. When he coached a local youth football team, he'd often wear his white coat. "As a black guy, I wanted them to see me and know as black and brown kids that they could be a doctor," Dr. Carson said. He'd drive his Porsche over for the same reason. "Who were the people in the neighborhood they'd see with money? The dope man. When they saw me with the Porsche, they'd wonder how did this guy get this shit? I liked math and chemistry as a kid and I was trying to show them that was a way out."

At the hospital, Dr. Carson partnered with Richmond High School, hosting some of the best biology students as interns for the summer. "They would rotate through the operating room, or hang out with me in the ER for the overnight shift," he said. Dr. Carson would encourage these high schoolers to make presentations to hospital executives and test them on different medical subjects. "They saw the good, the bad, and the ugly and what happens in their community," he said. "I wanted them to see how they could use their academic knowledge to help their community." When Dr. Carson was at DMC, he had seven or eight interns; now he has one or two at the clinic.

The clinic is limited in much more fundamental ways. It doesn't treat heart attacks or strokes, so these patients now have to travel to more distant hospitals in the event of an emergency. Before DMC closed, the average time from when an ambulance picked up a patient in San Pablo to when they arrived at the ER was 11 minutes and 24 seconds, according to data provided by the Contra Costa Emergency Medical Services agency. The year after DMC shut down, transport time increased to 27 minutes, 45 seconds. Even though the Kaiser hospital increased the capacity of its emergency department after

DMC closed in order to accommodate additional patients, ambulance transport times in Richmond also doubled. "Minutes count," said Dr. Carson. "In a stroke, you can lose millions of brain cells in one minute." In two recent cases, he said, local patients died on their way to hospitals that were further away. "I believe if DMC were still open, they would have had a chance," he said.

The pattern for patients in the East Bay is echoed more broadly across the country, according to Dr. Renee Hsia, an emergency room physician at UCSF who also researches health care policy. It took 4.4 minutes longer for victims of cardiac arrest in poorer areas to reach the hospital than in high-income areas, her research found. "Four minutes may not sound like much but it represents a significant increase in mortality," Dr. Hsia said.

When DMC was open and his son Alex had a severe asthma attack, Ali Essa could get him to the hospital from their home in San Pablo in a matter of minutes. Not long after it closed, Alex woke up coughing and throwing up at 2 a.m. "I thought I was dreaming but he grabbed my hand and I woke up," Essa said. "I tried to clean his face and I gave him two puffs from an aerator."

Alex continued to struggle for breath, and Essa knew he had to get his son to the hospital. A single dad, Essa bundled Alex and his older son into the car and headed for the Kaiser hospital in Richmond. Doctors there evaluated Alex's symptoms, but because he had previously been treated at a hospital in Oakland, they told Essa to take him there again. It was a thirty-minute drive away. "Of course I was praying and speeding," said Essa. "I had to do what I had to do. Even if I got a ticket I wasn't going to stop until I got to the hospital. I had to save his life." It was a harrowing ride, Essa said, but he managed to get Alex to Oakland in time and doctors were able to stabilize him. The experience has stayed with Essa. "It's not just about my son, it's about this community," he said. "When Doctors Medical Center was open, I felt safe."

Even when ambulances aren't delayed or diverted, the disappearance of DMC causes a rupture in how diseases are monitored and treated in Richmond, San Pablo, and other parts of western

Contra Costa County, where more than a quarter of a million people live. "We could provide ongoing care and coordinate with specialists," said Dr. Drager. "There's much less of that now. Care becomes sporadic and disorganized." And with DMC gone, other hospitals are struggling to keep up. "Our waiting time to see a doctor is up to ten hours," said Maria del Rosario Sahagun, who worked as an emergency room nurse at DMC and now is at the county hospital in Martinez, a forty-minute drive from San Pablo. "We've had to keep people in the ER for two days because there is no room upstairs. But we can't discharge them because they are sick."

Nordstrom or not, Dr. Carson thinks a new hospital may eventually come to western Contra Costa. It might not be a gleaming, light-filled facility like UCSF Mission Bay. But as more middle- and upper-middle-class people flee San Francisco and its outrageous home prices in search of more affordable real estate in the East Bay, this group will demand better care. "They're going to have to put in a hospital," he said. "Because white people are moving in. Gentrifying. Meghan doesn't want to go to an inner-city hospital that smells of piss and shit. She wants peace and quiet and a glass of white wine."

Unlike DMC, Twin Rivers Regional Medical Center in Kennett, Missouri, was a profitable hospital. It served much of surrounding Dunklin County. Roughly four hundred babies were delivered there every year, and 22,000 people visited its emergency room annually. A new surgeon had signed on and the town's doctors kept a steady flow of patients coming in. As a result, Twin Rivers earned about a million dollars in 2017. In the Missouri Bootheel, as the rural southeastern corner of the state that Twin Rivers served is known, that certainly counted as good money. But it wasn't enough for Community Health Systems, the for-profit hospital chain that owned it. And when Twin Rivers closed with little warning in June 2018, a county of thirty thousand people was left without a hospital.

The economic fault lines that split America don't just run between poor neighborhoods like San Pablo and the richer precincts in San Francisco where concierge doctors ply their trade. The division between rural areas like Dunklin County, Missouri, and prosperous cities and suburbs are just as profound, especially when it comes to health care. "It's another universe," said Dr. Mike Sarap, a surgeon in Cambridge, Ohio, a small town that's closer geographically and economically to stretches of Appalachia in nearby West Virginia than it is to tony Ohio suburbs like New Albany outside Columbus. "We're 180 degrees from concierge medicine."

And as wealth is increasingly concentrated on the coasts or in thriving cities like Nashville or Chicago, rural America finds itself outside the Velvet Rope. And hospitals, as well as doctors, are following the money. Since 2010, 107 rural hospitals have closed, with more than a dozen shutting down annually in recent years. "There are secular trends common to all rural hospitals," said George Pink, a professor of health policy and management at the University of North Carolina, Chapel Hill. "Rural populations are poorer, sicker, older and less likely to have employer-sponsored health insurance. They are more likely to be on Medicare, Medicaid, or are uninsured." For all the challenges facing facilities like DMC in San Pablo, on average, urban hospitals were twice as profitable as rural ones in 2016, according to Pink's research. In fact, Pink found, nearly 40 percent of rural hospitals lose money. And even profitable ones are being forced to shut their doors, as was the case in Twin Rivers.

For people in rural areas, where ambulance coverage is spread thin, that often means long drives on narrow roads during emergencies, sometimes in the middle of the night. While urban and rural hospitals face some of the same financial pressures, like a challenging payer mix, the impact is different. "Being able to jump the line is largely an urban phenomenon," said Katy B. Kozhimannil, who studies health policy at the University of Minnesota. In rural areas, she said, "Whether you're the owner of a multimillion-dollar farm or the agricultural worker in the field, there's only one hospital, if there's any hospital at all. In rural communities, access is a problem everyone faces and money can't buy you out of that challenge."

Nowhere is that more true than in the maternity ward. A baby can be born at any time, so facilities need to be open 24/7, which is expensive. Urgent care centers don't do deliveries. And with rural hospitals steadily closing, Kozhimannil found, locating a medical center to give birth in becomes much harder. By 2014, in more than half of all rural counties, there wasn't a single hospital that performed deliveries, forcing expectant mothers to take much longer trips when it was time to give birth. Poorer counties, like Dunklin in Missouri, were most vulnerable, with each $1,000 decline in household income associated with a 25 percent greater likelihood of maternity ward closure. In remote rural counties that lost hospital-based obstetrics departments, there was an increase in preterm births, the leading cause of infant mortality. "When a hospital closes, people are still going to give birth," Kozhimannil said. "It just transfers the risk from the hospital to the community and the individuals still living there."

As with so much in our divided health care system, the problem is compounded by low rates of Medicaid reimbursement. Nearly half of all babies in the United States are born to women on Medicaid, that is, to poor moms. The proportion is even higher at rural hospitals. Yet, Medicaid pays hospitals 50 percent less for deliveries than private insurance plans do. Still, as measly as Medicaid reimbursement may be, it's better for hospitals to get something rather than having to treat uninsured patients. Although the Affordable Care Act included provisions to expand the proportion of Americans covered by Medicaid, many Republican-led states in the South and Midwest rejected the offer. Missouri is one of those states, leaving more patients without any insurance and contributing to the closing of Twin Rivers.

"I study the effect of policies and programs on people who are not at the table to make those decisions," Kozhimannil said. "It's upsetting when it's purely a financial issue. There ought to be a policy solution to that." Alas, ought doesn't count for much in the Velvet Rope Economy.

The loss of a rural hospital doesn't just impose a heavy burden on patients. It also threatens the economic underpinnings of many places that don't have much else to count on these days. "The hospital is often the biggest employer in town," Kozhimannil said. "It keeps the laundromat open and probably the grocery store, too."

That was certainly the case in Kennett, Missouri. After an Emerson Electric plant closed in 2006, with many of the jobs going to Mexico, Twin Rivers Regional Medical Center was the town's economic lodestar. "We have a strong retail base and we're the regional hub in the Bootheel," said Jim Grebing, director of economic development for Kennett. "But retail and health care go hand in hand. People come in to see doctors or work at the hospital and shop. Eliminate the hospital and the whole thing starts to crack."

Even before Twin Rivers closed, Kennett and surrounding Dunklin County were part of an America that the long recovery which followed the Great Recession bypassed. Indeed, the recession never really ended in the Bootheel. Dunklin County's population declined by nearly 8 percent between 2010 and 2018, sinking to 29,423, according to the Census Bureau. At $32,348, the median income is roughly half the national average of $61,372. A quarter of residents live below the poverty line in this heavily agricultural region, and only 12.9 percent hold a bachelor's degree. All these factors contribute to a dismal picture of health in Dunklin—in a ranking of health outcomes in Missouri by the Robert Wood Johnson Foundation, it placed 111th out of 115 Missouri counties. Two other Bootheel counties—Pemiscot and Mississippi—were at the very bottom of the ranking.

In short, the Bootheel represents a part of the country that's as divided from more prosperous regions as San Pablo is from San Francisco or Palo Alto. And like the Bootheel itself, Twin Rivers hospital was buffeted by larger economic forces. In this case, it was the rise of the for-profit hospital. Founded as a county hospital in 1951, Twin Rivers was sold to a for-profit operator in the mid-1980s. The idea was that the county couldn't generate the revenue needed to navigate a rapidly evolving health care system—the hospital would be better off in the hands of private sector professionals who could guarantee its financial future. That was the theory, anyway. But when the county sold it, no one could have foreseen just how many hands would touch Twin Rivers.

The granddaddy of for-profit chains is the Hospital Corporation of America (HCA), now a publicly traded giant based in Nashville. Eyeing the fortunes its founders made by riding HCA's breakneck growth in the 1970s and 1980s, other entrepreneurs started for-profit hospital companies, many of them located not far from the mother ship in Tennessee. These private hospital chains waxed and waned in size, buying and selling hospitals like pieces in a game of medical Monopoly. Over the years, Twin Rivers had five different owners, some in quick succession.

"It's mind-boggling," said Joshua Nemzoff, a consultant who has spent the last forty years negotiating and advising on hospital deals. "People will leave bigger hospital companies and buy three dogs from the firm they left. The hospitals may not be making money but they can say they own hospitals and team up with a private equity firm." With fresh capital from these investors, the game would begin anew. If budget cuts and other efficiency measures allowed enough profit to be wrung out of the underperforming hospitals these entrepreneurs collected, there'd be an initial public offering which provided that much more money for acquisitions. Sometimes, even a veteran like Nemzoff could lose track. During a tour of one facility with a client who was hoping to sell, Nemzoff remarked that it looked familiar. "He laughed," Nemzoff said. "It turned out that I'd sold it to them six years before."

Community Health Systems, based south of Nashville in Franklin, Tennessee, followed just such a script. Two of its founders had worked at a spin-off of HCA, and they launched Community Health in 1985, buying their first hospital the same year. It's hard to imagine now but it made sense at the time, at least on paper: rural hospitals often had the local market to themselves, so there weren't rivals nearby who would compete for privately insured patients. Relative to today, Medicare reimbursement levels were fatter, a key consideration in rural areas where many patients are older. After an IPO in 1991, private equity firm Forstmann Little acquired Community Health in a $1.1 billion leveraged buyout in 1996. They brought in an experienced and ambitious new chief executive named Wayne T. Smith from a larger hospital chain, Humana.

Private equity owners usually don't stick around long—they're looking for a quick return on their investment. With impeccable timing, Community Health went public for a second time at $13 a share near the peak of the stock market bubble in mid-2000. The company continued to acquire hospitals, but by 2007 Smith was ready to hunt bigger game. Beating out a rival offer from Goldman Sachs's private equity arm, Community bought Triad Hospitals for $5.1 billion. Another HCA spin-off, Triad was a for-profit operator of rural hospitals and the acquisition doubled Community Health's revenues. But Smith wasn't done. In 2013, Community agreed to acquire Health Management Associates (HMA) in a deal worth $7.6 billion that made it the nation's largest for-profit hospital operator at the time. Twin Rivers and its 116 beds belonged to HMA, but it was now a speck in the universe of the combined company's two hundred hospitals and thirty thousand beds.

Unlike Triad, HMA owed about $3 billion in debt at the time of the acquisition, which ballooned Community's already sizable borrowing load. HMA had other problems, too, like an investigation by government regulators into its billing practices. Community Health would eventually pay hundreds of millions in fines to settle those claims, but even before that, it was clear Smith was in deep trouble. From a high of $52 a share in June 2015, Community stock was trading at $12 a year later.

"Community grew and grew and they bought one hospital after another," said Nemzoff. "When the hospitals didn't make as much money as Community hoped, they really ran into trouble. You can only reduce expenses so far. It's just like if you go and buy a big house but then you get fired and are only making 60 percent of what you used to make. All of a sudden you don't have enough money to pay the mortgage. It's not rocket science."

After earning $158 million in 2015, Community lost $1.7 billion in 2016 and another $2.5 billion in 2017. "Everything that could possibly go wrong went wrong," said Frank Morgan, an analyst with RBC Capital Markets. With no end in sight to the red ink and the company's debt rating sinking deeper into junk territory, Smith turned to the for-profit hospital chain playbook for a way out: cut costs, stop investing for the future, and sell or close hospitals. Capital expenditures at the company fell from $830 million in 2015 to $558 million in 2017. Over the same period, the hospital count in Community's network fell from 194 to 125, a reduction of nearly ten thousand beds. Smith was unloading hospitals as fast as he could but it still wasn't enough—by the time Twin Rivers was facing closure in mid-2018, Community was trading for about $3 a share.

In a statement, Community Health said the decision to close Twin Rivers "was primarily based on declining utilization," with inpatient admissions and emergency room visits having "dropped drastically between 2010 and 2017." Due to medical advances, the company said, more care could be administered without admission to the hospital, with 95 percent of patients treated at Twin Rivers receiving treatment on an outpatient basis. The company also said the failure to expand Medicaid in Missouri has made it more difficult for hospitals there "to cover fixed costs, labor and supplies," noting that the state has seen five rural hospitals close since 2014. As for the sale of so many facilities, the company said the divestitures have "proven to be a beneficial strategy for focusing our resources where they can be most effective. And the divestitures have been beneficial for many of the hospitals we've sold."

Back in Tennessee, Smith and other executives surely aren't losing sleep about the crisis in Kennett. They're paid too well for that. Between 2015 and 2017, as hospitals were being divested or shut down, Smith earned over $21 million. As if that weren't enough, he spent $175,000 on personal travel in the company's corporate aircraft. "They've devastated communities, destroyed shareholder value, and acted like pigs at the trough," said Steven Braverman, an investor who owned the stock in 2016 and 2017. "It's disgraceful."

Dale Lockhert never intended to stay in Kennett for more than a couple of years. When he and his wife, Amy, both doctors, moved there in 2000 from Detroit, the plan was to make some money in a place where the cost of living was low so they could pay off their student loans. But life was good in Kennett. "I like small-town living," said Dr. Lockhert. "It was a five-minute drive to the job, a five-minute drive to see the kids play soccer or basketball, and a five-minute drive to the gym." They'd go on vacation in St. Louis or Memphis or Seattle, see the crowds and traffic, and happily return to Kennett.

The Lockherts took over a medical practice in town but in 2011 Dale joined Twin Rivers as a hospitalist, overseeing admissions and treating patients in the hospital. From time to time, the couple would visit other towns and discuss moving but they'd always come to the conclusion that staying in Kennett was a better bet. Then Community Health came to town. "You could see a huge difference once they took over," said Dr. Lockhert. The message was clear: make more money.

Even though Twin Rivers was still profitable, in meetings administrators would compare the hospital's performance to the company's aggressive targets, and tell doctors and nurses they were falling short. Pressure increased to admit and keep patients overnight, even if the best course was to send them home. The more conditions doctors could document, the more could be billed to Medicare and Medicaid, so paperwork became a big burden. When doctors and nurses raised concerns, Dr. Lockhert said, "they told us that's okay, we can replace you. It was cold, businesslike. All these people had been there for all these years and they were ready to kick us to the curb." Some doctors and nurses took the hint and left, and turnover spiked.

As a general surgeon and former member of Twin Rivers' advisory board, Dr. Steve Pu watched these same developments with worry. As recently as 2010, Twin Rivers had made over $20 million a year. But after Community Health took over in 2014, the leadership at Twin Rivers had much less say in decisions big and small, according to Dr. Pu. That made it more difficult to recruit new doctors and get approvals for new investments. Twin Rivers only had shared rooms, and Dr. Pu and other staff wanted to turn a closed floor with offices into a new wing with private rooms in order to attract patients. "The only capital improvements were for things that were absolutely necessary or broken," Dr. Pu said.

As the financial situation at headquarters grew more dire, and efforts to integrate all the newly acquired hospitals into the Community system faltered, even more basic requests were vetoed at Twin Rivers. "We needed upgrades for cameras for colonoscopies or scopes for laparoscopic surgery," he added. "We didn't get them. There was just no investment." Upkeep of the hospital suffered amid the cuts and patients began to drift away. In 2016, the hospital suffered its first loss in twenty years. Meanwhile, the behavioral and psychiatric service, which was a moneymaker for Twin Rivers, was transferred to a newer and larger Community hospital in Poplar Bluff, Missouri. "That should have been a sign," Dr. Pu said.

Still, he and other doctors didn't see a closure on the horizon. "There were rumors," Dr. Pu said. "People weren't replaced and administrators were in Poplar Bluff more. Everybody assumed they would sell us." On April 30, Dr. Pu walked into the hospital and was called into a meeting with other senior doctors. They were handed a press release that was soon to go out announcing that Twin Rivers and Poplar Bluff were consolidating. Later that afternoon, a corporate representative from Community and the chief executive of Poplar Bluff delivered even worse news. "They told us we were being terminated in ninety days," Dr. Pu said. "I was told, 'Thanks for your service.' I took it personally. In a rural town, things are more personal, it's not cold like that usually. I spent thirty-four years serving that community." The hospital didn't even make the promised ninety days—Twin Rivers closed a month early on June 12, 2018.

The press release to announce the news did not use the word "close." Instead it was billed as a "consolidation" with Community's facility in Poplar Bluff. But Poplar Bluff isn't a neighboring town; it's more than an hour's drive from Kennett. There are smaller hospitals that are closer to Kennett, as well as urgent care centers in town, but they lack the equipment and staffing needed for more serious emergencies, according to Dr. Pu. In the event of a stroke or heart attack, the closest hospital that can administer clot-busting medication can be a thirty- to forty-five-minute ambulance ride away.

Think about that—under the best circumstances in Dunklin County, it's a minimum of thirty minutes before the effects of a blockage in a blood vessel in the heart or brain can be reversed. "You can't give clot-busters in an ambulance or at urgent care," said Dr. Pu. The nearest infusion center for chemotherapy is also about an hour's drive from Kennett, forcing cancer patients and their families to make that trek for every treatment. The same goes for the neonatal intensive care units that often mean the difference between life and death for a baby born prematurely. "For us, it's a catastrophe," said Grebing, Kennett's economic development director. "There's a loss of peace of mind."

Other doctors began to consider their options after the closure and look at other places to practice, but Dr. Pu was determined to stay. After fleeing from China following the Communist takeover in 1949, his parents moved to the United States and in 1968 his father came to Kennett to work as a doctor. "If you know anything about Asian culture, as the only son I was destined to practice medicine," he said. "I spent summers here working for my dad in the lab, and following doctors around. I never looked anywhere else. It was always about being a doctor in Kennett." Like the City College provost Tony Liss, Dr. Pu could have found a more financially stable place to work, but he had a deep connection with Kennett and its people. "They needed me and wanted me here," he said.

Before the hospital shut, Twin Rivers, with help from a federal grant, had reached a deal with a local medical school for residents to rotate through Kennett. "The vast majority of physicians end up staying close to where they trained," said Dr. Pu. "This was a way of augmenting the recruiting process but the entire program was scrapped when Twin Rivers closed. We're back to square one in terms of trying to get more physicians to the area."

To address that—and the lack of a hospital—Dr. Pu and Grebing began casting about for solutions. Immediately after the closure, in August of 2018, they got two new tax measures on the ballot in Dunklin County. A small sales tax would have funded the construction of a new hospital, while a property tax would have provided an ongoing stream of revenue to whoever would come in and run it. And as with school taxes and pay-to-play in Ohio, voters didn't believe the good of the community justified higher taxes. Both measures were voted down. "People didn't see the urgency of paying the additional taxes but this situation is not sustainable," said Grebing. "We have to have a facility and we're just trying to find another partner who is willing to invest. But we always come back to the roadblock of money."

In the meantime, some doctors in Kennett have decided to move on—reluctantly. Two months before the closure, Dale Lockhert had a heart-to-heart talk with his wife. "You know what," he told her, "we don't need to look anymore. This is the place we're going to stay for the rest of our lives. Let's stay here and retire." But when he lost his job at Twin Rivers, the couple had to reconsider. Dr. Lockhert and his wife eventually moved to Osage Beach, a tourist destination on the Lake of the Ozarks that's a four-and-a-half-hour drive from Kennett.

When the Velvet Rope Economy divides communities, it creates new winners as well as losers. Some more upscale middle-class communities extend their advantage. Resources flow there and new opportunities open themselves up to people who can take advantage of them. While not especially affluent, Poplar Bluff is better off than Kennett and Community Health Systems is now expanding there. Dr. Lockhert didn't have much choice, but in Osage Beach, his practice is in a more upscale area than at Twin Rivers in Kennett. "This place has everything," he said. "It's like the suburb of a nice city—restaurants, stores, outlet malls. The homes on the lake would blow you away and the boats would, too."

A few doctors are defying this trend. Dr. Todd Rumsey practiced as an obstetrician and gynecologist in Fort Wayne, Indiana, and was chairman of the board at Dupont Hospital there. He was one of the founders of Dupont, a modern facility that opened in 2001 as part of Fort Wayne's Lutheran Health Network. Wall Street considers Lutheran to be one of the crown jewels in Community's system, because unlike Twin Rivers it is *very* profitable.

But like a rich relative of the hospital in Kennett, Dupont couldn't escape the family drama at Community. "I don't think we ever compromised patient care but we stretched it as far as we could safely," said Dr. Rumsey. "There were fifty nursing positions open and a majority of the respiratory therapist positions were open. Community was unwilling or unable to invest and we reached a tipping point."

Dr. Rumsey, a sought after doctor in Fort Wayne, decided to leave Dupont. "I quit trying to serve both Community Health Systems and my patients as it was becoming mutually exclusive," he said. Dr. Rumsey moved to Cameron Memorial Community Hospital in small-town Angola, a thirty-minute drive north of Fort Wayne. Cameron is the only hospital in rural Steuben County, and Dr. Rumsey is one of only two obstetricians there, with the other nearing retirement. Working at a nonprofit hospital now, Dr. Rumsey doesn't miss the endless focus on profit margins and the pressure to beat the numbers that came to define life under Community. He also has more time to meet with moms-to-be and actually practice medicine. "They brought me in to grow the program at Cameron and attract new doctors," he said. "Community Health Systems isn't in the health care business. It's in the business of collecting health care dollars. The margin here is about meeting the needs of patients."

. . .

Public policy—in the form of inadequate reimbursement rates for Medicare and Medicaid patients—contributed to the closure of Twin Rivers and Doctors Medical Center. And government's role in raising the Velvet Rope extends far beyond health care—it plays out every day in other spheres, like the criminal justice system. Take the letter sent by the local prosecutor's office in Floyd County, Georgia, to a young woman charged with a crime. The missive resembled a sweepstakes come-on. "This is a one-time offer," it said, adding in bold underlined type, "You will not get another chance to enroll later." But in this case, the grand prize wasn't a $1 million jackpot, an all-expenses-paid vacation, or even a brand spanking new car. It was an offer to avoid criminal prosecution, and quite possibly, jail.

The recipient, who asked to remain anonymous, had been charged with one count of misdemeanor battery after a family scuffle. It was a first offense for her and the offer from the prosecutor in Floyd County seemed heaven-sent: attend twenty-four sessions in an anger regulation program and the charge would be dismissed. Even better, the whole case would be expunged from her record, like it never happened. There was just one problem—the pretrial diversion program, as alternatives to prosecution like this one are called, cost $690 and she didn't have the money.

She told the private firm that ran the anger management program about her money problems, but they weren't interested. "They told her there was nothing they could do," said Sarah Geraghty, who manages the impact litigation unit at the Southern Center for Human Rights in Atlanta. So the woman pleaded guilty and was sentenced to probation, but she still had to attend that same class. Only now she owed more than $1,000 because in addition to having to pay for the anger regulation sessions, she was looking at a fine of $300 plus additional supervision fees as part of her probation. And when the woman fell behind on those payments and failed a drug test, she ended up behind bars. "Diversion in some places is just one variation on the theme of justice for sale," said Geraghty. "There's really no pretense about it. If you have the money, you get into the program. If you don't have the money, you go into the criminal justice system."

Money has always carried advantages in the legal system—the ability to post bail, hire a better attorney, or pay a lawyer to appeal a conviction and stay out of prison in the meantime. But with local governments, police departments, and prosecutors' offices scrambling to find cash to fund their operations, defendants with means have a plethora of new ways to bend the arc of justice in their favor. Diversion is just one of them—there are many others, as we shall see, and they extend from the courtroom to the prison cell. What's more, some diversion programs like the one in Georgia are run by private, for-profit companies, heightening the temptation to extract fees and other charges from what is literally a captive audience.

As with many other elements of the Velvet Rope Economy, pretrial diversion began on a small scale, and was launched with the best of intentions. After a rise in juvenile crime in the 1940s and 1950s, courts sought out alternatives to traditional punishments. The goal was to avoid stigmatizing young offenders for the rest of their lives, especially if the crime was a first offense, said Joseph Zlatic, associate professor of criminal justice at Lindenwood University-Belleville in Illinois. A program of restitution, supervision, counseling, and substance abuse treatment when necessary could replace criminal prosecution or a jail sentence. With more progressive attitudes taking hold in the court system in the 1960s, diversion programs became available for adult offenders. After falling out of favor amid the war on drugs and calls to get tough on crime in the 1980s and 1990s, diversion made a comeback in the 2000s as worries about the impact of mass incarceration mounted.

But what really boosted diversion was a development that had nothing to do with progressive reforms or new theories about how best to combat crime. "The financial collapse of 2008 was a watershed moment," said Zlatic. "Public officials said, 'We can't continue to incarcerate the number of people that we have been. We simply can't afford it.'" The Great Recession had left state and local budgets in tatters. New sources of revenue were needed to fund court systems, prosecutors, and even the local jail, Zlatic said.

The confluence of these two forces caused prosecutors nationwide to create or expand pay-to-play, pretrial diversion programs. But absolution doesn't come cheap. In Maricopa County, Arizona, marijuana possession is a felony, but for $950 and participation in a three-hour seminar, the slate can be wiped clean. Regular drug tests are required for three months, sometimes as many as four a week, and there's an additional $15 charge each time you pee in a cup. Miss a drug test because of the inability to pay, and you risk being thrown out of the program and right back into court. *The Arizona Republic* reported that the Maricopa County Attorney's Office took in $1.6 million annually from the program between 2010 and 2016. In Kansas, people charged with drunk driving for the first time can pay roughly $1,000 in diversion fees and fines and avoid the usual forty-eight-hour jail sentence, said Patrick Lewis, an attorney in Olathe. "I always encourage clients to pay off court costs and fines because once it's paid off, your probation or diversion officer relaxes a bunch," Lewis said. "From speeding tickets on up, it's part of how they make their budget."

Deep in the heart of the Mississippi Delta, amid the cotton fields and country crossroads made famous by blues musicians, John Helmert practices law. He's more like a character out of a John Grisham crime novel than a courtly southern lawyer like Atticus Finch. "I don't need a highfalutin office," said Helmert, a divorced father of four who practices out of his apartment in Greenville. "I can meet clients in the courthouse or the library."

Helmert has represented indigent clients across the state, both in private practice and as a public defender, but he comes by his knowledge of poverty through experience. "I was poor growing up," he said. As a child, Helmert lived in a rural area near Gulfport and was mostly raised by his mother and grandmother. "My mother did a little bit of everything," he said. "I was fortunate I didn't need a lawyer but many people like me made bad choices and I wanted to help them." Being white, he said, protected him from what his poor black classmates faced. "If I were a black kid, I can tell you a dozen times when I would have been arrested," he said. "Because I was white, it never happened."

Helmert grew up in a family of four boys, and the four brothers took different paths. One became a preacher, another a pharmacist, and the third a police officer. With the latter, Helmert said, "we don't talk about law enforcement. I stay as far away from that with him as I can." After a stint in the Marine Corps and afterward running several grocery stores, Helmert went back to school, earning a law degree at age thirty-two. "If you remember how Marines are on the battlefield, that's how I am in court," he said. "My client tells me what the mission is and I don't back down." That said, Helmert is up against a larger institutional problem in the state when it comes to getting a fair shake for his clients. "It's a little known secret in Mississippi that it's illegal to be poor," he said. "If you commit a crime in Mississippi and you're poor, you're probably going to prison. If you're working at McDonald's you are not going to be able to complete pretrial diversion. You won't be able to afford it."

In recent years, amid strained budgets for prosecutors, pay-to-play diversion programs have become especially popular in Mississippi. But no single state official oversees all of Mississippi's diversion efforts—the district attorney or another government official in each of the state's twenty-two judicial districts can run the local program as they see fit. Diversion is typically an option for people charged with low-level offenses: marijuana possession or property crimes like auto theft or receiving stolen property. Monthly fees range from $125 to $250, according to Helmert, and participants must submit to regular drug tests, pay any fines and restitution charges imposed by the court, and attend meetings once a month with the local prosecutor's office.

Some programs are more demanding than others. In Mississippi's 16th Circuit in the eastern part of the state, the fee is $1,200, of which $200 must be paid by money order up front. At the time of completion, participants must be employed or enrolled in an educational program. Miss a meeting or fail a drug test and the program is terminated, with no refund for what's already been paid in. These requirements might not sound onerous for middle-class people, but they can be nearly impossible to fulfill for the poorest of the poor, said Helmert. For example, the 16th District includes rural Noxubee County, where 35 percent of the population is in poverty. Even getting to meetings can be tough for residents who don't own a car, said Helmert. Getting time off from shift work for random drug tests presents similar obstacles. Because diversion is a moneymaker, there's an incentive to steer people into the program even if they are likely to fail, Helmert said.

What's sad, said Spurgeon Kennedy, vice president of the National Association of Pretrial Services Agencies, is that the idea of diversion is noble. Keeping nonviolent defendants out of jail or sparing them from having a criminal conviction on their record benefits both these individuals and society at large. From where he grew up in Northeast Washington, D.C., Kennedy could see the dome of the Capitol but he perceived how far removed it was from the reality of his neighborhood. "I saw a lot of people I grew up with charged with minor offenses and they ended up with a criminal record," he said. Other friends went into law enforcement, Kennedy said, adding, "I used to joke with my family that my friends were either police officers or defendants."

Kennedy would spend twenty-five years working in Washington's pretrial services agency, and later help oversee research into pretrial options for the Department of Justice. When it works properly, he said, diversion can be life-altering. "People with money can avoid it but there is real collateral damage from a criminal conviction," he said. "Less chance of a job, less chance of getting an education, less chance of getting social services."

A few prosecutors are trying to make pretrial diversion fairer. In Hernando, Mississippi, District Attorney John Champion said that if someone is eligible for the diversion program, his office will make accommodations. "We will take anybody into the program," he said. "If they are truly destitute, we'll work with them. If they can't pay, I'm lenient. I fully understand the dynamics of my district. Good people make mistakes." Still, diversion fees help plug holes in his budget. While raising money is not the driving force behind the program, Champion said, "it is a method for us to raise money. The state of Mississippi doesn't fully fund us and we are monetarily strapped. They've given us these options. It is what it is."

The Salt Lake County district attorney in Utah, Sim Gill has tried to shift the focus away from money in his office's diversion programs. When the ability to pay is the determining factor, he said, "diversion is a macro commentary on the separation occurring between people who have wealth and those who don't." When he was a city prosecutor overseeing individual cases, he sought to make fines proportionate to the ability to pay. "If you're earning $1,000 a month, then a $500 fine has a different impact than if you're making $20,000 a month." Private companies that managed diversion programs were encouraged to offer sliding scales to participants. If they didn't, Gill would refer these candidates to county-run services. "As a prosecutor, I have incredible discretion and I challenged the for-profit mind-set," he said. "We talk about equality before the law and we have this notion that everybody will be treated the same way. But in application, the law can produce inequity."

At the Santa Ana Jail in Orange County, California, one group of prisoners is assigned to special cells where they don't mix with other inmates. It's not that these convicts are particularly dangerous. Most—but not all—are nonviolent offenders. Nor are they at risk for escape. Just the opposite—they're paying $110 a night for the privilege of serving out their sentences in comparatively comfy Santa Ana, instead of having to do hard time in the more dangerous county jail. Santa Ana is what's known as a pay-to-stay jail, one of more than twenty in the Los Angeles area that take in prisoners who'd rather be in a local lockup than the more fearsome county equivalent. "The tone is respectful and professional," said Christina Holland, the Santa Ana Jail administrator. "There's no yelling or screaming." Guards are instructed to be polite to their charges, calling prisoners Mr. and Ms., and asking them to perform tasks like cleaning the unit or organizing books in the library, rather than ordering them to do so.

"The county jails are dangerous," said Robert Schwartz, a well-known defense attorney in L.A. who steers clients to pay-to-stay facilities when he can. "They're dominated by gangs. Every competent lawyer knows what the risks are for clients in the county jail. A white, middle- or upper-middle-class guy who is not streetwise is truly a babe in the woods. A pay-to-stay jail is heaven on earth by comparison."

The *Los Angeles Times,* in an investigation with the Marshall Project, reported that there are almost two hundred beds available to paying customers in local jails in Los Angeles and Orange counties. Pay-to-stay programs in California mostly draw nonviolent offenders charged with drunk driving and misdemeanor drug offenses. But occasionally people charged with more serious crimes benefit. The newspaper found that pay-to-stay jails hosted dozens of people convicted of violent offenses like assault and battery, domestic violence, and sex crimes. Felons charged with the most serious crimes, like rape, murder, and armed robbery, are required to serve their sentences in state penitentiaries and are not eligible for pay-to-stay arrangements.

Perpetrators of financial fraud and other white-collar crimes can qualify, and there's been an increase lately in people charged with identity theft. "It's the internet crime du jour," said Schwartz. After conviction and sentencing, and with the approval of the judge, clients who would ordinarily go to the county jail can apply directly to local jails with pay-to-stay programs. Candidates supply the police report of their crime, the sentencing order from the judge, and a letter explaining why they are interested in pay-to-stay. "It's short," said Schwartz. "You don't have to tell your life story." Nonviolent offenders in good health are generally accepted, Schwartz said, and pay-to-stay inmates tend to be disproportionately white.

For local jurisdictions, jail for sale is popular for the same reason pay-to-play diversion programs have sprung up—they need the money. Most cities have dedicated websites that market their particular lockup, and officials don't consider the term pay-to-stay to be cheeky—it's frequently at the top of the page in capital letters. Police departments typically oversee the process of admission and aren't shy about boasting of the advantages of their hoosegow. "The Pay-to-Stay Program offers an alternative to serving time in the Los Angeles County Jail," the city of Hermosa Beach explains. "With the approval of the sentencing magistrate, men and women can serve their jail sentence in our clean and efficiently operated jail facility." Hermosa Beach is one of the more expensive jails—it charges $255 per day.

Just as pay-to-stay isn't a secret, neither are its origins. "We're a revenue-generating facility," said Holland, the Santa Ana Jail administrator. The city earns $80,000 to $100,000 annually from these inmates, and millions more providing cells for the U.S. Marshals Service and the Federal Bureau of Prisons. Most referrals come from attorneys who sometimes stop by for a tour before sending clients Holland's way. They usually like what they see, she said.

The difference between pay-to-stay at Santa Ana and hard time in a regular jail begins when people report to the facility. Initial booking can take up to four or five hours, but new inmates aren't handcuffed or locked to a chair as they might be elsewhere, said Holland. They can sit in the lobby, watch television, and make local calls for free. "They don't feel like they're in jail," Holland said. "It reminds me of the motor vehicle bureau."

Inside, it's different as well. Pay-to-stay inmates have a cell to themselves, or if they have to share one, it's only with another pay-to-stay prisoner. There's a 6:30 a.m. wake-up followed by breakfast, but guards will let prisoners sleep late if they wish. Most inmates spend their waking hours outside in the yard or in the dayroom, where there's a TV, a microwave, and board games, rather than being confined all day in their cells. "The cell door is open," Holland said. "If they want to go and lay down in their cell or read a book, that's okay." Inmates are locked down for the night at 9 p.m. The most distinctive element of the Santa Ana Jail experience is what is known as direct supervision. Guards are rarely out of sight and are trained to be approachable and treat prisoners with respect; in exchange, prisoners are expected to follow the rules and comply with any directions. "It's a little more humane," Holland said. "The whole philosophy is letting the inmate's behavior dictate how they are treated."

The divisions caused by wealth in the criminal justice system begin with pretrial diversion, but they don't end when inmates walk free. Long after incarceration, they persist in a web of fines and fees that keep the poor entangled in the system even as wealthier people move on with their lives. Christina Kovats spent seven years behind bars after driving under the influence of opiates and causing a crash in which her passenger, an elderly woman she was taking care of as an aide, was severely injured. Kovats, a mother of four, gave birth to her youngest child after she was jailed in 2010 and didn't see the baby girl again for more than a year.

When she walked out of the maximum security unit of the Indiana Women's Prison in 2017, Kovats was assessed a fee of $4,000 to cover court costs, using a public defender, and to cover a charge for her probation. That was in addition to $6,000 in restitution and $2,500 to reinstate her driver's license. "It was an astronomical amount that I knew was hanging over my head," she said. Earning $8.50 an hour as a stylist in a hair salon, there was no way she could pay off all that debt in a reasonable amount of time, but falling behind meant violating her probation and risking a return to jail. Before she was able to pay to get the new driver's license, she had to travel two hours by bus each way to get to work.

"It's hard to understand the terror," she said. "I don't ever want to return to that life in prison." Random drug tests, sometimes as many as three times a week, are a condition of her probation but cost $13 each. She will be on probation through 2033. "The fines and fees were almost a rent payment in itself," she said, detailing the choices she has to make. "Do you eat or pay the fees? Do you buy gas to drive and see your kids or pay for a drug test? Even though I finished my prison term, I have to keep paying."

Like diversion programs or pay-to-stay in many towns, jail systems in many states help cover the overhead by burdening inmates with hundreds or even thousands of dollars in charges after they leave. "The population in the criminal justice system is politically vulnerable and the system is opaque so jails can raise fees without scrutiny," said Alexandra Natapoff, a professor of law at the University of California, Irvine.

Recently, that has begun to change. In 2018, two attorneys with extensive experience in government, Joanna Weiss and Lisa Foster, founded the Fines & Fees Justice Center to draw attention to the issue. Meanwhile, groups like the American Civil Liberties Union, Civil Rights Corps, and the Southern Center for Human Rights have challenged the way state and local governments attempt to collect fees. Arguing they are prohibited under the equal protection and due process clauses of the Fourteenth Amendment, as well as an Eighth Amendment ban on "excessive fines," these groups have had some success.

The Supreme Court ruled decades ago in *Bearden v. Georgia* that it was unconstitutional to jail someone because of the inability to pay, but left enough room for judges to conclude that the people before them are unwilling, rather than unable, to pay. Despite the Constitution and legal precedents like *Bearden,* said Ms. Foster, municipalities hungry for money have continued to push the limits of the law. "Every day we learn about something new," she said. "It's like playing whack-a-mole."

Foster spent ten years as a Superior Court judge in California and later headed the Department of Justice's Office for Access to Justice. Most people inside the Velvet Rope scarcely know about the likes of fees for diversion programs or jail stays, she said. "As a judge I understood we were imposing fines and fees," she said. "But I blithely assumed people who couldn't afford to didn't pay and nothing happened."

What opened her eyes was a 2015 report by the Justice Department that concluded that the Ferguson, Missouri, police department systematically and intentionally discriminated against black residents. "Ferguson's law enforcement practices are shaped by the city's focus on revenue rather than by public safety needs," the report concluded. As a percentage of Ferguson's budget, law enforcement fees rose from 12 percent in 2011 to 23 percent in 2014. In one case, a woman who illegally parked her car only once ultimately paid $550 and served six days in jail when she missed a court date and was unable to pay. "The idea that the justice system is hurting people and keeping them from leading productive lives just made me furious," Foster said. "It was personal." She coauthored a Department of Justice letter to state chief justices across the country saying it was the department's view that many fines and fees were unconstitutional, violated federal law, and were causing significant harm. Many courts responded positively, she said, but soon after Donald Trump took office, the Justice Department rescinded the letter.

Not long before her release, while she was in a college program for prisoners, Christina Kovats won a $1,000 award for a paper she wrote on the history of the Indiana Women's Prison. Her instructor was proud and it was a bright spot in a life marked by poverty, addiction, and bad choices. Kovats savored the honor but the $1,000 went to pay restitution. Now she is living in a halfway house, which costs her $550 a month, and with her debt to society paid, she is slowly paying down her debt to the state of Indiana. She was accepted into Marian University in Indiana while in prison, and hopes to eventually go back to school and earn a degree in human resources. "I take responsibility for my actions," she said. "But I expected a chance to move beyond it."

Indeed, Kovats spent seven years in jail because of what she did, and no one else is to blame. But her current travails aren't due to her mistakes. They are the product of government policy. Whether it's diversion programs, pay-to-stay jails, or crippling fines and fees, they stem from the same root. "The more people have tried to shrink government, the more they've tried to offload the costs of the criminal justice system onto poor people," said Ernie Lewis, executive director of the National Association for Public Defense. The same could be said of the health care system, where low rates of Medicare and Medicaid reimbursement cause hospitals to close, leaving those without means to do without care.

Indeed, unlike the corporate decisions that shape life inside the Velvet Rope, the divisions outside are frequently the direct result of actions by public officials, from the White House on down to the judge at the cash-strapped local municipal court. And in the past when private companies like Community Health didn't act in the best interest of patients, the government was there to regulate them and serve as a counterbalancing force. But as deregulation became the norm in Washington, private firms have much more latitude to do as they please.

"It's not by accident," said Jason Corburn, director of the Institute of Urban and Regional Development at the University of California, Berkeley. "These are conscious policies at the federal, state, and local level." But only the less fortunate feel the full impact. "Wealthy communities are able to insulate themselves," he added. "We allow people to have a first-class line at the airport or a separate entrance at sporting events. Now it's being repeated at the community level."

8.

Isolation

nside New Jersey's Burlington Center Mall it is silent, save for the drip-drip-drip of water falling from the ceiling and forming a puddle in front of the former T-Mobile outlet. In the middle of the deserted atrium, where shoppers once congregated, empty wooden racks and shelves lay abandoned. All that remains of Flaming Wok and Famous Japan are turned-up chairs on vacant tables in the food court. Nearby a forlorn sign announces New Restaurant Coming Summer 2013.

This Ozymandias-like setting is what is known as a dead mall. Others call them ghost boxes or gray fields. To most observers, they are a monument to shifting spending habits, the rise of online retailing, or the preference of millennials for more authentic, urban experiences. These factors play a role, to be sure, but the real story is more complex. Because up the road, the upscale Cherry Hill Mall is thriving, anchored by a Nordstrom and dotted with high-end shops like Armani Exchange, Williams-Sonoma, and an Apple store.

At Burlington, the anchor stores were decidedly middle-class emporiums like Sears, J.C. Penney, and Macy's. Now they are closed and sealed up like sarcophagi. Burlington's intended audience was the once vast American middle class, and as it has shrunk, their once busy gathering places have emptied. In Burlington's case, 1.5 million square feet of retail space has been left to rot, spread out over nearly a hundred fallow acres.

Whether it's a mall, a department store, a restaurant chain, or a main street in a small town, for businesses serving the middle class, the terrain has grown more desolate. As outlets close, the retail experience is devolving into a world of designer boutiques and dollar stores. And for all but the rich, that means a fraying of community with the loss of both places to see others as well as spots to mix with others not like you.

Think of it like a barbell: with incomes stagnant for all but the top earners, consumers and the businesses that cater to them have clustered around one end or the other. More economically homogenous neighborhoods are propelling the split: in nine out of ten metropolitan areas surveyed by Pew, the proportion of middle-class families living in them shrank between 2000 and 2014. "It mirrors demographics," said Glenn Brill, a managing director at FTI Consulting who tracks the real estate market. "The portion of the population that is considered middle-class is peeling off, one way or the other. As a result, retail has broken to a large extent into a high and low."

This has fostered a sense of isolation that is profoundly changing the way an increasing number of people live, work, shop, and eat. There is an erosion of what economists and sociologists call social capital, and the effect on communities is as profound as the loss of financial capital. Robert Putnam, the Harvard professor of public policy, defines social capital as "connections among individuals—social networks and the norms of reciprocity and trustworthiness that arise from them."

Social capital is what binds people together in societies. It creates a sense of common purpose and all-encompassing interests, and as social capital erodes, citizens are cut off from one another. Not all of the loss of social capital is caused by economic factors. Some of it may be caused by a cultural trend toward greater individualism. As Putnam points out, television, the rise of the two-career family, and generational changes are also responsible. More recently, technological innovations like the internet and the rise of social media, which replace face-to-face contact, have played a significant role, too.

Economic forces are speeding the process, though. Consumers may pay less at big box discounters and dollar stores, but the savings come with a social cost. And as local institutions like the independent grocer, hardware store, or community bank wither amid competition from national chains, there are fewer ways for people to use and benefit from the social capital they have, said Charles Tolbert II, a professor of sociology at Baylor University. It's like a one-two punch: as the middle class ebbs, their social capital is diminished, and there are fewer institutions to help them make use of what's left.

Many scholars see social capital as an abstract force of unity that operates at the society-wide level, but Tolbert's studies of independent banks suggest it is an individual financial asset, too, one that provides direct economic advantages even in an otherwise merit-based, capitalistic economy. "If I've faithfully sat in the pews at church on Sunday morning, or in the bleachers at Little League or volunteered in the PTA, maybe it helps that the loan officer knows me when I go to the local bank to get a mortgage," Tolbert said.

Institutions like banks and stores are less focused on people without means, and devote more resources to attracting the most affluent customers. The upshot is that it's much easier for the wealthy to take advantage of the social capital they possess, the way a bank assigns a relationship manager to customers who maintain a high balance. On the other hand, about eight million poorer American households lack a bank account, and 29 percent of consumers don't have a credit card. That makes it much harder to access so much of what's dynamic in the economy today—Uber, Seamless, Amazon, and many new retail outlets. Concerned about the effect on lower-income consumers, Philadelphia banned cashless stores in early 2019 and similar proposals are under consideration in New York and New Jersey. "Things that make life simpler for a huge swath of the population are not available if you don't have a credit or debit card," said Benjamin Keys, a professor at the University of Pennsylvania's Wharton School. "It's almost like an invisible velvet rope and it's one more way in which people are isolated."

As retail outlets become more stratified—or disappear entirely—everyday interactions grow rarer and society itself becomes more atomized. And with fewer meeting places for people in different classes, there's less room for empathy and understanding in the culture. In their prime, malls were about much more than shopping. Although they were blamed, not unfairly in some cases, for killing downtowns, in other ways malls replicated the function that a main street used to serve. Families would come to shop there on weekends, running into friends and neighbors and letting their kids savor a little freedom in a safe environment.

In suburbia, malls became a rare example of quasi-public space, said Ellen Dunham-Jones, a professor at the Georgia Tech School of Architecture and director of its urban design program. "The focus has always been on building really great private space in the suburbs," she said. "Everyone loves their home but in general, the public realm was never as celebrated."

For teenagers coming of age in the 1970s, 1980s, and 1990s, the mall was not unlike a public square or main street where their parents and grandparents once socialized. "I remember reading Archie and Veronica comic books and thinking: 'Where was our soda shop?'" said Dunham-Jones. "The food court was as close as we got. Today, teenagers are hanging out on Facebook."

When Burlington Center Mall opened in 1982, it drew visitors from near and far. The governor of the state at the time, Thomas H. Kean, was there for the ribbon cutting and shoppers mobbed the place. "It was brand-new and modern and cool," said Deirdre Ryan, who first visited Burlington as a ten-year-old, not long after its debut. The centerpiece in the atrium was a bronze, life-size statue of an elephant known as Petal. When she was a teenager, Ryan's parents would let her and a friend roam the mall on their own before meeting up at Petal afterward. "We were given some money and usually ended up at a store which just sold stickers, or in the food court," said Ryan, who grew up in nearby Bordentown, New Jersey, and is now forty-six. "Going to the mall was a treat, it was something to look forward to."

Over time, though, Cherry Hill Mall and its fancier stores began to lure customers with deeper pockets. "There's a perception that Cherry Hill is more affluent," said Brian Carlin, the mayor of Burlington Township. "There are those in the community who called the Burlington Mall a flea market between three anchors." In 2007, seven people were arrested in a gang fight that briefly closed the mall and some shoppers concluded that the area wasn't safe. The recession took its toll on the Burlington Center Mall, and was soon followed by a wave of department store closings, with Macy's shuttering in 2010, followed by J.C. Penney in 2014, and Sears in 2018.

Malls don't die quickly. It is a drawn-out process, with its own rhythms and hierarchies. In the healthiest malls, more expensive national apparel and footwear shops dominate, like Abercrombie & Fitch, Brooks Brothers, and Cole Haan. When these retailers pull out, they are replaced by respectable but less elite tenants like Foot Locker and Kay Jewelers as well as mom-and-pop stores and health clubs. In the tertiary stage, when shoppers can sense things are going downhill, massage parlors and beauty salons move in. Both of the latter were represented as the end approached in Burlington, along with a food pantry, another sign of the mall's deteriorating socioeconomic status. Different owners cycled through, each proposing different plans that went nowhere. Old stores closed, and it became harder and harder to attract new ones.

When Deirdre Ryan moved back home in 2008 after living in Massachusetts and California, she almost didn't recognize the Burlington Mall. "It was so sad," she said. "It wasn't the mall my friends and I grew up with. It didn't bring in the clientele. It was just depressing and they didn't invest in it."

After water pipes burst during a deep freeze in January 2018 and damaged the electrical system, the mall's owners shut it down. Sears's 300,000-square-foot store, which was attached to the mall but in a separate building, hung on until September 2018. Emblematic of the middle-class consumer, Sears itself went bankrupt the following month. There was one survivor—the sculpture of Petal the elephant. Beloved by residents, it was rescued in February 2019 after a fundraising campaign by the Rotary Club of Burlington and moved to an outdoor promenade near the Delaware River.

The surrounding area suffered as a result of Burlington's closure, said Rose Mary Burden, who could drive from her home in Columbus, New Jersey, to the mall in about six minutes. "It's really disappointing that the mall is closed," said Burden. "As a single mom of three, it would be a major convenience if there were a mall nearby with an Old Navy or a Macy's." The closest malls to her home are a half hour's ride away so with Burlington gone, she does most of her shopping on the internet. "I just don't have time to drive to the mall," said Burden, who is forty-seven. "I do miss the experience of going shopping and looking through windows. But when I order new outfits or shoes for my kids, most of the time I resort to buying them online."

Kim Parker of Hammonton, New Jersey, also misses the mall. She marked several milestones in her life there, buying her prom dress, her engagement ring, and her wedding dress all at Burlington. "I definitely would rather buy at the mall," said Parker, who is forty-five. "It left a hole as far as a place to go for a couple of hours and walk around and shop. You didn't have to spend a lot of money if you didn't want to."

The phenomenon that played out in New Jersey is being replicated across the country, according to DJ Busch, managing director at Green Street Advisors. The reason? Richer consumers have been the overwhelming beneficiaries of rising prices for stocks and other financial assets, a development economists term the wealth effect. Middle-income shoppers, dependent on salaries or the value of their homes, haven't enjoyed a comparable increase in net worth or income, Busch said.

As with retailers, the mall landscape is divided among winners and losers, without much room in between. Of the one thousand or so malls in the country, 37 percent are dead or dying, according to Green Street, which tracks the real estate industry. Known as Class C or D malls, these centers are marked by low occupancy rates and the loss of one or more anchor tenants. And with department stores closing—Sears and sister company Kmart closed more than 225 stores in 2018—more malls are falling into the endangered category. "Class C and D malls are doomed," said Busch. "There is very little use for them as retail ventures. The land could have a higher and better use for something other than retail."

At least fifty malls in the U.S. are like Burlington—flat out dead and closed for business. When they are close to big cities, some deceased malls are being torn down and replaced with fulfillment centers for online retailers like Amazon. That's an example of what the economist Joseph Schumpeter called creative destruction and it is a natural outgrowth of a healthy, evolving economy. And in the last few years, there has been an uptick in the number of properties marked for demolition.

But many other now vacant shopping centers resemble Frederick Towne Mall in Maryland, which closed down in 2013. The place has steadily deteriorated, as anyone can see in one of a series of YouTube shorts on dead malls by filmmaker Dan Bell. He found broken windows, trash-filled corners, and, on a 2:30 a.m. night tour inside, eerie neon lights that glow in the otherwise pitch-black hallways. "The city has been dealing with this mall for a long time," said Richard Griffin, Frederick's economic development director. It lies on the west side of Frederick, where the Washington suburbs end and rural Maryland begins. Once the most valuable piece of property in Frederick, it was valued at over $40 million by the state. By the time a local doctor purchased the moldering property in 2017, it traded hands for a little over $6 million. The owner dreams of making it a retail mecca again but there have been no takers, according to Griffin.

Frederick Towne Mall is likely to have more company in the

years ahead. Even among Class B malls, which account for another third or so of malls, the outlook isn't rosy. "It's binary," Busch said, which means there's a 50 percent chance they will end up like their Class C and D counterparts. To resuscitate them would require enormous amounts of capital but in many cases it's doubtful anyone would want to invest for the future. Class A malls are the healthiest, marked by luxury tenants and anchors and high sales per square foot. In addition to better demographics, these fancier malls have other advantages in an age of easy online shopping. "The higher the degree of luxury of an item for sale, the more someone will want to see it in person before making a purchase," Busch said. Upscale malls are selling something else, too, according to Dunham-Jones. "The really high-end malls give you the experience of luxury," she said. "Perfumed air. Marble floors and valet parking."

Just as wealth is increasingly concentrated, so are the shops that depend on it. "You can't force retailers to go into a neighborhood or a community where buying power doesn't exist because they will fail," said Christopher Zahas, a real estate economist and urban planner in Portland, Oregon. "Retailers like to go where there's investment and to be near other successful stores. They thrive on each other."

Indeed, that's evident when online-only retailers seek out brick-and-mortar locations for the first time. The decision by digitally native companies like eyeglass merchant Warby Parker or Casper, the mattress maker, to open stores where consumers can touch and feel the merchandise has been hailed as a salvation for the beleaguered mall industry. But Green Street found it to be another case of winner-take-all: when internet retailers go from being a virtual presence to actually renting out space, they overwhelmingly flock to A++ malls, the elite of the elite.

As all but the top-tier malls fade, so has their value to investors. The real estate market has basically written off the value of Class B, C, and D space, according to Busch. Class A outlets equal 25 percent of total malls but they account for 80 percent of the sector's market value. Although department store closures hurt the entire mall industry, they were concentrated among the 290 stores in Class B and Class C malls that shut down in 2018. Only fifty department stores closed at Class A malls. And the closures were concentrated in areas of the country that have struggled economically.

For all the purported pressure from the internet on mid-tier chains like Sears or Macy's or J.C. Penney, online purchases account for just 10 percent of all retail activity, according to the Census Bureau. More significant is how shoppers are flocking to one end of the barbell or the other. "Where there is high income, there is growth," said Chaim Katzman, a veteran real estate investor and mall owner. In the wake of the financial crisis of 2008–09, Katzman owned about two hundred malls in the U.S. and began pruning his portfolio, selling off properties in smaller markets where he felt growth prospects were limited. "We decided to really concentrate on improving our demographics," Katzman said. For example, he sold off malls in less urbanized areas of the Southeast, but kept his property in Buckhead, an upscale Atlanta neighborhood. Katzman also scooped up what he calls "trophy assets" in the places that would ultimately benefit most from the long post-recession recovery—cities like New York, Los Angeles, and San Francisco.

In a metaphor for how retail and the broader economy have evolved in the past decade, Katzman watched what happened when Loehmann's, a legendary source of bargains for generations of women from all different classes, went bankrupt in 2014. The massive property he owned in Manhattan's Chelsea neighborhood, where Loehmann's had been for decades, was left vacant. In its place came Barneys, a store that stands for luxury the way Loehmann's once did for discounts, where a Prada coat or a Chanel bag can sell for thousands of dollars.

There are ways of predicting what fate lies in store for a specific mall. At Green Street Advisors, the best indicator is what is known as a TAP score, short for Trade Area Power. It's based on four factors—household income, population, education, and cost of living—and it's a kind of shorthand for which side of the Velvet Rope a particular property is located. The higher the score, the more likely a particular mall will be healthy. For example, the prosperous Mall at Short Hills in New Jersey is rated A++ and carries a TAP score of 93. A-rated malls typically have a TAP score of more than 70. Burlington Mall, which is D-rated, has a TAP score of 48, putting it almost exactly in the middle of the American socioeconomic matrix.

That's a dangerous place to be, according to Mark Cohen, director of retail studies at Columbia Business School. "The middle class is being hollowed out," he said. "The bifurcation of the consumer space is emblematic of that. Whether it's brick and mortar or online, wealthier people are shopping with abandon. They have tremendous discretionary buying power. With the middle class and the lower classes living paycheck to paycheck, consumers are going downmarket."

Cohen ticks off the names of middle-class department stores that once anchored malls and shopping centers but are dead or dying: Sears. Mervyn's. Abraham & Straus. He worked at all three but got into retailing by accident. After graduating from Columbia University with a degree in electrical engineering in 1969 and then earning an MBA there two years later, Cohen was accepted into a training program at Abraham & Straus in New York City. "When I joined, my family wanted to conduct an exorcism," he said. "Why is this math and science kid going to work for a department store?"

For Cohen, it was a way to earn some money while preparing to interview at companies where he could make use of his engineering degree, like IBM. "As trainees, we were thrown into the fray but I found it exhilarating," he said. "Out of thirty-seven of us on the first day, there were three of us left when the program ended." Cohen started out as a men's dress shirt and tie buyer and worked his way up the ladder at one middle-class chain after another before running Sears Canada from 2001 to 2004. These stores, like the malls they occupied, were more than a place to shop, he explained. They were places where middle-class people, especially women, could gather and find a like-minded community of fellow shoppers, much as their better-off peers might still be able to find in a Manhattan boutique or an elite retailer for the one percent like Bergdorf Goodman.

Salespeople were full-time employees and knew their customers well, with each knowing the other's family milestones and building a connection beyond the cash register. "Department stores and malls were where the middle class shopped and were the center of the universe from a commerce point of view," Cohen said. "There was a human connection between the customers, the merchandise they bought, and the people who sold it to them. The human connection, for the most part, is gone now."

So has the ability to live a middle-class life as a store salesperson. Garrick Brown, vice president of retail intelligence at Cushman & Wakefield, the real estate broker, analyzed the employment costs associated with full-time employees at 150 publicly traded retailers between 1985 and 2015. He found that after adjusting for inflation, wages had declined by 30 percent. "If you want customer service, you have to go high end," he said. "If you go into most department stores today, there's no one on the floor, just two clerks behind a register with a long line of people waiting."

There was exactly one rack of clothes left in the last hour at the last Loehmann's store in Manhattan on the day it closed its doors forever. When I visited, the mood was reminiscent of a wake, or better yet, a shiva call. Women circled the lone rack, eyeing labels, holding up skirts and blouses for size before reluctantly putting them down, as if they wanted to walk out the door with one final bargain after shopping at Loehmann's for decades. Downstairs, the beloved Back Room had already been stripped bare of clothing. All that remained were boxes of hangers and metal racks priced at $10 each, along with a fluorescent floor lamp marked "this fixture for sale." Even boxes of white-and-black Loehmann's shopping bags in various sizes were available for purchase although there were no buyers in sight.

"I started going to Loehmann's forty years ago in the Bronx with my mother and grandmother," Allene Feldman, an Upper West

Sider, told me as she fought back tears. Bargain hunting drew the Feldmans to Loehmann's of course, but that wasn't the heart of the appeal. Instead it was the shared experience, both among the generations in her family and among the women of different classes and races who tried on their finds in the communal dressing room and offered strangers unvarnished advice, sometimes solicited and sometimes not. Penny Fuller, another Upper West Sider scanning what little was left, admitted she didn't need to shop at Loehmann's anymore and in her fur coat and expensive bag, she wouldn't have been out of place at Barneys. But, like Feldman, Fuller too craved what she called the communal experience. "We used to try on a dress and ask, 'What do you think?'" she said. "That's missing elsewhere."

It is Steve Maksin's final day as the owner of Burlington Center Mall and although he's made a fortune on it, he isn't feeling nostalgic. "It's yesterday's snow," he said, eyes wandering over one vacant storefront after another. "This is what was viable thirty years ago. There is no use for it in the modern economy. It needs to be razed to the ground." There is money to be made on dead malls, as it turns out, but not by the people who live, work, or shop nearby. A Brooklyn-based vulture investor, Maksin buys up the distressed debt of dying malls, takes over the properties, and tries to redevelop them or, if he can, flip them to another investor for a hefty profit. Not that it's easy. "It's fraught with danger," he said. "Don't do this at home."

Buying a dying mall can be like catching a falling knife, he explained. When anchors leave or vacancy levels rise, provisions in the leases of the remaining tenants allow them to renegotiate with the landlord and pay less. "They say, 'We will pay $40 per square foot, or $30 or $10,'" he said. "Tenants have tasted blood and they will go to the mall owner and say this rent is too high. The rental structure collapses." Then there is the cost of upkeep, which is why Maksin let Burlington close rather than fix the pipes that burst in early 2018. In his malls, it costs hundreds of thousands of dollars just to keep the lights on. Every time it snows in the Northeast, Maksin has to shell out hundreds of thousands more to clear all those parking lots.

Burlington Center Mall was already terminal when Maksin's firm, Moonbeam Capital Investments, bought it for $3.4 million. The previous owner had paid $10.5 million in 1999, but that was before the Great Recession struck and Macy's left. Maksin picked up the mall at a foreclosure auction in 2012. It was 60 percent occupied at the time, and Maksin felt it was a good redevelopment play. What he didn't know was that it would take seven years.

Mall leases are notoriously complicated but Maksin is trained as both an accountant and lawyer, and he has been able to master the intricacies of the process. "There's hidden time bombs as well as hidden treasure," he said. For example, anchor tenants have veto power over redevelopment plans, which can trip up real estate investors looking for a quick buck. As long as Sears was open at Burlington, Maksin couldn't shut down the mall and position it for another purpose. He was patient, however, buying the former Sears and J.C. Penney parcels in Burlington only after those stores had given up the ghost. Sears originally wanted $7 to $8 million— Maksin waited them out and paid $1.7 million. Once he controlled the entire property, not just the mall itself, his firm was in a much stronger position to market it as a potential site for warehouses or offices.

Maksin savors the wheeling and dealing that comes with buying and selling dead malls. A native of Kiev, Maksin got his start supplying Soviet souvenirs like busts of Lenin, Red Army medals, and other tchotchkes to tourists. It was the mid-1980s and glasnost was under way in the Soviet Union. Maksin sensed opportunity. "We'd trade stuff for sneakers and jeans and sell it at a tremendous markup," he said. "As I made more money, I realized I was not living in a free country."

Maksin's grandmother had immigrated to the U.S. years earlier and while visiting her in 1989, he defected and sought political asylum. He turned Vsevolod, his very Slavic first name, into a middle name, and called himself Steven. He enrolled at Kingsborough

Community College, took English as a second language, and won a scholarship to New York University's Stern School of Business. After working for an accounting giant, he cofounded a currency trading firm on Wall Street; when that was sold in 2010, Maksin turned to real estate. Despite his success, he still lives in Brighton Beach, a Russian immigrant enclave, rather than move to Park Avenue or Las Vegas. He owns homes in both. "My roots, my family, my mother and my love of the ocean made me stay," he said.

After the 2008 market meltdown, the financial landscape was bleak. "I named the firm Moonbeam because we would be a light in the darkness," he said. There was more than enough darkness to go around. Malls were in free fall and with backing from wealthy families and private equity investors, Maksin began buying up properties that other potential buyers considered roadkill. Sometimes, Maksin has discovered, there is life after death for malls. A vacant shopping center in Las Vegas that he owns is now used by the police force to train new recruits. "I don't have to spend as much on security," he said. At an Orlando mall, the motor vehicle department has moved in, along with the tax collector's office. He's eyeing other potential tenants like medical offices or local colleges that need new teaching space.

But the best scenario is when Moonbeam can sell to a deep-pocketed investor like Clarion Capital Partners, a New York–based private equity firm with billions under management. Maksin had been talking to Clarion for years about Burlington but once Sears departed and Moonbeam bought that property, the biggest obstacle to redevelopment was out of the way. Clarion paid Maksin more than $22 million for the Burlington Mall in February 2019, three times the total amount he put in. As of this writing, Burlington was still sitting abandoned, although there's talk of replacing it with warehouses or other commercial space. But it's no longer Steve Maksin's problem. "Is this a great business or what?" he said.

Whatever happens to Burlington Center Mall, it will live on at a website called Deadmalls.com. It features hundreds of dead or dying properties, with contributors posting photos and videos of malls in various states of decay along with recollections of better days. Take ShoppingTown, a Moonbeam property near Syracuse that is rated C- by Green Street Advisors and has a TAP score of 53, putting it well within the danger zone. Sears, the only remaining anchor at Shop- pingTown after J.C. Penney, Macy's, and Dick's Sporting Goods all left, shut down in 2018. On Deadmalls.com, there's an obligatory video of gated-up stores, lonely tiled corridors, and a desolate food court. "I hate going there now because it reminds me too much of *Dawn of the Dead*," one poster wrote.

Jack Thomas, one of the three mall fanatics behind the site, filmed the video from ShoppingTown and when he's not at his job working with the developmentally disabled, he's traveling the coun- try trying to get into abandoned shopping centers. Perhaps because they represent something larger in American life—the decline of the middle class, fewer shared experiences, and increased isolation— dead malls have become a meme. There is a particularly spooky scene in the movie *Gone Girl* set in a dead mall and Thomas's web- site drew more than 235,000 unique visitors in 2018. Like beached whales, dead malls draw fascination as well as dismay. "Everybody loves an apocalypse-type scenario," he said. "We're exploring this forbidden place. We aren't doing this to expose or trash a place. We want to preserve the memories."

In tiny Blue Hill, Nebraska, Thramer's Food Center isn't just a place to shop. It doubles as a restaurant—the only one in town— and for the rural community's 936 residents, the grocery store is a place to run into neighbors, hear the latest news, and exchange gossip. Homebound seniors can call in a list of items on Thursday and have them delivered the next day. And on the second Tuesday of each month, members of Blue Hill's Community Club gather to plan events like the annual July 4th parade plus celebrations for chil- dren and families on Christmas and Halloween.

When academics talk about institutions that promote social capital in a community, places like Thramer's Food Center are what they have in mind. But ever since the spring of 2017, owner Tim Thramer has worried that his grocery's days are numbered. That's when a Dollar General opened on the edge of town, one of 1,315 stores the company opened in the United States in 2017, or nearly four per day. Like most dollar stores, Dollar General doesn't offer fresh fruit and vegetables or meat, and most of its offerings cost less than $10.

But the competition has forced Tim Thramer to rethink how long his store can continue to offer up groceries, as well as social capital, in Blue Hill. If Thramer's Food Center closes, the nearest full-service grocery is a twenty-two-minute drive away in Red Cloud, the childhood home of writer Willa Cather. "I'll stay here and fight till the end but I'm fairly certain I'm the last owner of this business," Thramer said. "Dollar General is one of the nails in the coffin."

By targeting low-income consumers in rural America and poorer sections of big cities, dollar stores have found fertile ground. The two largest chains, Dollar General and Dollar Tree, have over thirty thousand outlets, more than Walmart and McDonald's combined. Analysts expect them to continue to open four stores a day into the foreseeable future, and Dollar Tree sees room for an additional ten thousand locations. The contrast with the rest of retail is telling—dollar stores are opening four times faster than other retail outlets, and their sales are growing at two to three times the rate the economy is expanding. Nearly 65 percent of dollar store customers earn less than $50,000, with the largest portion making less than $25,000.

"The economy is continuing to create more of our core customer," Dollar General's chief executive, Todd Vasos, told *The Wall Street Journal* in 2017. "We are putting stores [in areas] that perhaps five years ago were just on the cusp of probably not being our demographic and it has now turned to being our demographic."

Dollar stores do offer lower prices for some goods than grocery stores but they take a social and economic toll. When dollar outlets drive out grocery stores, shoppers who don't want to drive long distances must settle for less healthy packaged, canned, and processed foods and forgo fresh meat, fruit, and vegetables. On the north side of Tulsa, Oklahoma, a predominantly African American neighborhood, there are dozens of dollar stores but not a single full-service grocery store, according to a December 2018 report by the Institute for Local Self-Reliance (ILSR).

The study found that dollar stores largely bypassed more affluent, white neighborhoods and concentrated in census tracts with both a greater percentage of black residents and households living in poverty. Independent grocery stores had historically avoided these neighborhoods because banks were reluctant to provide credit, said Stacy Mitchell, co-director of the Institute for Local Self-Reliance. Meanwhile, the big supermarket chains preferred to invest elsewhere. Now, the prevalence of dollar stores discourages new, full-time grocery stores from opening, and getting a loan remains a challenge. "These dollar stores aren't merely a symptom of economic distress," Mitchell said. "They are causing it."

Dollar General has been especially aggressive in expanding into rural towns in the Midwest that Walmart would consider too small. As their numbers have grown, independent grocery stores have been folding. Twenty years ago, there were 1,200 grocery stores in Nebraska, said Kathy Siefken, executive director of the Nebraska Grocery Industry Association. Today there are five hundred, and the pace of closings has increased as more dollar stores pop up. Ten more grocery stores closed in the state in 2018, Siefken said, all in rural communities where dollar stores had recently opened. Paradoxically, food deserts are popping up in a state that's part of the breadbasket of America.

"When a Dollar General comes into a community, they don't sell perishable items," Siefken said. "They take the easy way out and sell products they don't have to worry about going bad." (Many do stock milk.) And with profit margins already thin at grocery stores—about 1.5 percent—few independents can compete with the purchasing power and prices available to a company with $25 billion in revenue.

There is also an impact on small-town economies, many of which have been suffering for years as young people move away and the farm sector is pinched by weak commodity prices. Traditional small-town groceries employ fifteen to seventeen people, according to David Procter, director of the Center for Engagement and Community Development at Kansas State University. Dollar stores tend to employ about half as many, he said. At local stores, profits go back into the community and this creates what economists call a multiplier effect, as those dollars stay and circulate. But when a giant corporation moves in, profits are sucked out and go to a far-away headquarters and distant shareholders.

Procter spends nearly one third of his time working with grocery store owners and local officials to devise strategies to keep stores open. Once a week, he hears from a community where a dollar store is about to open. Leaders and local businesses want to know what their options are. In some cases, they turn to the local zoning board or elected officials and try to prevent the dollar store from opening. More commonly, they try to persuade residents to support the independent grocery by shopping there. "They're fighting pretty powerful forces," Procter said. "When we started surveying rural grocery stores in 2008, the biggest competitive challenge was Walmart. We don't hear that much about Walmart now. In the last three years, it's been Dollar General."

There are other ramifications—grocery stores tend to be located downtown and are a vital source of foot traffic for other businesses, like pharmacies, restaurants, or hardware stores. Dollar stores are usually located on highways or busy roads just outside of town. Without a downtown presence, it changes the dynamic on Main Street.

The social impact cannot be underestimated. Local service clubs like Rotary International and Kiwanis International use these stores as a meeting place, much as Blue Hill's Community Club gathers in Tim Thramer's market. In Perry, Kansas, there was a small library in one corner of the grocery where residents could check out books. The store closed in late 2018, five years after Dollar General arrived.

When nearby towns lost independent supermarkets, population declines followed, said Wayne Ledbetter, a county commissioner in Jefferson County, which includes the town of Perry.

Although Dollar General does make local donations and supports a literacy foundation that provides community grants, small-town residents say the chain is less generous than many independent grocery stores. "When we asked Dollar General for a donation to help with our fall festival, which is our biggest fundraiser, we got a big fat zero," said Paula Hladky, who is active in the Perry community. "It doesn't matter how we present it to them. They always say it doesn't match their mission. Dollar General takes what they can get, and they give us nothing in return."

In a statement, Dollar General insisted its stores are a force for good, not economic harm, in the communities where they operate.

"We believe the addition of each new Dollar General store presents positive economic growth for the communities we proudly serve," the company said. "We believe our small-box footprint and product assortment helps our customers stretch their budgets, particularly on items such as paper and cleaning products, which often are offered at much higher prices in both large and small grocery stores.

"Our stores provide customers with both alternative and complementary options to items sold in larger-box grocers and retailers, including many components of a healthy diet such as milk, eggs, bread, cheese, frozen and canned vegetables, proteins and more," Dollar General added.

In Blue Hill, Tim Thramer has no plans to close his store but he's had to make some tough choices. He's already cut two part-time workers as sales have dipped and he's donating less to charity. "We help with the booster club at schools, churches, the fire department, and community events like July 4th," Thramer said. "We sell food at a discount or at cost and donate cash. I've been cutting back and being more choosy. Not because I want to but because I have to."

.   .   .

Dollar stores are not new. Dollar General traces its roots to Depression-era Kentucky, and got its start in small towns there and in neighboring Tennessee, where it is still headquartered. But the dollar store category boomed after the Great Recession and never looked back. While other parts of retail have struggled, Dollar General and Dollar Tree have become Wall Street darlings. "Dollar stores, in a sense, truly legitimized themselves as stocks and as a retail channel during the downturn in 2008 and 2009," said Vincent Sinisi, a Wall Street analyst who covers the sector. "When things were so bad, the stigma came off dollar stores." An influx of new customers followed the recession, with formerly middle-class shoppers no longer able to afford anything but a dollar store.

At Dollar General, about 75 percent of sales come from what are called consumables—everything from packaged food and soda to soap, shampoo, toilet paper, and diapers. Dollar General has tended to focus on rural areas, although it is beginning to move more heavily into urban neighborhoods. Dollar Tree is more suburban, and Family Dollar, which is owned by Dollar Tree, got its start in cities and is more prevalent there. Dollar General and Family Dollar have a similar mix of products for sale, mostly consumables like packaged food, cleaning supplies, snacks, and personal care items. At Dollar Tree, everything is generally priced at $1 or less.

In the interview with *The Wall Street Journal,* Todd Vasos explained how the dollar store shopping cycle works. The average Dollar General customer "doesn't look at her pantry or her refrigerator and say, 'You know, I'm going to be out of ketchup in the next few days. I'm going to order a few bottles,'" he said. "The core customer uses the last bit of ketchup at the table the night prior, and either on her way to work or on her way home picks up one bottle."

Much as they are busy inside the Velvet Rope, the deep pockets of private equity funds are also active outside, whether in the guise of mall-focused Moonbeam Capital or, in Dollar General's case, Kohlberg Kravis Roberts. The investment firm bought the chain for over $7 billion in 2007 and brought in new management while retooling its supply chain and other infrastructure, said Peter Keith, an analyst with Piper Jaffray. The timing couldn't have been better—when the economy tanked the following year, Dollar General and KKR were perfectly positioned to reap the rewards. KKR managed to take Dollar General public again in November 2009, when the rest of the stock market was barely out of its recession-era funk.

"This is when the group got the attention of Wall Street investors," said Keith. "If you were a portfolio manager, these stocks had accelerating fundamentals when everything else was getting killed." Dollar General would soar 422 percent in the next ten years, compared with a 160 percent gain for the Standard & Poor's 500. Meanwhile, J.C. Penney lost 96 percent of its value over the same period while Sears embarked on its decade-long journey into bankruptcy.

More recently, with the economy finally beginning to gather speed and deliver salary increases to lower-paid workers, a new worry erupted on Wall Street. Would the good times be bad news for dollar stores? If their core customers had a little more cash in their pocket, some investors worried, they might buy more discretionary items, which dollar stores stock less of. "For many investors, dollar stores are a counter-cyclical investment," said Keith. In a conference call with investors in December 2018, Vasos sought to reassure them that Dollar General shoppers were still struggling. "While the economy appears to be doing well, we know that our core customer is always challenged," he said.

Keith said he doesn't see much risk that Dollar General customers will suddenly start trading up and he rates the stock a buy. "These customers can't spend $150 on food for the week," Keith added, echoing Vasos's view that shoppers will make small purchases when they can afford it, rather than stock up. "People spend more right around the first of the month when government subsidy checks begin to arrive and SNAP cards are funded," Keith said. Since dollar stores are cheap to open and operate, the company can continue to move into smaller and smaller towns, Keith added. "We do think they have a very compelling store growth strategy," he said. "They can really lock down that town that can only support one dollar store."

A few independent grocery store owners, like Diana Hahn in Park River, North Dakota (population: 1,403), are fighting back. Hahn's husband, Randy, who runs the meat department, started smoking his own hams and bacon and selling homemade beef jerky, drawing new customers from miles around. "We found a niche," she said. "We're always at community events. That's not something a big corporation is going to do."

And when a Dollar General opened in her town in the state's Red River Valley in February 2018, she was ready. Prepared for a 10 to 20 percent drop in sales, she immediately cut two part-timers, as well as her advertising and donation budgets. She had talked to other grocery stores, and the cuts were the quickest steps she could take. One advantage Hahn also had was that the nearest Walmart was an hour away. Plus, grocery stores in some nearby towns had already died, and their residents were traveling to her store to shop. "They're very loyal to us because they know what it's like to not have a grocery store," Hahn said. "What's bad for one person is good for someone else, that's just the way life is. We're not going anywhere."

It's not an easy fight, though, and isolation stalks many small towns as one shop after another closes. Forty years ago in Ravenna, Nebraska, the downtown boasted a movie theater, two grocery stores, a liquor shop, and several restaurants, said Kim McDowell, who was born and raised there. One bar remains open, there isn't a full-service, sit-down restaurant left, and the movie theater and grocery stores are gone. "I remember when this town was alive at night," she said. "Now you go and it looks like a ghost town."

After high school, McDowell went to college in Kearney, a larger town of more than thirty thousand about a half hour's drive away, but she missed Ravenna, no matter how small it was. While working as a cashier in a local supermarket in Kearney, she met her husband-to-be, Paul, who worked in the produce department. When a grocery store in Ravenna came up for sale in 1996, they jumped on it. Ravenna Super Foods opened just days before July 4th, an auspicious sign, they thought.

The store survived local economic setbacks like the closing of a dairy plant, and layoffs by the Burlington Northern Santa Fe railroad that cuts through downtown. Customers would come to shop in the century-old, redbrick-fronted building and linger for coffee and conversation. "They'd stick around for half an hour and we'd sit there and talk to them," Paul McDowell said. "That's what created the hometown atmosphere." He also became more involved in local affairs, serving as president of Ravenna's Chamber of Commerce and the local economic development corporation.

When Dollar General opened a location in Ravenna in 2016, Kim McDowell said she had a bad feeling, but initially sales didn't suffer too much. After six months, they were off just a few percentage points. "We hung in there pretty good but it just kept going down," Paul McDowell said. "Perishables were fine but where they hammer you is soap, paper products, Pepsi, and Coke. We just couldn't compete on price."

By 2017, the grocery was bleeding money but the McDowells weren't ready to call it quits. They turned to their retirement savings account and pulled out over $100,000 to keep their store open. But when the compressors in the freezer section blew—replacing them would cost $30,000—the McDowells were reluctant to drain their savings further. There were only ten employees left in the store, down from a peak of thirty, but making payroll was becoming impossible. As much as it pained them, the McDowells closed their store in January 2019. Longtime patrons embraced them and cried as they made their final purchases.

Kim is now working at a title and escrow company in Kearney, while Paul took a job as an assistant manager at a supermarket there. Used to being his own boss, at fifty-five, Paul is now the oldest employee in the store by roughly twenty years. "It's difficult on so many levels," he said. "You have no idea. But I have a lot of knowledge and experience that I want to share." Despite having raised three daughters in Ravenna, and built a myriad of local connections, with both of them now at jobs in Kearney, the McDowells are thinking of leaving Ravenna. "I don't want to because I like the small-town community," Paul McDowell said. "I tried everything I could do. I never would have left if we could have made it work."

Like Mark Zuckerberg years later, Samuel Beall III's career in business began with a side hustle in college. The setting was not the Harvard Quad in Cambridge, Massachusetts, though; Beall got his start in Knoxville at the University of Tennessee and the product was pizza, not social media. It was the late 1960s, and while other students were protesting the Vietnam War or journeying to Woodstock, Sandy Beall, as he is known, was running three Pizza Hut franchises on the side to pay his way through school.

Sandy Beall's father, Samuel Beall Jr., was an engineer who worked on the Manhattan Project and helped develop the atomic bomb. But the younger Beall's interests lay elsewhere. "I was never much of a student," he recalled. "I always worked, whether it was engraving jewelry or stringing tennis rackets." His passion, however, was food and he dreamed of owning a restaurant. When the owner of the Pizza Hut franchises he managed in Knoxville died and willed Beall some money to open his own place, he seized the opportunity.

But first, Beall was advised to go north to New York City to get ideas for the new restaurant. Beall wasn't going to find them in Knoxville, a Bible Belt town that didn't boast much of a nightlife and where restaurants had long been forbidden to serve alcohol. When he arrived in Manhattan, two new venues that essentially created the swinging singles scene on the Upper East Side, T.G.I. Friday (the original, not the later franchised chain) and Maxwell's Plum, immediately caught Beall's eye. Not far away, he also discovered an older watering hole famous for its burgers and everyman setting, P.J. Clarke's.

"I took bits and pieces from each one," Beall recalled. The name of his new venture, Ruby Tuesday, was inspired by T.G.I. Friday with a little help from the Rolling Stones single. The boisterous separate bar and singles-oriented atmosphere there resembled Maxwell's Plum, and the burgers and old bric-a-brac on the walls came straight out of P.J. Clarke's. "There was nothing like it in Knoxville," Beall said. "It was a redneck version of Maxwell's Plum."

The city had just dropped its ban on serving alcohol in restaurants and Beall secured what was only Knoxville's second commercial liquor license. The new bar and grill was a hit from the time it opened in 1972. Beall soon dropped out of college to manage the place full-time, but not before persuading his fraternity brothers to invest in new locations. Ruby Tuesday expanded into Chattanooga, Nashville, and Memphis before venturing elsewhere in the South like Alabama, Georgia, and Florida. Before long Beall was cutting the ribbon at a new Ruby Tuesday every nine months.

By the mid-1980s, Ruby Tuesday was part of a publicly traded company, and the chain continued to grow like kudzu, moving out of the South and into other parts of the country. "You had demand from middle America," he said. "Middle-class people had time to sit down and enjoy a meal. You could get a real hamburger with quality cheeses on a great bun. It was quality, fun food." While other full-service chains like Cheesecake Factory occupy big spaces, Beall deliberately kept Ruby Tuesday on the smaller side, with no more than thirty-five tables. There were urban Ruby Tuesdays, but for the most part, Beall said, "I wanted it to be a neighborhood place with reasonable prices in smaller markets." Malls were a favorite venue.

The chain prospered right through the economic boom of the 1990s and into the mid-2000s. Unemployment was low, and soaring home values created a middle-class version of the wealth effect. "One year, we opened a Ruby Tuesday every five or six days somewhere in America," Beall said. "It was insane but we were able to do that in the 1990s." Ruby Tuesday was soon the largest full-service restaurant chain in the eastern United States. And Beall became one of the richest men in Tennessee, as shares of Ruby Tuesday soared from below $5 to more than $30 a share.

Then came the Great Recession. Beall had endured downturns before in the early 1980s and early 1990s, and again after the tech bubble burst in 2000, but those were bumps in the road compared to what followed. The collapse in 2008 and 2009 was entirely different. Many Ruby Tuesday customers stopped going out entirely, and the ones who could still afford it were going to cheaper casual chains with $5.99 dinner specials, or to fast food joints like Wendy's. The stock sank to $2 a share.

Beall tried the only strategy he thought might work—move Ruby Tuesday upscale with better food and nicer interiors, and attract more affluent customers who could still afford to dine out. The company spent $100 million overhauling the decor at its nine hundred restaurants, stripping out the fake Tiffany lamps and bric-a-brac and going with leather, dark wood, and sleek surfaces. Lobster tails were added to Ruby Tuesday's menu, along with a better wine selection. It flopped. New diners looking for something a little fancier never arrived, and sales continued to soften. "The customer base wasn't brought along with these changes," said Steve Rockwell, a veteran restaurant industry analyst who served as an executive at Ruby Tuesday from 2008 to 2010. "The more affluent customer wasn't convinced or even aware of the changes that were made to the brand."

Shares of Ruby Tuesday remained depressed and hedge fund managers turned up the pressure but nothing worked. After forty years at Ruby Tuesday, Beall had had enough. "The hedge funds thought they had all the answers," he said. He stepped down in 2012, and his successor abandoned the upscale strategy and added more fried food to the menu. But something larger was afoot than decor or dining options, said Aaron Allen, a restaurant industry consultant. "Consumers didn't have as much money after the recession and they went to fast food and never came back," he said. Faster, cheaper options like Panera Bread and Chipotle took away market share. "America is so busy now and time dictates so much of what you eat," Beall said. Indeed, with money tight, many people in Ruby Tuesday's demographic have to work longer hours to make ends meet, precluding a sit-down meal at a full-service restaurant.

One group of Americans, however, still has time to enjoy a

leisurely meal: the affluent. Except they flock to chains with white tablecloths and extensive wine lists, like Ruth's Chris Steak House and Capital Grille. These and other more expensive eateries attract diners from a much smaller segment of the population than those who flocked to Ruby Tuesday but that's been more than enough to power growth. Between 2012 and 2019, shares of the company that owns Ruth's Chris Steak House tripled as earnings surged.

Ruby Tuesday's sales continued to dive, with business falling by 10 percent annually between 2013 and 2018. A private equity investor bought the company for $3 a share in 2017, and management has continued to close restaurants. All told, the number of Ruby Tuesday outlets fell to 544 in 2018 from 945 in 2007. Much like dead and dying malls, many of these holdouts are outside the more prosperous areas where Ruth's Chris Steak House is concentrated. "They built a lot of locations in more rural southern markets where economic activity just dried up," Rockwell said. "Demographics are fluid. What was a great location for Ruby Tuesday may not be so today because the community has changed."

If you thought that was the end of the Beall story, though, think again. During the fat years at Ruby Tuesday, Sandy Beall poured money into a sprawling 4,200 acre property called Blackberry Farm that he and his wife had purchased in 1976 in the Great Smoky Mountains of eastern Tennessee. Always a foodie at heart, even if Ruby Tuesday's offerings could never be confused with gourmet fare, Beall began to host family and friends for luxurious meals at Blackberry Farm. Sam Beall, Sandy's eldest son, was also drawn to the kitchen at a young age, and by his early teens was working the line at Ruby Tuesday. He, too, wanted to open a restaurant, but his vision was the opposite of the mass formula his father had discovered in New York City and exported around the country two decades earlier.

"I knew there was something different for me and I knew it from day one," Sam Beall told me in an interview before his death in a skiing accident in 2016. After training at the California Culinary Academy and apprenticing with legendary chef Thomas

Keller at the French Laundry restaurant in Napa Valley, Sam Beall returned to Blackberry Farm and created what would ultimately become an ultra-exclusive resort for the burgeoning ranks of the wealthiest foodies. Now overseen by Sam's widow, Mary Celeste Beall, Blackberry Farm is thriving and weekends sell out six to eight months in advance. Rates for the hotel's sixty-eight rooms start at $1,095 for a historic room with a king-sized bed and go up to about $10,000 a night for a five-bedroom home on the property. All meals are included, and with a three-night minimum in many instances, the typical stay costs between $5,000 and $10,000 for food and accommodations.

Unlike Ruby Tuesday, Blackberry Farm recovered quickly from the 2008–09 recession and has been adding high-end extras ever since. There's a bottle-lined wine tunnel where guests can peruse a myriad of vintages. All told, Blackberry Farm's cellars contain 160,000 bottles. At a spa called the Wellhouse, guests can enjoy a revitalizing duo scalp and foot massage ($180), a lavender and vanilla bourbon body drench ($290), or a two-and-a-half-hour, full-body treatment that combines seasonal plants, flowers, and herbs and is inspired by the natural rhythms of the farm ($480). In early 2019, the Bealls opened a sister resort next door called Blackberry Mountain, constructed with local stone and wood and offering thirty-six additional rooms.

On Blackberry Farm's website, there is no sign of Ruby Tuesday fare like the Spicy Jalapeño Pretzel Burger and Louisiana Fried Shrimp. In contrast to his father, Sam Beall told me he was never focused on the mass market. "We don't go to chain restaurants and I don't eat anything that doesn't come from the season in our area, even when I'm out," he said. "It's a different way of life, more mindful, more real, more sustainable."

It's also a much more expensive way of life than customers at Ruby Tuesday could ever conceive of, and price isn't the only difference. Blackberry Farm is healthy, artisanal, small-scale, and available only to a well-heeled and sophisticated few. "It's like comparing a

Prius to a Rolls-Royce," said Rockwell, who has visited both Blackberry Farm and Ruby Tuesday.

Sandy and Sam Beall's journeys reflect seismic shifts in who drives economic growth in America and around the world today, which cohorts are growing and which are shrinking, and how businesses cater to them. The trajectories of Ruby Tuesday and Blackberry Farm also speak to social capital, who has it and who does not. While Ruby Tuesday's customers trade down to a cramped, in-and-out meal at Wendy's, the elite gather with friends and enjoy a five-course dinner at Blackberry Farm. Or they can expand their social networks and horizons with group activities at the resort, taking pottery-making lessons, playing organized paintball games, and bonding in yoga classes.

The rarefied lifestyle of Blackberry's guests has little in common with how most Americans live, while Ruby Tuesday in its prime was a reflection of the then American majority, the broad middle class. That's fine with Sandy Beall. His own tastes have changed. Burgers built his fortune, but Beall has moved on. "I don't eat much fried food or red meat," he said. "I have three hamburgers a year. I used to have three a week and I haven't had fries in a year." Unlike Ruby Tuesday, which is a shadow of its former self, Blackberry Farm seems set to endure. "It's family and it's forever," he said. "Whether it's Blackberry or Hermès, there is great brand loyalty. I wanted to create something my great-grandchildren could have."

For retailers and restaurants, demographics is destiny. At a real estate company, it might mean keeping a mall with a high TAP score open, while shuttering properties elsewhere. Or Ruth's Chris Steak House selecting an upscale neighborhood for its newest restaurant, even as Ruby Tuesdays close in less prosperous areas. Changing demographics are now deepening this divide—as wealth and poverty become more concentrated, business abandons areas that were once in the middle. There have always been rich and poor neighborhoods, to be sure. But there were also places where people of different classes lived together, if not always side by side, then at least street by street.

These neighborhoods are losing ground, according to research by Sean Reardon, who studies the impact of poverty and inequality on education at Stanford University, and Kendra Bischoff, a professor of sociology at Cornell. In 1970, 65 percent of families lived in middle-income neighborhoods; by 2009 only 42 percent did. The proportion of families living in affluent areas more than doubled, as did the proportion in poorer ones.

"Most families increasingly live in neighborhoods that are more homogenous economically than they were in the past," Reardon said. This polarization has lifelong consequences. Isolated from better-off peers, children growing up in poor neighborhoods are less likely to complete college, earn less once they enter the workforce, and are more likely to become single parents. When children are raised in uniformly wealthy enclaves, Reardon said, "it may limit their understanding and empathy for the life experiences of most of America. When we don't have empathy, it makes it harder to feel like we have shared problems in society. It's easy to feel like those are someone else's problems."

Widening regional economic gaps parallel that local shift. Between 1865 and 1980, there was a convergence in incomes between different parts of the country, said Ed Glaeser, a professor of economics at Harvard. In poorer regions, earnings grew faster off a lower base, reducing disparities. That process largely stopped in the 1990s, according to Glaeser. Despite that, more Americans seem stuck in place. "It feels like we are much less fluid as a country and there is a sclerosis of American economic geography," Glaeser said. The housing market adds to the immobility. With real estate prices having exploded in the most prosperous parts of the country, while staying flat or dropping elsewhere, it's not as if a family in the Rust Belt can sell their home and buy an equivalent place in Seattle, San Francisco, or Boston. Both middle-class and poorer Americans are increasingly locked in place, and as they become more isolated, demographics deteriorate further, worsening the problem.

Neighborhoods and the places we shop aren't the only spaces that are becoming more segmented. In the workplace, where employees of different classes traditionally labored together, a caste system has developed. Forty years ago at the headquarters of a successful company, the executives, the cafeteria workers, and the janitors all worked for the same employer. When the firm did well and grew, all benefited, though some of course benefited more than others. There was a shared sense of purpose, even if the only tangible sign was an invitation to the holiday party or a turkey at Thanksgiving. The executives are still there but now the cafeteria worker is employed by a food services firm and the janitor works for an outside cleaning company. "They've been Balkanized," said David Autor, a professor of economics at MIT. "As far as executives are concerned, you're not really coworkers any longer. You might as well be a robot."

The end result is more than just isolation among individuals. The country, and the institutions that govern it, begin to fray. "When the middle class starts to crumble, people increasingly see themselves as different from others," Ganesh Sitaraman, a law professor at Vanderbilt University, told *The Atlantic* in 2017. "They sort themselves by wealth, by education level, and the result is that there's an increasing fracturing of society, a loss of the solidarity that comes with having a large middle class. And that can be very destructive to a republic."

This is where we are headed but the isolation goes both ways. Whether it's the cruise ship passenger in their elite hideaway, the concierge doctor's patient, or the favored guest at Blackberry Farm, the wealthiest among us are isolated, just as the less privileged are at the dying mall and the dollar store. The difference is that the rich can still opt for a more connected life; everyone else is on their own.

Conclusion

· · · · · · · · · · · · · ·

The first thing Jody Hoffer Gittell notices when she boards a
Southwest Airlines flight is what she doesn't have to do: endure
the long walk past first-class passengers luxuriating in oversize
seats as she makes her way down a cramped aisle to the back of the
plane. Alone among the major carriers, Southwest doesn't offer first
or business class. It's one size fits all in the cabin, and it's precisely
why she chooses to fly Southwest whenever she can. "Once you're
on board, everyone is the same," she said. "I like the feeling that
everyone matters and there aren't any gradations in how much they
matter. It creates a sense of community even if it is a very short-term
community."

Velvet Ropes aren't entirely absent at Southwest. In 2007 it
began allowing passengers to pay for early boarding—but otherwise it has stuck to the egalitarian vision sketched out by its founder,
Herb Kelleher, when the airline was launched in the early 1970s.
There are no fancy lounges for elite frequent fliers or extra charges
for more legroom—not even assigned seats—and passengers are
permitted to change reservations without a fee, regardless of what
they spent on the ticket. Nor do fliers have to pay to check a bag or
even two. "They were founded on an ethic of mutual respect and
regard for all," said Gittell, a professor of management at Brandeis
University who authored a book on the carrier, *The Southwest Air-*

lines Way. "It's not just window dressing—it's core to their business model."

Southwest's approach isn't merely the story of a successful company that respects and values its customers. It serves as an object lesson as well. In this book, we've explored how tiered our society has become, who has been included and who has been excluded, and how corporations and government alike have fueled that process. But Southwest's example shows that the Velvet Rope Economy is not a fait accompli. More equitable options exist for consumers and citizens—and companies and institutions can succeed if they offer them.

The key is for businesses, political leaders, and above all, American citizens, to confront the problem and demand more egalitarian alternatives. The stakes are high. Because the choice isn't just about having a better flight, or a more pleasant interaction in the other realms we've surveyed, like tourism, medical care, insurance, and education. It goes to the heart of what kind of society we want to live in and whether the social fabric tears further and unravels or is mended.

Barring a revolution—and I'm certainly not calling for that—Velvet Ropes will not disappear. "The economics are too powerful," said Bill George, a professor at Harvard Business School who served as the chief executive of Medtronic, a medical device maker. Customers who order one hundred widgets will most likely get a better price than those who buy ten, he said, and they might be wined and dined as well. The key, he explained, is that it's possible to reward the best customers while still serving all customers well.

It's a delicate balance but there are huge rewards for businesses that manage to strike it successfully. Indeed, at Starbucks, Target, and Best Buy there is no Velvet Rope, and they are among the best performing companies of the last quarter century. The barista might know your name if you order a latte every morning at your local Starbucks, but that drink won't arrive any faster than it will for a patron who's there for the first time. The billionaire and the barista wait on the same line at Best Buy.

To put it in the language of this book, ease and access should be a standard operating procedure, not the preserve of a select few. Take the bank or the cable company—both have the resources to answer all calls quickly, not just the ones from people with a high customer lifetime value. Envy can be minimized as a marketing tool, and exclusivity shouldn't mean a cattle-car-like experience for anyone not in the front of the plane or the elite frequent-flier club. I'm not advocating the elimination of skyboxes at stadiums, or the practice of charging more for seats closer to the action. But roped-off sections that prevent fans from walking down to the field to get an autograph, as we saw at Yankee Stadium, are a bridge too far.

But that's just scratching the surface. As a society, we need to recognize that we've let public institutions like hospitals, fire departments, state colleges, airports, and libraries suffer from decades of underinvestment. Rebuilding them would blunt some of the extremes in inequality that now disfigure American society. Seeing the physician or taking a trip could be a pleasant experience even if you don't go to a concierge doctor or belong to the Private Suite. Homeowners would be able to rely on the local fire department instead of having to hire private firefighters.

Pulling down the Velvet Rope isn't just good for the community—it can prove to be very good business. Southwest is the most profitable airline in the history of the American aviation industry, having made money for forty-six years in a row. Unlike American, United, and Delta, the carrier never filed for bankruptcy and its stock has vastly outperformed its peers since the company went public in 1977. Southwest's profit margins are 50 percent higher than its competitors' and the airline has the healthiest balance sheet in the industry, according to Rajeev Lalwani, an analyst who tracks the company for Morgan Stanley. "Customers love the egalitarian approach and they now have this incredibly well-regarded brand," he said. "It's worked. That's why they are not going crazy segmenting the cabin."

Southwest's distinctive path stands in sharp contrast to the rest of the industry—which helps explain its success. At other airlines today, one aviation consultant said, "If you want a cheap ticket, you're going to be in a bad seat and you better pack lightly." Southwest's alternative approach grew out of its roots as a discount airline ferrying passengers between Love Field in Dallas and other Texas cities in the 1970s. The airline business was highly regulated at the time, and fares had to be approved by a federal board—unless flights were intrastate. Herb Kelleher, a San Antonio lawyer, saw an opening. And after almost four years of lawsuits by bigger competitors trying to prevent Southwest from ever getting airborne, the airline went into service with three planes in 1971.

It was an era when the middle class was at its height and inequality was low, at least in relation to where it had been in the past and where it would be in the future. Kelleher's goal wasn't to lure corporate travelers away from American or Pan Am. It was, as he put it, to get people out of their cars and give them a chance to take advantage of a mode of travel that heretofore had been mostly reserved for the jet set.

There is a personal element to Southwest's radically different trajectory, too, and it shows what happens when executives like Kelleher turn early lessons into corporate values. In an article in *Fortune,* Kelleher described how his mother taught him that positions and titles were adornments and didn't signify people's underlying value. "I learned firsthand that what she was telling me was correct, because there was a very dignified gentleman in our neighborhood, the president of a local savings and loan, who used to stroll along in a very regal way up until he was indicted and convicted of embezzlement," he recalled. "She taught me that every person and every job is worth just as much as any other person and any other job."

But it wasn't enough to treat customers that way; if it were really going to be put into practice, that spirit had to be extended to employees within the organization. The sense of equality started at the top at Southwest, with a nonhierarchical management style. There was a genuine sense that employees were partners, said Ann Rhoades, who headed up human resources and training at the airline in the late 1980s and early 1990s. Once a quarter, the top twelve officers in the company would each have to spend a day working alongside front-line employees. "One time as a flight attendant, I spilled Bloody Marys all over," Rhoades recalls with a shudder. "The Monday after, I got a note from Herb telling me I was never going to work as a flight attendant again." When crews stay overnight in different cities, some airlines have been known to book better hotels for pilots than for flight attendants. At Southwest in the early years, everyone stayed at the same place.

Many of the practices established under Kelleher, who stepped down as chairman in 2008, endure. Pilots sometimes help flight attendants clean the cabin to speed the turnaround process. Workers at all levels, from ramp agents and baggage handlers to flight attendants and pilots, can fly for free to attend company parties. "If you really want it to be egalitarian, then everyone has to feel like they are in it together," said Charles O'Reilly III, who teaches at Stanford University's Graduate School of Business. From the beginning, employees at Southwest have been encouraged to use humor with passengers, to break down barriers and make sometimes onerous flights more bearable.

Until 2007, passengers boarded according to when they checked in for the flight, so seating was first-come, first-served. If you wanted a better seat, all you had to do was show up earlier. Southwest turned the lack of assigned seats into an advantage because it allowed passengers to board more quickly and planes spent less time on the tarmac as a result. "There is something seductive about finding ways to squeeze more margin out of customers," said O'Reilly. By finding ways to boost productivity instead—like quicker turnarounds and takeoffs—Southwest found a more customer-friendly way to make money. As a Harvard Business School case study recounts, "Southwest sent observers to the Indianapolis 500 to watch pit crews fuel and service race cars. The airline recognized that pit crews performed, in a different industry and at much faster speeds, the same functions as airplane maintenance crews." With those lessons and other steps, Southwest was able to reduce turnaround times by 50 percent.

To be sure, it's not always corporate greed that fosters segmentation. Sometimes, consumers themselves are responsible. Southwest's decision to allow those willing to pay to move to the head of the line was prompted by customer demands. Ann Rhoades was among the Southwest executives who helped launch JetBlue in 2000 and their initial impulse was to adhere to the egalitarian model, too, she said. But in the last decade, JetBlue has introduced Even More Space seats that customers could purchase, along with Mint, its version of business class. "Those of us from Southwest weren't used to it and we said, 'Are you sure we want to separate people?'" she said. "But customers told us this is what they wanted. It was a customer accommodation."

In trying to find a balance between a capitalist economy and egalitarian ideals, there are inevitable conflicts that are not easy to resolve. Indeed, they go to the heart of the American experiment itself. In the Declaration of Independence, the founders declared that the idea that "all men are created equal" was a self-evident truth. But later in the very same sentence, "the pursuit of happiness" is defined as an unalienable right. The impulse to pay to jump the line is always going to be there; just how far it goes is ultimately up to all of us and according to the social norms we enforce.

Egalitarianism can seem downright countercultural. Jody Hoffer Gittell grew up on a farm in a Mennonite community in Pennsylvania Dutch country. "It was about humility and everyone having equal value," Gittell said, qualities she still believes in as a management expert. It explains why Gittell prefers Southwest. But egalitarian values don't have to lead to practices as old-fashioned as those of the Amish. Southwest's place as the most successful airline in American history proves that.

Curbing the extreme stratification found in the travel and leisure sector, whether it's cruise ships, hotels, or sporting activities, is a taller order. On board ship, classes go back a long way, and the return to more segmented liners has proven to be a hit with many customers. Hotels, too, have enjoyed great success by offering many different levels of accommodation within the same property, even as Airbnb has given travelers new budget options.

But there are intriguing exceptions. There is no popular leisure sport with more elite connotations than golf. The best courses in the country usually belong to private clubs, with old-money membership rolls and initiation fees that run into the six figures. Annual dues cost tens of thousands more. Mike Keiser had a different vision. He wanted to create a golf resort on the rugged Oregon coast that would hark back to the origins of the game in Scotland and Ireland. In those countries, the sport's best venues remain accessible for ordinary players and that's the case at Bandon Dunes, which he founded in 1999. *Golf Digest* ranks it among the top one hundred courses in the country, alongside peak Velvet Rope private clubs like Augusta National and Winged Foot. Anyone can play at Bandon Dunes, which overlooks the Pacific Ocean, and Keiser has kept the cost of a round of golf to $135 in the off-season. There are other top courses where the public can play, like Pebble Beach in California, but a game there costs nearly $600—year round. "I could charge more but I want it to be affordable," said Keiser. "I'm making money. I don't need to make more money and I'm fine with breaking even in the winter."

Keiser made his fortune by starting a company that turned recycled paper into greeting cards. It reached $100 million in revenues before he sold it to a private equity firm. Not that he's a fan of private equity firms. If one of them acquired Bandon Dunes, he said, "they would almost assuredly borrow a ton of money to buy it, then increase the rates big-time." Bandon Dunes is aimed at the retail golfer, not the corporate player on an expense account. "There are no expensive spas here with facials and pedicures," Keiser said. If they prefer, guests can carry their own bags instead of hiring a caddy, which isn't an option at many of the top private clubs.

Friends were skeptical when he set out to create a great course for the Everyman golfer, but the resort has proven to be a huge hit. There are four full-size courses now at Bandon Dunes, up from one when it opened, and all of them made *Golf Digest*'s top 100 ranking. "Golf was harmed when it became aspirational and therefore expensive," Keiser said. "If I charged more, I'd lose a lot of loyal golfers. I'm a populist and would rather have a full house."

At Lambeau Field, home of the Green Bay Packers, the best seats in the house aren't behind glass in a carpet-lined skybox with faux-leather swivel chairs. The fans who are closest to the action sit on metal benches that take up the first sixty rows in from the field, all around the stadium. The Packers trace their name to the team's founding, when the owners of a meatpacking plant in this Wisconsin town on Lake Michigan contributed the money for uniforms and equipment. A century later, football is a multibillion-dollar business but Green Bay hasn't strayed as far from its blue-collar history as have many other teams. "We could definitely generate more money from the stadium if we wanted to but we made a conscious choice not to," said Mark Murphy, the president and chief executive officer of the Green Bay Packers. "I look at ticket prices for the Super Bowl and I do worry the sport is becoming less affordable for blue-collar or middle-class families."

A decade ago, the team was preparing to launch a $300 million renovation and expansion of the stadium, which opened in 1957, and Murphy had some big decisions to make. The general admission benches in what's known as the lower bowl featured the best views of the game, but replacing them with a smaller number of expensive club seats could yield millions in new revenues for the team. At the same time, expansion plans called for more than eight thousand new seats and earmarking them all for premium seating would yield millions more. The demand was evident—there are more than 130,000 names on the waiting list for season tickets at Lambeau Field. Even if only 10 percent were prepared to pay what fans elsewhere did for personal seat licenses, the renovation would help pay for itself. "It was a very short discussion," said Murphy. "If you sit in the bowl, you're having the same experience that fans did when they watched Vince Lombardi coach in the 1960s. We didn't want to take away from what makes Lambeau Field special."

The lower bowl was left untouched and the vast majority of the new seats went to general admission fans. While personal seat licenses at stadiums in other cities can cost tens of thousands of dollars, prices for the equivalent in Green Bay were set at a uniform $2,100. And for current holders of season passes, the cheapest package for each season costs $278. "People who can afford anything they want or people who really have to stretch to pay for tickets are sitting side by side at Lambeau Field," said John Bergstrom, a business owner in Neenah, Wisconsin, who spent two decades on the Packers' board of directors. "They want to sit on that bench and be part of that crazy experience."

Like Southwest, the home of the Green Bay Packers is not entirely without Velvet Ropes. There are clubs for elite fans and skyboxes and cushier premium seats available. But they don't impinge on everyone else's experience—much of the elite seating is located high up in the stadium, where the view isn't nearly as good as it is down in the bowl. And although there are premium dining options, most concession stands are operated by nonprofits like Boy Scout troops, church groups, and high school team boosters that take home a share of the profits. "We're not completely pure," said Murphy. "But there's a balance we try to strike. We want to be as affordable as possible."

Murphy had a Velvet Rope experience of his own. After playing eight seasons for the Washington Redskins as a safety, he received season tickets at the old home of the team, Robert F. Kennedy Memorial Stadium. The seats were in the upper deck, but they offered good views of the action. When the Redskins moved to what is now known as FedExField outside Washington in 1997, Murphy was still in the upper deck but now there was a huge premium section in between him and the game. "You felt like you were so far from the field," he said. "In newer stadiums, they put boxes and suites in prime locations and bump everyone else. It informed a lot of my thoughts on how you want to treat season ticket holders."

His scruples have not hurt the Packers' standing in the league. Although the population of Green Bay and its environs makes it the smallest football market in the country, the team has won four Super Bowl championships and is valued at $2.6 billion, according to *Forbes*. What allows Murphy to make the decisions he does is that the Green Bay Packers are fan-owned, with more than 300,000 shareholders. To pay for the renovation, there was a stock offering in 2011 and the shares, priced at $250 each, were quickly snapped up. "It's a very different culture than the typical NFL team," said Murphy. "Any profit we make we put back into the stadium, and invest in our players and facilities. We don't have the profit motive the way owners of other teams do."

That shows in ways large and small. Both regular fans and elite ticket holders get to stand close up as the players charge from the locker room and onto the field before kickoff. To secure these spots, winners are chosen at random in a free drawing and there is a free lottery to get onto the field for pregame practice, too. VIP parking isn't located any closer to the field than regular parking. You won't see field-level clubs or the kind of "Tequila Bunkers" found at Levi's Stadium. Murphy has also sworn off giving naming rights to a corporate sponsor, forgoing $20 to $30 million in revenue annually to retain the stadium's original name. "Lambeau Field is like taking a time machine going back to an era when people actually treated each other with respect," said Andy Dolich, the sports consultant who worked for the San Francisco 49ers and other teams. "For football fans, this is their shrine, their temple."

Treating all individuals better, rather than just the ones who can pay more, is one way of curbing the effects of the Velvet Rope Economy. But if the goal is a more cohesive society, where inequity is diminished and social capital augmented, then businesses also have to work at the macro level, explicitly considering the needs of the communities in which they operate.

The Itasca Project in Minneapolis–St. Paul shows how that can be done. Every Friday morning at 7:30, a dozen or so of the most powerful men and women in the Twin Cities gather in a conference room at the offices of McKinsey & Company, the consulting giant. Executives from the biggest companies in town are there; so are government officials and representatives of major philanthropies. They form the Working Team of the Itasca Project, a private civic initiative by about seventy-five local leaders aimed at boosting growth and development in the region, while tackling the toughest social problems. The larger group includes additional business leaders, as well as the mayors of Minneapolis and St. Paul and officials from the state university system.

Think of it as Establishment 2.0: more diverse and solution-minded than the establishment of old, to be sure, but every bit as powerful. "This isn't about a group of senior executives dictating from a conference room what they think should be done," said Tim Welsh, a vice chairman of U.S. Bank and a former McKinsey senior partner who helped found Itasca in 2003. "We're all in this together and have to help each other." Nor are Itasca's members insular—they seek out community input even as they set the agenda.

In late 2015, a young black man, Jamar Clark, was shot and killed by police in north Minneapolis, a predominantly African American neighborhood. Black Lives Matter and other groups organized demonstrations, and violence erupted. To business leaders, it felt like a turning point in Minneapolis, a city that prides itself on tolerance and comity. "Itasca said we've got to help address this issue," Welsh explained. "This has to calm down and we need to provide jobs and opportunities in north Minneapolis." Working with members of the community, local groups, and government agencies, Itasca set out to invest in the area, using money from public and private sources. The plan called for a new corporate headquarters and health care facility, improved transportation infrastructure, and job placement and training. "No one can remember this level of investment since the 1930s," said Welsh. "This is patient capital. We're not looking for immediate returns."

Although they typically work behind the scenes, Itasca members have been willing to step into the public eye. More than a decade ago, after a downtown bridge spanning the Mississippi River collapsed, killing 13 people and injuring 145, it was obvious that new investment in roads and public transit was necessary. But Tim Pawlenty, the Republican governor at the time, vetoed a proposed increase in gas and sales taxes to fund $6.6 billion in transportation improvements. He had made a no-new-taxes-pledge and none of his previous vetoes had been overridden. Itasca, however, was able to move the debate beyond the usual left-right dynamic.

James R. Campbell, a prominent local banker who was another cofounder of Itasca, donned a hardhat and fluorescent vest and stood with union leaders on the capitol steps to rally support. He and other business executives made the case to Republican lawmakers that traffic jams and long commutes were bad for employers and employees alike. More time on the road meant less time workers could be at their desks or with their families. In the end, six Republican legislators defied the governor and the veto was reversed by a two-vote margin. "I can't overstate the importance of the Itasca Project leadership on the transportation issue," said Chris Coleman, the former mayor of St. Paul. "There's no question it changed the trajectory of the debate." In other cities, the elites may prefer to just pay to use a faster lane, but Itasca shows a different outcome is possible.

Again and again in this book, we've seen how the educational system has contributed to inequality. It might be IvyWise giving people with the deepest pockets the most access to the Ivy League, or pay-to-play fees keeping poorer students on the sidelines. The children of the rich dominate at colleges like Columbia and the University of Chicago and enjoy first-class teaching facilities, while many poor and middle-class students have to make do at New York's City College or Chicago State. Elite graduate schools have become a principal gateway to the upper middle class, but tuition at the best law and medical programs tops $60,000. These professional schools, in particular, have become bulwarks of income inequality rather than engines of mobility.

A few individuals and institutions are trying to change that and help others get past the Velvet Rope. Dr. Rafael Rivera, associate dean for admissions and financial aid at New York University's School of Medicine, is one of them. A radiologist by training, Dr. Rivera was raised by his aunt and grandmother in Brooklyn, New York. His family depended on food stamps. Before winning a scholarship to Cornell, he worked in a shoe factory and at a Burger King during high school. He stayed at Cornell for his medical degree, but when he emerged from all those years of schooling, he faced a crushing amount of debt, both in the form of student loans and credit card obligations. Rivera applied for debt forbearance to gain some breathing room but the interest on what he owed continued to accumulate. It took him roughly a decade to pay it off. "This discourages a significant number of people from pursuing their dream," he said. "You're always worried that the rug will be pulled out from under you."

Dr. Rivera and Dr. Robert I. Grossman, the chief executive of NYU Langone Health, were determined to try something new. It took more than a decade, but at the ceremony in 2018 when first-year medical students begin their training and receive their white coats, school officials had a surprise announcement. NYU's School of Medicine would no longer charge tuition—for any of the ninety-two medical students in the incoming class. "When we dropped the bomb it was awesome to see," Dr. Rivera said. "There were tears of joy. You could see the financial weight lift from their shoulders." A dedicated fund of $650 million, raised from donors, generates enough income annually to make tuition a memory at NYU's medical school, regardless of the student's need.

Some were skeptical of the decision to aid all students, not merely low-income ones. But it was an academic life raft for the often overlooked middle class. "There's a group in the middle that need-based aid doesn't reach," Dr. Rivera said. "We've been need-based for years and look at the level of indebtedness." Before the program was launched, nearly 60 percent of NYU's medical students owed money when they graduated, with an average debt load of $168,000.

Freeing young doctors from debt is only one objective of the program. Dr. Rivera hopes it will encourage students to consider lower-paying specialties they might not otherwise have thought about, like pediatrics and family medicine. The simplicity and scope of the offer was also intended to increase both racial and socioeconomic diversity. It's working: applications from African Americans for a place in the class of 2023 more than doubled. More students from low- and middle-income families also sought admission. "This is a moral imperative," said Dr. Rivera. "I hope other medical schools see what we did and it will start a sea change." So far, the only one to do so is Kaiser Permanente's new medical school in California, which said in early 2019 that students in the first five classes would not have to pay tuition.

NYU's program is an outlier in terms of professional schools, but on the undergraduate level, there has been more progress, for middle-class households in particular. At Princeton, which has a $26 billion endowment, tuition is waived for students from families that earn up to $160,000. Harvard and Yale, whose endowments are even larger, have similar formulas. Top schools with much smaller endowments, like Rice University in Houston, are following suit. In the fall of 2018, Rice announced it would be tuition-free for families earning up to $130,000. "There are mental velvet ropes," said David Leebron, the president of Rice. "People will say, 'College is not for us. It's for rich people.' We wanted to go to the heart of that problem."

The experiences of Southwest, Bandon Dunes, the Green Bay Packers, the Itasca Project, and NYU's medical school highlight valuable lessons for limiting the reach of the Velvet Rope Economy.

First, individual leaders matter—if they are willing to set their own course. Herb Kelleher had a different vision for Southwest, and wasn't afraid to do away with things that had been taken for granted at other airlines. When the Packers renovated Lambeau Field, Mark Murphy resisted a trend that has overtaken just about every other sports venue in the country. Before Bandon Dunes opened, Mike Keiser said, "Everybody I knew thought it was a crazy speculation, including me."

Second, culture matters. Kelleher imbued the Southwest organization with his egalitarian impulse and the executives who followed him have maintained that culture ever since. The Green Bay Packers embody the small-town spirit. Even before Itasca, businesses in the Twin Cities were active in the community and generous donors to charity, promoting a more locally minded model of capitalism.

A third lesson is not to let the perfect be the enemy of the good. NYU has been criticized for not attaching more strings to its financial aid policy, like only waiving tuition for doctors who agree to practice in underserved communities. But not everyone can commit to that before starting medical school, and it would have muted the impact of the program. There is premium seating plus clubs for elite fans at Lambeau Field, but it doesn't define the experience. Southwest does permit passengers to pay to go to the front of the line but that's a long way from having nine different groups waiting to get on the plane or five different sections in the cabin.

Fourth, it's possible to be inclusive and hugely successful. Bandon Dunes is on the verge of opening a fifth course, and draws top-notch golfers. The Packers have sold out every game they've played since 1960, and fans wait thirty years for a shot at a season ticket. Southwest has outearned its competitors for decades, and although it is half the size of American Airlines, it is worth twice as much in terms of market capitalization. "It's a fundamentally different approach," said Ryan Buell, a Harvard Business School professor. "Southwest is perennially ranked highest in customer satisfaction and it doesn't treat some customers worse so someone else can feel better."

In the winter of 2018, Ryan Buell went with his family to the Universal theme park in Orlando. At Harvard, Buell studies service industries, and he was shocked as he saw customers who paid to jump the line speed by everyone else. "It felt so obnoxious and unfair," he said. "The experience of the majority of customers is being undermined by the experience of elite customers. There is a better approach."

What would that look like? "You can treat everyone fairly and build differentiation on top of that," Buell said. "When you build inequity into your service model, it becomes a zero-sum game." A key factor, he said, is a willingness to say no to customers. Southwest could easily create a section with more legroom and charge more for it, but it would go against the culture of the company. Just as important, Buell said, it would complicate a very efficient boarding process that is key to getting planes off the ground quickly and back into the air.

A major obstacle to fairer—and better—treatment for consumers is conventional business wisdom on how to run service industries. Less contact between employees and customers, it was thought, equaled more efficiency. In the 1960s, management scholars even termed customers "environmental disturbances," and argued they should be separated from a company's core processes, according to Buell. "When customers can see the hidden worker behind the scenes, they perceive more effort went into the service they receive," Buell said. "When employees can see the people they are helping, the work is more meaningful and they are willing to exert more effort."

Finally, consumers can say no, too, and vote with their feet. Buell's hotel stay in Orlando came with front-of-the-line passes but he and his family decided to wait with everyone else. Sticking with a hardworking family physician, rather than seeing a concierge doctor, is more equitable and won't harm your health. You don't have to stay in the ship-within-a-ship on your next cruise. You might actually meet new people and broaden your horizons by traveling with everyone else. Patronize an independent grocery store instead of a chain dollar store, and add to, rather than subtract from, social capital. If you donate money to an educational institution, consider setting aside a portion for a school that doesn't have a multibillion-dollar endowment, like New York's City College or Chicago State. Support local tax increases when the beneficiary is the public school system, the community hospital, the fire department, or public transit.

Government can help, too, in a myriad of ways. One tax cut after another benefiting the rich over the last forty years has exacerbated rising inequality, as have regulatory policies that favor the interests of the biggest companies over those of consumers. Tax cuts aimed at the middle class would boost their spending power, and, in turn, draw more businesses back to serving them. The middle class could certainly use the help—at $97,000, the median net worth of American families in 2016 was $40,000 lower than where it had been before the recession in 2007. To find the money, Washington could raise taxes on capital gains to the level of ordinary income, leveling the playing field for the 50 percent of Americans who don't own stocks at all. Closing tax loopholes that benefit private equity firms and hedge funds would reduce the degree to which they concentrate wealth.

Expanding Medicaid to all fifty states and lifting Medicare reimbursement rates would benefit rural hospitals and big-city public health care facilities alike. It would also help beleaguered family doctors earn more, diminishing the appeal of concierge medicine. Forty percent of Americans make less than $15 an hour. More aid to community colleges and public university systems, as well as broader apprenticeship opportunities, would allow workers stuck in these low-paying jobs to earn much more. So would raising the federal minimum wage, which is currently set at $7.25. Tighter regulation of the airlines by Washington would protect passengers from the most abusive practices when they fly. New investments in airports and roads would reduce congestion and delays, lessening the need for alternatives like the Private Suite or Blade. Pooling a portion of the funds raised by PTAs, like Portland does, would reduce disparities between public schools.

Business leaders also need to recognize that they've taken the Velvet Rope model too far. If these incremental steps aren't taken, the end result will be more radical action. In the face of growing economic inequality, prominent Democrats have called for massive tax increases on the rich, including a tax on wealth, not just income. Decades of wage stagnation, especially for less educated workers, have empowered populists' appeals to anger and resentment on the right. Capitalism exists with the consent of democracy, and the more the vast majority find themselves not just outside the Velvet Rope but treated with disdain, the system itself is threatened.

It's up to all of us—including those well ensconced inside the Velvet Rope—to create a less segmented society, where Americans from different walks of life actually meet one another and find common ground. If they do, maybe there will be more talking, and less shouting, in public life. It won't be easy. There are huge profits to be made in the Velvet Rope Economy, and the temptation there is always to raise the cordons even higher. That's the way things are going. But it doesn't have to be that way. There's room enough for all of us inside the Velvet Rope.

Acknowledgments
....

They say that success has a thousand fathers (and mothers), and when it comes to an undertaking as massive as writing a book, I can say it's absolutely true. This project grew out of my initial reporting on inequality as an economics correspondent for *The New York Times*. My editor, Tom Redburn, and I realized that inequality wasn't simply a matter of some Americans having more money than others, or wealth being concentrated to a greater degree than in the past. Side by side, Americans of different classes were being treated differently, even as they participated in the same experiences. In other cases, the rich scarcely knew what obstacles ordinary Americans faced every day. They could buy their way out.

From two initial Velvet Rope stories—one on concierge medicine, the other on cruise ships and the leisure industry—Tom and I saw that this phenomenon was transforming the economy. The Velvet Rope Economy was something everyone could relate to but no one had articulated. I want to thank Tom for helping me come up with the initial vision for what would become this book. Later, after retiring from the *Times,* Tom was a steady source of help, advice, and feedback as the book took shape.

Kris Puopolo, my editor at Doubleday, is another person who provided critical guidance along the way and helped turn this from a proposal into reality. She provided just the right balance of encouragement and pressure to keep the project on track. Her enthusiasm was the perfect antidote for when my energy flagged.

Even before Kris entered the picture, my agent, Andrew Wylie, gave me the confidence to believe this could work. Andrew was patient as my proposal went through inevitable delays, and was always there to help and advise. I want to thank him for believing in me when others didn't.

I owe a huge debt of gratitude to my editors at *The New York Times,* beginning with Dean Baquet, Carolyn Ryan, and Rebecca Blumenstein. But the person at the *Times* who made this book possible was Ellen Pollock, the business editor, who was more than generous about giving me the time I needed to finish this project. Kevin McKenna, Vikas Bajaj, and Dean Murphy were similarly patient and enthusiastic along the way—thank you! I also appreciate the support I received from friends at the *Times* like Patricia Cohen, Conor Dougherty, Nathaniel Popper, and John Schwartz.

Mark Duggan and Adam Gorlick from the Stanford Institute for Economic Policy Research (SIEPR) were great hosts when I spent two weeks there as a fellow, writing the introduction and tapping into the wisdom of some of the top thinkers at the university.

Friends were a great help, too. Jared Mintz was always there with good ideas, as was Mike Laskawy. Elizabeth Brooks and Paul Nagle provided a home away from home during my frequent visits to the ground zero of the Velvet Rope Economy, San Francisco. Liz and Paul were great sounding boards and sources of feedback as they read chapters. Paul provided the germ of the idea that grew into the section on club teams in the Exclusion chapter.

She is not here to have seen this come to fruition, but I want to thank Rachel Mintz, of blessed memory, for her crucial help. She first suggested I look at professional sports and stadiums, beginning with Yankee Stadium. It was an angle I hadn't thought of, and it would power one of my favorite chapters in the book, Exclusivity.

I want to thank the figures in the book who took the time to give me an insider's view into how the Velvet Rope functions in their organizations, and were forthright in discussing its nuances and implications. These include Dr. Jordan Shlain and Dr. Ethan Weiss in medicine, Gerry Cardinale and Chad Estis in the world of sports, Gavin de Becker at the Private Suite, Kat Cohen and Merrily Bodell of IvyWise, Dan Berkowitz at CID Entertainment, Caryn Seidman-Becker of Clear, Scott Hudgins of Disney, Rob Wiesenthal at Blade, Mark Murphy of the Green Bay Packers, Rudd Davis at BlackBird, and Sandy Beall at Blackberry Farm.

Others opened doors and lent their expertise as I was reporting on a host of different sectors. I'm lucky to have had the help of Rob Zeiger, Kevin Sheehan, Max Muhleman, Al Guido, Dick Kinzel, Bruce Laval, Leonard Sim, Steve Brown, Steve Maksin, Duncan Dickson, John Bergstrom, Jody Hoffer Gittell, Adam Borgos, Robert Poole, Dick Fredericks, and David Hablewitz.

For the second section of the book, I had some critical help in understanding the places where privilege doesn't hold sway. Some of these people showed me how institutions suffer as a result of inequality; others told me in deeply personal terms of how it affected their own lives or those of their children. I was fortunate to get the perspectives of Michael Klein, Amy Glenn, Kevin Reed, Mike Sagas, Kajsa Reaves, Tony Liss, Nicole Brooks, Kathy White, Eric Zell, Dr. Desmond Carson, Dr. Dale Lockhert, Dr. Steve Pu, John Helmert, Christina Kovats, Tim Thramer, Diana Hahn, and Kim and Paul McDowell. And my in-laws Sandy Carol Drescher and Dr. Edward Drescher were there to help and cheer me on, as was my brother-in-law, Clayton Carol.

Dr. Ira Dosovitz provided critical advice and support that helped me get through the Sisyphus-like writing process and deliver the completed manuscript. Along the way, my mother, Eleanor K. Schwartz, was always there with a copy editor's pen to help improve my prose.

But the biggest thank-you of all goes to my wife, Annalise Carol. Without complaint, she put up with countless nights when I worked late or on Sundays when I was writing. My younger daughter, Lily, was born a month after I signed the contract for the book, and she really didn't get to know me for a while but I hope to make it up to her. Like her mom, my older daughter, Willow, was a trooper throughout. Annalise was the one who shouldered the load of getting them to bed, and afterward helped me get through the moments of self-doubt that plague every author. Annalise, I will be forever grateful to you for your love, support, and confidence that I could do this.

Notes

·········

INTRODUCTION

3   "With growing inequality": Interview with Michael J. Sandel.

3   Sandel examined these: Michael J. Sandel, *What Money Can't Buy: The Moral Limits of Markets* (New York: Farrar, Straus & Giroux, 2012).

4   "This is my life": Interview with Nick Hanauer.

5   "Be pampered throughout your cruise": ncl.com.

6   And Discovery Cove: Michael J. de la Merced, "Sea World Stake, Long Held by Blackstone, Is Sold to Chinese Firm," DealBook, *New York Times,* March 24, 2017, nytimes.com.

6   Just over 17 percent: "Income and Poverty in the United States: 2017," U.S. Census Bureau, Report Number P60-263, census.gov.

6   The evidence of this trend: Raj Chetty, Michael Stepner, and Sarah Abraham, "The Association Between Income and Life Expectancy in the United States, 2001–2014," *JAMA: The Journal of the American Medical Association* 315 (April 26, 2016): 1750–66.

7   "The companies, having proved": Robert B. Ekelund Jr. and Robert F. Hebert, *The Secret Origins of Modern Microeconomics: Dupuit and the Engineers* (Chicago: University of Chicago Press, 1999), 217.

8   Expanding upon Dupuit's ideas: Interview with Robert B. Ekelund Jr.

8   Although it never really disappeared: Kelcie Willis, "McDonald's McRib to Return for 35th Anniversary," *Atlanta Journal-Constitution,* November 2, 2017.

10   Since the early 1970s: Three leading experts on inequality, Thomas Piketty, Emmanuel Saez, and Gabriel Zucman, estimate that pretax average income among the top one tenth of one percent grew by 4.3 percent annually between 1980 and 2014, lifting it from $1.4 million to just over $6 million. Among the top 10 percent, pretax income rose annually by 2.4 percent. By

contrast, among the other 90 percent of Americans, pretax income increased by less than one percent a year over the same period. A recent survey by the Federal Reserve found that 51 percent of Americans would be unable to come up with $2,000 in the event of an emergency.

And when it comes to total wealth, the widening of inequality is even more striking. Saez, an economics professor at Berkeley and a leading expert on inequality, estimates that the top one percent of American households now control 42 percent of the nation's wealth. That's up from less than 30 percent two decades ago. The top 0.1 percent accounts for 22 percent, nearly twice the proportion in 1995.

For the reference to income see: Thomas Piketty, Emmanuel Saez, and Gabriel Zucman, "Distributional National Accounts: Methods and Estimates for the United States," *Quarterly Journal of Economics* 133, no. 2 (2018): 553–609.

For the reference to wealth see: Emmanuel Saez and Gabriel Zucman, "Wealth Inequality in the United States Since 1913: Evidence from Capitalized Income Tax Data," *Quarterly Journal of Economics* 131, no. 2 (2016): 519–78.

10 By definition the one percent: Interview with Geoff Yang.

10 A study in 2017: Chuck Collins and Josh Hoxie, "Billionaire Bonanza, the Forbes 400 and the Rest of Us," Institute for Policy Studies, November 2017.

11 Goldman Sachs initially owned: Ben Klayman, "Yankees, Cowboys and Goldman form Sports Services Co.," Reuters, October 20, 2008.

11 Goldman sold its investment: Interview with Gerry Cardinale.

11 "Our team was sitting around": Interview with Yang.

12 "This is where companies": Interview with Steven Fazzari.

12 Among the most powerful: Interview with Emmanuel Saez.

12 There's a dichotomy: Interview with Yang.

13 A January 2018 Gallup poll: Gallup News Service, "Gallup Poll Social Series: Mood of the Nation," January 2–7, 2018.

14 Meanwhile, according to a survey: Pew Research Center, "The Partisan Divide on Political Values Grows Even Wider," October 5, 2017.

14 To make it into: Piketty, Saez, and Zucman, "Distributional National Accounts: Methods and Estimates for the United States," 553–609.

CHAPTER 1: ENVY

22 "Airlines paved the way": Interview with Michael Bayley.

22 As coach passengers pile into: Interview with Alex Dichter.

22 As if soft leather: "Emirates Unveils Brand New Cabins for Its Boeing 777 Fleet," Media Centre, Emirates.com.

23 The need to openly display: Interview with Russell Belk.

24 This isn't theoretical: Katherine A. DeCelles and Michael I. Norton, "Physical and Situational Inequality on Airplanes Predicts Air Rage," *Proceedings*

of the National Academy of Sciences of the United States of America 113, no. 20 (May 2, 2016): 5588–91.

24   Even a little air rage: Daniel Victor and Matt Stevens, "United Airlines Passenger Is Dragged from an Overbooked Flight," *New York Times,* April 10, 2017.

25   Dr. Dao eventually received: Lauren Zumbach, "A Year After a Passenger Was Dragged Off a United Flight, Everyday Indignities Remain," *Chicago Tribune,* April 9, 2018.

25   "I was working with": Interview with Niels van de Ven.

26   "Benign envy seems to": N. van de Ven, M. Zeelenberg, and R. Pieters, "Leveling Up and Down: The Experiences of Benign and Malicious Envy," *Emotion* 9, no. 3 (2009): 419–29.

26   Russell Belk, the business professor: Interview with Belk.

27   "It's about transparency": Interview with David Clarke.

27   That's obvious from: Press Release, "Royal Caribbean Reports Record 2018 Results and Provides Forward Guidance," Royal Caribbean, January 30, 2019.

28   Delivering that kind of: Royal Caribbean, 2018 Proxy Statement, p. 45.

28   As a result: anesi.com.

29   Richard Fain, Royal Caribbean's chairman: Interview with Richard Fain.

29   "For a long time": Interview with Adam Goldstein.

32   "It was prime": Interview with Bob Schillo.

32   As far as Royal Caribbean: Interview with Goldstein.

33   Microsoft's former chief executive: Paula Rooney, "Microsoft's CEO: 80-20 Rule Applies to Bugs, Not Just Features," *CRN,* October 3, 2002.

33   Studies have shown: Marvin E. Wolfang, Robert M. Figlio, and Paul E. Tracy, "The 1945 and 1958 Birth Cohorts: A Comparison of the Prevalence, Incidence and Severity of Delinquent Behavior," Center for Studies in Criminology and Criminal Law, University of Pennsylvania, 1982, p. 16.

33   In the health care system: Ian K. Kullgren, "Does 20% of the Population Really Use 80% of Health Care Dollars?," *Politifact,* at the Poynter Institute, February 23, 2012, politifact.com.

35   "When an industry": Interview with Steve Tadelis.

35   "At the low end": Interview with Clarke.

35   That's the story behind: Interview with Arnaud De Bruyn.

36   In academia, equity theory: J.S. Adams, "Toward an Understanding of Inequity," *Journal of Abnormal and Social Psychology* 67 (1963): 422–36.

37   "Most customers prefer imposing": R. Butori and A. De Bruyn, "So You Want to Delight Your Customers: The Perils of Ignoring Heterogeneity in Customer Evaluations of Discretionary Preferential Treatments," *International Journal of Research in Marketing* 30 (2013): 358–67.

38   On its travel blog: Jennifer Wu, "Why You Should Consider Cruising in The Haven," "Chasing the Sun," Norwegian's Official Travel Blog, August 11, 2016, ncl.com.

38   The danger of malicious envy: Interview with Bayley.

38   "We are giving suite guests": Interview with Lisa Lutoff-Perlo.

38   Just listen to: Interview with Kevin Sheehan.

40   With the launch: Interview with Andy Stuart.

40   "We are living": Interview with Thomas Sander.

41   But the genius: Tim Winship, "Airline Frequent Flyer Miles, 30 Years Later," ABC News, May 25, 2011.

41   "In the early 1980s": Interview with Aarti Ivanic.

42   "At the high end": Interview with Bjorn Hanson.

42   United Airlines, for example: Scott McCartney, "What the Airline Knows About the Guy in 14C," *Wall Street Journal,* June 20, 2018.

42   "There's been a confluence": Interview with Robert Palmatier.

45   On the other hand: Interview with Gary Loveman.

45   "If you're a student": youtube.com.

45   "Companies prey upon": Interview with Joseph Nunes.

46   "Status matters because": Xavier Drèze and Joseph C. Nunes, "Feeling Superior: The Impact of Loyalty Program Structure on Consumers' Perception of Status," *Journal of Consumer Research* 35, no. 6 (2008): 890–905.

50   "When that Porsche": Interview with Gary Leff.

51   "Rule clarity diminishes": Lena Steinhoff and Robert W. Palmatier, "Understanding Loyalty Program Effectiveness: Managing Target and Bystander Effects," *Journal of the Academy of Marketing Science* 44 (2016): 88–107.

52   While studies like: Interview with Palmatier.

52   "I teach in an environment": Interview with Russell Lacey.

CHAPTER 2: EXCLUSIVITY

58   The basic fighting group: Maria Konnikova, "The Limits of Friendship," *The New Yorker,* October 7, 2014.

59   Since Dunbar's research: W.-X. Zhou, D. Sornette, R.A. Hill, and R.I.M. Dunbar, "Discrete Hierarchical Organization of Social Group Sizes," *Proceedings of the Royal Society B: Biological Sciences* 272 (February 17, 2005): 439–44.

59   In a 2016 paper: P. Mac Carron, K. Kaski, and R. Dunbar, "Calling Dunbar's Numbers," *Social Networks* 47 (October 2016): 151–55.

61   "The bread and circuses": Robert C. Trumpbour and Kenneth Womack, *The Eighth Wonder of the World: The Life of Houston's Iconic Astrodome* (Lincoln: University of Nebraska Press, 2016).

61   "Hofheinz boasted that": Interview with Benjamin D. Lisle.

62   It was September 1985: Interview with Jim Nagourney.

63   They also explain: Dennis R. Howard and John L. Crompton, *Financing Sport* (Morgantown, WV: FiT Publishing, 2018).

65   The most extreme: Interview with Victor Matheson.

66   Muhleman came up with: Interview with Max Muhleman.

67   "We didn't have time": Interview with Tamera Green.

67   As Aaron Gordon noted: Aaron Gordon, "The Creator of Personal Seat Licenses Hates Them as Much As You Do," *Vice,* December 28, 2015.

67   "We knew we had": Interview with Muhleman.

68   Between 1990 and 1994: Howard and Crompton, *Financing Sport*: 138–43.

69   "I was uneasy": Interview with Chad Estis.

69   The arena's eventual price tag: Howard and Crompton, *Financing Sport*: 140.

70   "We segmented from premium": Interview with Mike Rawlings.

72   That represents a high-water: Howard and Crompton, *Financing Sport*: 423.

72   "I said to Jerry": Interview with Gerry Cardinale.

74   "The Cowboys rewrote": Interview with Al Guido.

74   But according to Roger Noll: Interview with Roger Noll.

76   At the old Candlestick Park: Interview with Andy Dolich.

77   "Presto!" *Forbes* wrote: Mike Ozanian, "The Most Valuable Teams in the NFL," *Forbes,* September 14, 2015.

77   "If someone offered me": Interview with Jonathan Coslet.

78   For Cardinale, holding that trophy: Interview with Cardinale.

79   "Businesses create subsets": Interview with Noll.

82   "In many respects": Interview with John Collins.

82   If those invite-only tents: Interview with Dan Berkowitz.

84   "I was obsessed": Interview with Keith Petrower.

84   In his memoir: "Mo Rivera: Old Yankee Stadium Had Far Better Atmosphere Than New One Does," CBSNewYork/AP, May 7, 2014.

85   "There are a lot": Interview with Fred Harman.

85   "When you yell": Interview with David Smith.

CHAPTER 3: EASE

87   "I didn't want people": Interview with Dick Kinzel.

89   "The premium customer": Interview with David Clarke.

89   "If you look": Interview with Todd James Pierce.

90   "Disney has perfected": Interview with Robert Niles.

91   Lines had bedeviled Disneyland: "Disneyland Gates Open: Play Park on Coast Jammed—15,000 on Line Before 10 a.m.," *New York Times,* July 19, 1955.

92   "You have to manage": Interview with Steve Brown.

93   Laval made a name: Interview with Bruce Laval.

95   "It favors the people": Interview with Martin Lewison.

96   In 2017, Disneyland welcomed: 2017 Theme Index and Museum Index: The Global Attractions Attendance Report, Themed Entertainment Association.

99   whose price has risen: Interview with Lewison.

99   Keeping FastPass free: Interview with Scott Hudgins.

100   There's even a helpful chart: universalorlando.com.

100   "It's not a childlike": Interview with Niles.

101   Universal's corporate culture: Interview with Duncan Dickson.

101   "Quite a few people": Interview with Leonard Sim.

102   For clients like Universal: Interview with Brown.

104   "When situations like these": Duncan Dickson, Robert C. Ford, and Bruce Laval, "Managing Real and Virtual Waits in Hospitality and Service Organizations," *Cornell Hospitality Quarterly* 46 (February 1, 2005): 52–68.

105   "They don't want": Interview with Adam Borgos.

106   Exploiting the disabled: Jeff Rossen and Josh Davis, "Undercover at Disney: 'Deplorable' Scheme to Skip Lines," *Today,* NBC, May 31, 2013, today.com.

106   In a 2012 *Esquire* article: Tom Junod, "The Water-Park Scandal and Two Americas in the Raw: Are We a Nation of Line-Cutters, or Are We the Line," *Esquire,* September 5, 2012, esquire.com.

108   Although he lives: Interview with Kinzel.

109   "He looked at me blankly": Interview with Rudd Davis.

109   Khosla told me: Interview with Vinod Khosla.

109   "There's a danger": Interview with Eric Klinenberg.

110   While BlackBird uses fixed-wing: Interview with Rob Wiesenthal.

110   In March 2018: Dan Primack, "Blade Raises $38 Million to Build Flying Taxi Infrastructure," *Axios,* March 22, 2018, axios.com.

110   In early 2019: "On-Time Performance, Flight Delays at a Glance," Bureau of Transportation Statistics, U.S. Department of Transportation, transtats.bts .gov.

115   Blade's online blog: blade.flyblade.com.

115   Wiesenthal's chutzpah earned him: Ivanka Trump, *The Trump Card: Playing to Win in Work and Life* (New York: Touchstone, 2009).

116   At ninety-three of the top one hundred: David Koenig and Scott Mayerowitz, "Airlines Carve U.S. into Markets Dominated by 1 or 2 Carriers," Associated Press, July 14, 2015, apnews.com.

116   "People can walk in": Interview with Evan Licht.

117   "My family's been going": Interview with Harley Saftler.

117   "Blade is the only way": Interview with Janet Sousa.

117   "The roads are at capacity": Interview with Rob Benz.

118   When he heard about: Interview with Robert Poole.

120   She had first promoted: Interview with Heidi Stamm.

120   In fact, a 2014 study: Mark Burris, Negin Alemazkoor, Rob Benz, and Nicholas S. Wood, *Research in Transportation Economics* 44-C (2014): 43–51.

120   The reason for the decline: Interview with Mark Burris.

120   Other academic studies: "A Highway for All: Economic Use Patterns for Atlanta's Hot Lanes," Southern Environmental Law Center, 2013, southern environment.org.

121   "How does this help": Interview with David Hablewitz.

122   Putnam is the author: Robert D. Putnam, *Bowling Alone: The Collapse and Revival of American Community* (New York: Simon & Schuster, 2000).

CHAPTER 4: ACCESS

123   Dr. Weiss only devotes: Interview with Dr. Ethan Weiss.

123   Jordan Shlain is what most of us: Interview with Dr. Jordan Shlain.

125   On average, it takes: Merritt Hawkins, "Survey of Physician Appointment Wait Times," 2017.

125   The number of annual office: Stephen M. Petterson, Winston R. Liaw, Robert L. Phillips Jr., David Rabin, David S. Myers, and Andrew Bazemore, "Projecting U.S. Primary Care Physician Workforce Needs: 2010–2025," *Annals of Family Medicine* 10, no. 6 (November–December 2012): 503–9, annfammed.org.

125   From a single practice: Interview with Dr. Howard Maron.

126   Dr. Harlan Matles joined: Interview with Dr. Harlan Matles.

126   John Battelle, a healthy: Interview with John Battelle.

127   "You have no idea": Interview with Matles.

127   An internist who takes: Interview with Shlain.

129   Twenty years later: Interview with Charisse Fazzari.

133   "You don't get better care": Interview with Dr. Henry Jones III.

133   "This is something": Interview with Joe Leggio.

133   In its maternity ward: Interview with Barbara Osborn, Northwell Health.

135   He joined CNN: Interview with David Sager.

136   Called Private Health Management: Interview with Leslie Michelson.

142   At Bucknell, the crush: Melissa Korn, "Some Elite Colleges Review an Application in 8 Minutes (or Less)," *Wall Street Journal,* January 31, 2018, wsj .com.

142   Top public universities: Don Jordan, "More Than 65,000 Apply for Incoming Freshman Class," *University Record,* June 12, 2018, record.umich.edu.

142   In the mid-1990s: Office of Budget and Planning, The University of Michigan.

142   At Georgia Tech: Ibid.

142   In 2017, Dartmouth put: Clare Lombardo and Elissa Nadworny, "College Waitlists Often Waste Would-Be Students' Time," National Public Radio, April 5, 2018, npr.org.

143   In 2016, according to: Staff of the Cooperative Institutional Research Program, "The American Freshman: National Norms for Fall 2016," and "The American Freshman: National Norms for Fall 1996," Higher Education Research Center at UCLA, heri.ucla.edu.

143   Jared Kushner's father: Daniel Golden, "The Story Behind Jared Kushner's Curious Acceptance into Harvard," *ProPublica,* November 18, 2016, pro publica.org.

143   When emails from Sony: wikileaks.org.

143   In March 2019: Jennifer Medina, Katie Benner, and Kate Taylor, "Actresses, Business Leaders and Other Wealthy Parents Charged in U.S. College Entry Fraud," *New York Times,* March 12, 2019.

144 And that's late: IvyWise: Interview with Merrily Bodell.

145 "These are the people": Interview with Bodell.

147 "Let's say we have": Interview with Kat Cohen.

149 These days, many colleges: Harvard Financial Aid Initiative, Harvard University, college.harvard.edu.

149 They are scouring the country: "Affordable for All," Princeton University, princeton.edu.

149 They generally pay: "Number of International Students in the United States Reaches New High of 1.09 Million," Institute for International Education, November 13, 2018; Annual Report, Institute for International Education, 2000, p.widencdn.net.

151 For others, IvyWise suggests: sumac.stanford.edu.

152 Finally, he would submit: tcr.org.

152 "Schools are savvy": Interview with Meghan Riley.

154 Over the last few years: Raj Chetty, John N. Friedman, Nicholas Turner, and Danny Yagan, "Mobility Report Cards: The Role of Colleges in Intergenerational Mobility," NBER Working Paper No. 23618, Revised Version (July 2017), opportunityinsights.org.

154 At Yale: nytimes.com.

155 "What's being bought": Interview with Richard Reeves.

CHAPTER 5: SECURITY

157 Fires in northern California: Evan Sernoffsky, "Where the Blazes Began," *San Francisco Chronicle,* October 22, 2017, sfchronicle.com.

158 "On the way up": Interview with Dick Fredericks.

160 "God forbid we should": Interview with Mark Heine.

161 Her district includes: Christopher Weber, "Insurers Dispatch Private Firefighters in California," Associated Press, December 21, 2017.

162 "We have to have": Interview with Cecilia Aguiar-Curry.

162 "Municipal fire departments": Interview with Carroll Wills.

162 During the first twelve hours: Joaquin Palomino and Kimberley Veklerov, "Wine Country Requested Hundreds of Engines in Firestorm's First Hours. Less than Half Came," *San Francisco Chronicle,* November 17, 2017, sfchronicle.com.

162 However, after several years: Karen Brainard, "State Suspends Fire Fee in Cap-and-Trade Deal," *San Diego Union-Tribune,* July 31, 2017, sandiegouniontribune.com.

163 "When you have something": Interview with Steve Leveroni.

163 Some are ordinary homes: Interview with David Torgerson.

164 "You can't protect": Interview with Amy Bach.

165 And as each wildfire season: Leslie Scism, "As Wildfires Raged, Insurers Sent in Private Firefighters to Protect Homes of the Wealthy," *Wall Street Journal,* November 5, 2017, wsj.com.

165   In a few cases: Jackson Landers, "In the Early 19th Century, Firefighters Fought Fires . . . and Each Other," Smithsonian.com, September 27, 2016, smithsonianmag.com.

165   "We do offer": Interview with Fran O'Brien.

166   But PURE chief executive: Interview with Ross Buchmueller.

168   In a 2017 Federal Reserve: "Report on the Economic Well-Being of U.S. Households," Federal Reserve, May 22, 2018, federalreserve.gov.

168   "If you file a big": Interview with Bach.

168   "Never wait a second": Interview with Gavin de Becker.

169   It told readers: Gavin de Becker, *The Gift of Fear: And Other Survival Signals That Protect Us from Violence* (New York: Dell, 1997).

171   Besides its own terminal: Heathrow "VIP: Frequently Asked Questions," heathrowvip.com.

173   "It used to be far easier": Interview with Jack Keady.

173   Nearly 87 million: LAWA Comprehensive Annual Financial Report-FY 2018, Los Angeles World Airports, p. ii, October 30, 2018, lawa.org.

173   A massive $14 billion: "LAX Modernization at a Glance," Los Angeles World Airports, lawa.org.

173   Transportation industry advocates: Martin Romjue, "Leading Industry CEOs Advocate for Airport Access," *LCT Magazine,* September 27, 2018.

173   "I've spoken to people": Interview with Michael DiGirolamo.

178   "A customer doesn't buy security": Interview with Caryn Seidman-Becker.

181   "We've revolutionized the bomb shelter": Interview with Gary Lynch.

181   "We're the REI": Interview with Roman Zrazhevskiy.

182   "They look at the numbers": Interview with Tom Gaffney.

183   These fears: Interview with Anna Bounds.

CHAPTER 6: EXCLUSION

187   These include the property: Nothingbuthouse.com, "25 Most Expensive Homes in Columbus, Ohio," nothingbuthouse.com.

187   The mayor of New Albany: Interview with Sloan Spalding.

188   Costs were rising: "New Albany School Levy Fails," *Columbus Dispatch,* October 28, 2014, dispatch.com.

189   "There was a sense of community": Interview with Michael Klein.

190   "There was a tremendous amount": Interview with Kevin Reed.

191   "It's disconcerting that parents": Interview with Kajsa Reaves.

192   "We've privatized school sports": Interview with Sarah Clark.

192   Almost 30 percent: "Pay-to-Participate: Impact on School Activities," *Mott Poll Report* 33, no. 5 (March 18, 2019), C.S. Mott Children's Hospital, mott poll.org.

192   "If schools are charging": Interview with Bruce Howard.

192   As a result: Interview with Howard Fleeter.

193   Years of inadequate support: Interview with Ryan Gallwitz.

194   "I had kids crying": Interview with Amy Glenn.

194   "We barely fielded": Interview with John Townsend.

195   All told, with registration: Interview with Susan Eustis.

195   "It's the gentrification": Interview with Jay Coakley.

196   Those days are fading: Interview with Mark Hyman.

196   The dream of an athletic scholarship: Interview with Tom Farrey.

196   Sports scholarship awards: Ibid.

197   But just 5.5 percent: "Estimated Probability of Competing in College Athletics," NCAA Research, ncaa.org.

197   "You're looking at $6,000": Interview with Stephanie Roell.

198   "It's not like I was duped": Interview with Mike Sagas.

199   "There was a lot of pushback": Interview with Tim Schulz.

200   Dev Pathik, who heads up: Interview with Dev Pathik.

201   The city of Westfield: Interview with T.J. Land.

201   Participation in team sports: *State of Play: 2018 Trends and Developments,* Sports & Society Program, Aspen Institute, aspeninstitute.org.

201   Tom Farrey, who oversaw the study: Interview with Farrey.

202   About 85 percent: Enrollment Data for P.S. 191, the Riverside School for Makers and Artists, Student Information Repository System, New York State Department of Education, 2017–18, data.nysed.gov.

202   By contrast, nearly two thirds: Ibid., P.S. 87, William T. Sherman School.

202   But unlike New Albany: New York State School Funding Transparency Forms, InfoHub, NYC Department of Education, infohub.nyced.org.

202   What makes the difference: IRS Form 990, 2016–2018, Candid, formerly GuideStar and Foundation Center.

202   In the best year at P.S. 191: Interview with Kajsa Reaves.

202   Indeed, across town: Kyle Spencer, "Way Beyond Bake Sales: The $1 Million PTA," *New York Times,* June 1, 2012, nytimes.com.

203   "In short, wealthy parents": Catherine Brown, Scott Sargrad, and Meg Benner, *Hidden Money: The Outsized Role of Parent Contributions in School Finance,* Center for American Progress, April 8, 2017.

203   "We expected there would": Interview with Scott Sargrad.

203   Donating—heavily—to the PTA: Interview with Ashlyn Aiko Nelson.

203   It's a mind-set: Ashlyn Aiko Nelson and Beth Gazley, "The Rise of School-Supporting Nonprofits," *Education and Finance Policy* 9, no. 4 (October 2014): 541–66.

204   Parents in wealthy towns: Brown, Sargrad, and Benner, *Hidden Money: The Outsized Role of Parent Contributions in School Finance.*

204   Many parents in disadvantaged schools: Interview with Dennis Morgan.

205   In third grade: Riverside School for Makers and Artists—New York State Report Card [2017–2018], New York State Education Department, data.nysed.gov.

205   Meanwhile, at P.S. 87: P.S. 87, William T. Sherman—New York State Report Card [2017–2018], New York State Education Department, data.nysed.gov.

206   "If parents can afford": Interview with Kristy Sanchez.

206   The principal of P.S. 191: Interview with Lauren Keville.

207   "there are some schools": Quoted in Ben Chapman, "Law Would Make City Reveal PTA Fundraising Information," *New York Daily News,* September 25, 2018, nydailynews.com.

207   Once local school: Interview with Dan Ryan, All Hands Raised.

207   "I have no problem": Interview with Morgan.

208   It was part of: Anemona Hartcollis, "Bloomberg Gives $1.8 Billion to Johns Hopkins for Student Aid," *New York Times,* November 18, 2018.

209   At Johns Hopkins: Ibid.

209   City College has more than twice: Fall 2017 census data, CUNY Central Office.

209   "Hopkins is already": Interview with Tony Liss.

209   Ranked by their ability: "CUNY Again Dominates Chronicle's Public College Social Mobility Rankings," Press Release, City University of New York, August 20, 2018, 1.cuny.edu.

209   "It's the engine of mobility": Interview with Stephen Brier.

209   It's also massive: David W. Chen, "Dreams Stall as CUNY, New York City's Engine of Mobility, Sputters," *New York Times,* May 28, 2016, nytimes.com.

209   For more than 125 years: Interview with Brier.

210   More than half: Ibid.

211   Designed by architect Renzo Piano: "Columbia University Dedicates Its 17-Acre Manhattanville Campus, Establishing Its Academic and Civic Aspirations for a Century to Come," Press Release, Columbia University, October 24, 2016, manhattanville.columbia.edu.

211   And with a deep pool: Columbia—Financial Aid & Educational Financing: Facts and Figures, cc-seas.financialaid.columbia.edu.

211   City College's endowment: Interview with Liss.

212   "Inequality is being exacerbated": Interview with Clifton Conrad.

212   Endowments are growing fastest: Interview with Caroline M. Hoxby.

212   At the University of Michigan: Cost of Attendance, Office of Financial Aid, University of Michigan, finaid.umich.edu.

212   In forty-five states: Michael Mitchell, Michael Leachman, Kathleen Masterson, and Samantha Waxman, "Unkept Promises: State Cuts to Higher Education Threaten Access and Equity," Center on Budget and Policy Priorities, cbpp.org.

213   "Some days I didn't": Interview with Nicole Brooks.

213   More than two thirds: 2017–2018 Fact Book, Chicago State University, csu.edu.

213   Like much of: Julie Bosman, "Chicago State, a Lifeline for Poor Blacks, Is Under Threat Itself," *New York Times,* April 9, 2016, nytimes.com.

214   At one point: Rick Seltzer, "'Nail in the Coffin' for Chicago State?," *Inside Higher Ed,* October 5, 2016.

214   "There was a sense": Interview with Philip Beverly.

214   From more than 7,000: Chicago State University—University Profile, csu.edu.

214   "It's very bleak": Interview with Ann Kuzdale.

214   By June 2019: Campaign progress, University of Chicago Campaign, Inquiry & Impact, campaign.uchicago.edu.

215   "It's all of a piece": Interview with Brier.

215   In the 1980s: Claire Cain Miller, "The Relentlessness of Modern Parenting," *New York Times,* December 25, 2018, nytimes.com.

215   "There is no society": Interview with Coakley.

CHAPTER 7: DIVISION

216   At its groundbreaking: Louise Chu and Juliana Bunim, "UCSF Breaks Ground on State-of-the-Art Mission Bay Medical Center," University of California, San Francisco, ucsf.edu.

216   Five years later: "UCSF Medical Center at Mission Bay Opens, Welcomes 131 Patients," University of California, San Francisco, ucsf.edu.

216   It's a working-class city: QuickFacts, San Pablo, U.S. Census Bureau, census .gov.

216   Next door: QuickFacts, Richmond, U.S. Census Bureau, census.gov.

217   Only 10 percent: Interview with Kathy White.

218   Henry J. Kaiser: about.kaiserpermanente.org.

218   "This was a perfect storm": Interview with John Gioia.

218   Even as cutting-edge: Interview with Michelle Ko.

219   The life expectancy: Jason Corburn, Shasa Curl, and Gabino Arredondo, "A Health-in-All-Policies Approach Addresses Many of Richmond, California's Place-Based Hazards, Stressors," *Health Affairs* 33 (November 2014), healthaffairs.org.

220   With the opening: History of Richmond, ci.richmond.ca.us.

220   "Community leaders decided": Interview with Eric Zell.

222   "Kaiser and its hospital": Interview with Sharon Drager.

222   One of them: Victoria Colliver, "Zuckerberg, Wife Give $75 Million to S.F. Hospital," *San Francisco Chronicle,* February 6, 2015, sfgate.com.

222   Marc Benioff, the founder: Jill Tucker, "Benioffs Donate Another $100 Million to Children's Hospitals," *San Francisco Chronicle,* April 8, 2014, sfgate .com.

223   "The companies that lease": Interview with Mark Howe.

223   Howe's campaign worked: Victoria Colliver, "A Year After Hospital Closed, 250,000 in Contra Costa Struggle for Care," *San Francisco Chronicle,* April 20, 2016, sfchronicle.com.

224   "It's like they pulled": Interview with Desmond Carson.

225   Before DMC closed: "Average Transport Time, Pre- and Post-DMC Closure," Contra Costa Emergency Medical Services.

226   The pattern for patients: Interview with Renee Hsia.

227   "I thought I was dreaming": Interview with Ali Essa.

227   "Our waiting time": Interview with Maria del Rosario Sahagun.

227   Roughly four hundred babies: Jack Healy, "It's 4 a.m. The Baby's Coming. But the Hospital Is 100 Miles Away," *New York Times,* July 17, 2018.

227   As a result: Interview with Dr. Steve Pu.

228   "It's another universe": Interview with Dr. Mike Sarap.

228   Since 2010: Interview with George Pink.

228   "Being able to jump": Interview with Katy B. Kozhimannil.

229   By 2014: P. Hung, C. Henning-Smith, M. Casey, K. Kozhimannil, "Access to Obstetric Services in Rural Counties Still Declining, with 9 Percent Losing Services, 2004–14," *Health Affairs* 9 (September 2017): 1663–71.

229   In remote rural counties: K. Kozhimannil, P. Hung, C. Henning-Smith, M. Casey, and S. Prasad, "Association Between Loss of Hospital-Based Obstetric Services and Birth Outcomes in Rural Counties in the United States," *JAMA: The Journal of the American Medical Association* 319, no. 12 (March 27, 2018): 1239–47.

229   Nearly half of all babies: Anne Rossier Markus, Ellie Andres, Kristina D. West, Nicole Garro, and Cynthia Pellegrini, "Medicaid Covered Births, 2008 Through 2010, in the Context of the Implementation of Health Reform," *Women's Health Issues* 23 (September–October 2013): 273–80.

230   "We have a strong": Interview with Jim Grebing.

230   Dunklin County's population declined: QuickFacts, Dunklin County, U.S. Census Bureau, census.gov.

230   All these factors: County Health Rankings & Roadmaps, Missouri, Robert Wood Johnson Foundation, countyhealthrankings.org.

231   Over the years: Interview with Dr. Pu.

231   "It's mind-boggling": Interview with Joshua Nemzoff.

232   After an IPO: Milt Freudenheim, "Forstmann to Acquire Community Health for $1.1 Billion," *New York Times,* June 11, 1996.

232   In 2013, Community agreed: Michael J. de la Merced, "Community Health Agrees to Buy H.M.A. for $3.6 Billion," *New York Times,* July 30, 2013.

233   "Everything that could possibly": Interview with Frank Morgan.

233   Capital expenditures at the company: 2018 Form 10-K, Community Health Systems Inc., chsnet.gcs-web.com.

233   "was primarily based": Statement to author from Tomi Galin, senior vice president, corporate communications and marketing, Community Health Systems.

233   Between 2015 and 2017: 2016–2018 Proxy Statements, Community Health Systems Inc.

234   "They've devastated communities": Interview with Steven Braverman.

234   "I like small-town living": Interview with Dale Lockhert.

235   As recently as 2010: Interview with Dr. Pu.

238   "I don't think": Interview with Dr. Todd Rumsey.

239   Take the letter sent: Interview with Sarah Geraghty, Southern Center for Human Rights.

240   The goal was to avoid: Interview with Joseph Zlatic.

241   In Maricopa County: Shaila Dewan, "Caught with Pot? Get-Out-of-Jail Program Comes with $950 Catch," *New York Times,* August 24, 2018, nytimes .com.

241   *The Arizona Republic* reported: Megan Cassidy, "If Prop. 205 Passes, Maricopa County Attorney's Office Funds from Marijuana Diversion Program Would Dry Up," *Arizona Republic,* October 26, 2016, azcentral.com.

241   In Kansas, people charged: Interview with Patrick Lewis.

241   "I don't need": Interview with John Helmert.

242   In Mississippi's 16th Circuit: Pre-Trial Diversion brochure, District Attorney's Office, 16th Circuit Court of Mississippi, docs.wixstatic.com.

243   For example: QuickFacts, Noxubee County, Mississippi, U.S. Census Bureau, census.gov.

243   What's sad: Interview with Spurgeon Kennedy.

243   In Hernando, Mississippi: Interview with John Champion.

244   When the ability to pay: Interview with Sim Gill.

244   At the Santa Ana Jail: Jennifer Steinhauer, "For $82 a Day, Booking a Cell in a 5-Star Jail," *New York Times,* April 29, 2017, nytimes.com.

245   "The tone is respectful": Interview with Christina Holland.

245   "The county jails": Interview with Robert Schwartz.

245   *Los Angeles Times*/Marshall Project: Alysia Santo, Victoria Kim, and Anna Flagg, "Upgrade Your Jail Cell—for a Price," *Los Angeles Times,* March 9, 2017, latimes.com.

246   "The Pay-to-Stay Program": hermosabch.org.

247   "It was an astronomical amount": Interview with Christina Kovats.

248   "The population": Interview with Alexandra Natapoff.

248   "Every day we learn": Interview with Lisa Foster.

249   "Ferguson's law enforcement": Investigation of the Ferguson Police Department, Civil Rights Division, U.S. Department of Justice, March 4, 2015, justice.gov.

249   She coauthored: finesandfeesjusticecenter.org.

250   "The more people have tried": Interview with Ernie Lewis.

250   "It's not by accident": Interview with Jason Corburn.

CHAPTER 8: ISOLATION

252   More economically homogenous: "America's Shrinking Middle Class: A Close Look at Changes Within Metropolitan Areas," Pew Research Center, May 11, 2016, pewsocialtrends.org.

252   "It mirrors demographics": Interview with Glenn Brill.

252   Robert Putnam, the Harvard professor: Robert Putnam, *Bowling Alone: The Collapse and Revival of American Community* (New York: Simon & Schuster, 2000).

253   And as local institutions: Interview with Charles Tolbert II.

253   On the other hand: 2017 FDIC National Survey of Unbanked and Under-
       banked Households, Federal Deposit Insurance Corporation, fdic.gov; Art
       Swift, "Americans Rely Less on Credit Cards Than in Previous Years," Gal-
       lup News, April 25, 2014, news.gallup.com.

253   Concerned about the effect: Scott Calvert, "Philadelphia Is First U.S. City to
       Ban Cashless Stores," *Wall Street Journal,* March 7, 2019, wsj.com.

253   "Things that make life": Interview with Benjamin Keys.

254   In suburbia: Interview with Ellen Dunham-Jones.

254   When Burlington Center Mall: Sam Wood, "Burlington Center Mall in
       South Jersey Closes Down; A Resurgence Seems Elusive," *Philadelphia In-
       quirer,* January 12, 2018, philly.com.

254   "It was brand-new": Interview with Deirdre Ryan.

255   "There's a perception": Interview with Brian Carlin.

255   After water pipes burst: Danielle DeSisto, "Burlington Center Mall Closed
       After Water Pipes Burst; Sears Still Open," *Burlington County Times,* Janu-
       ary 9, 2018.

256   Beloved by residents: Lisa Broadt, "Petal the Elephant Headed to New
       Home in Burlington City," *Burlington County Times,* February 1, 2019.

256   The surrounding area: Interview with Rose Mary Burden.

256   "I definitely would rather": Interview with Kim Parker.

256   The phenomenon that played: Interview with DJ Busch.

257   Of the one thousand: Green Street Advisors, U.S. Mall Outlook, February 1,
       2019.

257   The place has steadily: youtube.com.

257   "The city has been dealing": Interview with Richard Griffin.

257   By the time a local doctor: Mallory Panuska, "Frederick Towne Mall Site
       Sells for More Than $6 Million," *Frederick News-Post,* February 24, 2017.

258   "You can't force": Interview with Christopher Zahas.

259   For all the purported: Quarterly Retail E-Commerce Sales, News Release,
       U.S. Census Bureau, March 31, 2019, census.gov.

259   "Where there is high income": Interview with Chaim Katzman.

260   That's a dangerous: Interview with Mark Cohen.

261   "If you want": Interview with Garrick Brown.

261   "I started going": Interview with Allene Feldman.

262   "We used to try": Interview with Penny Fuller.

262   "It's yesterday's snow": Interview with Steve Maksin.

265   "I hate going": deadmalls.com.

265   "Everybody loves an apocalypse-type": Interview with Jack Thomas.

266   That's when a Dollar General: 2018 Form 10-K, Dollar General Corporation.

266   "I'll stay here": Interview with Tim Thramer.

266   The contrast with the rest: Interview with David Gordon, research director
       at Edge by Ascential.

266   Nearly 65 percent: Interview with Darhsan Kalyani, senior industry analyst,
       IBISWorld.

266 "The economy is continuing": Sarah Nassauer, "How Dollar General Became Rural America's Store of Choice," *Wall Street Journal*, December 15, 2017, wsj.com.

267 On the north side: Marie Donahue and Stacy Mitchell, "Dollar Stores Are Targeting Struggling Urban Neighborhoods and Small Towns. One Community Is Showing How to Fight Back," Institute for Local Self-Reliance, December 6, 2018.

267 Independent grocery stores: Interview with Stacy Mitchell.

267 Twenty years ago: Interview with Kathy Siefken.

268 Traditional small-town groceries: Interview with David Procter.

269 When nearby towns: Interview with Wayne Ledbetter.

269 "When we asked": Interview with Paula Hladky.

270 Dollar General traces: newscenter.dollargeneral.com.

270 "Dollar Stores, in a sense": Interview with Vincent Sinisi.

270 The investment firm bought: Interview with Peter Keith.

271 KKR managed to take: "Dollar General I.P.O. Is Priced at $21 Per Share," Dealbook, *New York Times*, November 13, 2009.

272 "We found a niche": Interview with Diana Hahn.

272 Forty years ago: Interview with Kim McDowell.

273 "They'd stick around": Interview with Paul McDowell.

273 Longtime patrons embraced: Erika Pritchard, "Small Town Grocery Stores Are Closing at an Alarming Rate, Including Ravenna Super Foods. One Common Factor in the Closures? Dollar General," *Kearney Hub*, February 18, 2019.

274 "I was never much": Interview with Sandy Beall.

276 "The customer base wasn't brought": Interview with Steve Rockwell.

276 But something larger: Interview with Aaron Allen.

277 All told, the number: Jonathan Maze, "Ruby Tuesday Closes Another 15 Locations," *Restaurant Business*, April 3, 2018, restaurantbusinessonline.com.

277 "I knew there was": Interview with Sam Beall.

280 In 1970, 65 percent: K. Bischoff and S.F. Reardon, "Residential Segregation by Socioeconomic Status, 1970–2009," *US2010: America in the First Decade of the New Century* (New York: Russell Sage, 2014): 208–33, brown.edu.

280 "Most families increasingly live": Interview with Sean Reardon.

280 Isolated from better-off peers: scholar.harvard.edu.

280 Widening regional economic gaps: Interview with Ed Glaeser.

281 "They've been Balkanized": Interview with David Autor.

281 "When the middle class": Rebecca J. Rosen, "Can the Country Survive Without a Strong Middle Class?," *The Atlantic*, March 21, 2017, theatlantic.com.

CONCLUSION

283 "Once you're on board": Interview with Jody Hoffer Gittell.

284 "The economics are too powerful": Interview with Bill George.

285   Southwest is the most: "Southwest Reports Fourth Quarter and Annual Profit; 46th Consecutive Year of Profitability," Southwest Airlines, January 24, 2019, investors.southwest.com.

285   Southwest's profit margins: Interview with Rajeev Lalwani.

286   "I learned firsthand": Katrina Brooker and Alynda Wheat, "The Chairman of the Board Looks Back," *Fortune,* May 28, 2001, archive.fortune.com.

286   There was a genuine: Interview with Ann Rhoades.

287   "If you really want": Interview with Charles O'Reilly III.

287   As a Harvard Business School: James L. Heskett and W. Earl Sasser Jr., "Southwest Airlines: In a Different World," HBS Case Collection, Harvard Business School, April 2010.

289   *Golf Digest* ranks: Ron Whitten, "America's 100 Greatest Golf Courses," *Golf Digest,* January 2019.

289   "I could charge more": Interview with Mike Keiser.

290   "We could definitely generate": Interview with Mark Murphy.

291   "People who can afford": Interview with John Bergstrom.

291   Although the population: "Sports Money: 2018 NFL Valuations," *Forbes,* September 20, 2018, forbes.com.

292   "Lambeau Field is like": Interview with Andy Dolich.

293   "This isn't about": Interview with Tim Welsh.

294   But Tim Pawlenty: Nelson D. Schwartz, "In the Twin Cities, Local Leaders Wield Influence Behind the Scenes," *New York Times,* December 28, 2015.

294   He and other business executives: Interview with James R. Campbell.

294   "I can't overstate": Interview with Chris Coleman.

295   "This discourages a significant": Interview with Dr. Rafael Rivera.

295   It took more than a decade: David W. Chen, "Surprise Gift: Free Tuition for all N.Y.U. Medical Students," *New York Times,* August 16, 2018.

296   So far, the only one: Abby Goodnough, "Kaiser Permanente's New Medical School Will Waive Tuition for Its First 5 Classes," *New York Times,* February 19, 2019.

296   At Princeton, which has: admission.princeton.edu.

296   "There are mental": Interview with David Leebron.

297   "It's a fundamentally different": Interview with Ryan Buell.

299   The middle class could: Survey of Consumer Finances, Federal Reserve, 2016, federalreserve.gov.

299   To find the money: "Changes in U.S. Family Finances from 2013 to 2016: Evidence from the Survey of Consumer Finances," *Federal Reserve Bulletin* 103 (September 2017), federalreserve.gov.

299   Forty percent of Americans: Irene Tung, Yannet Lathrop, and Paul Sonn, "The Growing Movement for $15," National Employment Law Project, nelp.org.

Index

·········

About the Author

Nelson D. Schwartz writes about economics for *The New York Times,* where he has worked for more than a decade. Before his current beat, Schwartz covered Wall Street and banking and served as European economics correspondent in Paris from 2008 to 2010. In 2014, Schwartz was the recipient of the *Times*'s annual Nathaniel Nash Award for the reporter who "best excels in business and economic news."

A graduate of the University of Chicago, he worked for ten years at *Fortune* magazine before joining the *Times.* He is a native of Scarsdale, New York, and lives with his family on the Upper East Side of Manhattan.